Culture, Economy and Politics

New Directions in Cultural Policy Research

Series Editors: **Eleonora Belfiore**, University of Warwick, UK, and **Anna Upchurch**, University of Leeds, UK

New Directions in Cultural Policy Research encourages theoretical and empirical research which enriches and develops the field of cultural policy studies. Since its emergence in the 1990s, the academic field of cultural policy studies has expanded globally as the arts and popular culture have been re-positioned by city, regional, and national governments, and international bodies, from the margins to the centre of social and economic development in both rhetoric and practice. The series invites contributions in any of the following: national and international cultural policies, arts policies, the politics of culture, cultural industries policies (the 'traditional' arts such as performing and visual arts, crafts), creative industries policies (digital, social media, broadcasting and film, and advertising), urban regeneration and urban cultural policies, regional cultural policies, the politics of cultural and creative labour, the production and consumption of popular culture, arts education policies, cultural heritage and tourism policies, and the history and politics of media policies. The series will reflect current and emerging concerns of the field such as, for example, cultural value, community cultural development, cultural diversity, cultural sustainability, planning for the intercultural city, cultural planning, and cultural citizenship.

David Hesmondhalgh, Kate Oakley, David Lee and Melissa Nisbett
CULTURE, ECONOMY AND POLITICS
The Case of New Labour

Lachlan MacDowall, Marnie Badham, Emma Blomkamp and Kim Dunphy
MAKING CULTURE COUNT
The Politics of Cultural Measurement

Clive Gray
THE POLITICS OF MUSEUMS

New Directions in Cultural Policy Research
Series Standing Order ISBN 978–1–137–53305–0 (hardback)
(*outside North America only*)

You can receive future titles in this series as they are published by placing a standing order. Please contact your bookseller or, in case of difficulty, write to us at the address below with your name and address, the title of the series and the ISBN quoted above.

Customer Services Department, Macmillan Distribution Ltd, Houndmills, Basingstoke, Hampshire RG21 6XS, England

Culture, Economy and Politics

The Case of New Labour

David Hesmondhalgh
University of Leeds, UK

Kate Oakley
University of Leeds, UK

David Lee
University of Leeds, UK

Melissa Nisbett
King's College London, UK

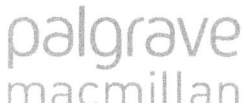

First published 2015 by
PALGRAVE MACMILLAN

Palgrave Macmillan in the UK is an imprint of Macmillan Publishers Limited, registered in England, company number 785998, of Houndmills, Basingstoke, Hampshire RG21 6XS.

Palgrave Macmillan in the US is a division of St Martin's Press LLC, 175 Fifth Avenue, New York, NY 10010.

Palgrave Macmillan is the global academic imprint of the above companies and has companies and representatives throughout the world.

Palgrave® and Macmillan® are registered trademarks in the United States, the United Kingdom, Europe and other countries.

ISBN 978–1–137–42637–6

This book is printed on paper suitable for recycling and made from fully managed and sustained forest sources. Logging, pulping and manufacturing processes are expected to conform to the environmental regulations of the country of origin.

A catalogue record for this book is available from the British Library.

A catalog record for this book is available from the Library of Congress.

Contents

Figures, Tables and Boxes

Acknowledgements

This book is based on a research project, *Cultural Policy under New Labour*, funded by the UK Arts and Humanities Research Council under its Standard Research Grants Scheme, and held at the University of Leeds. The grant ran from January 2012 to December 2013. David Hesmondhalgh was the principal investigator, Kate Oakley and David Lee were the co-investigators and Melissa Nisbett was the research fellow appointed to support the project. The research and writing were a team effort, with each chapter led by a different author (or two). Most of the interviews were conducted by Melissa, but all of us were involved in some of them, either jointly with Melissa or alone. Our thanks to Andreas Rauh Ortega for help in preparing the bibliography, and for other assistance.

We are grateful to all the interviewees, who gave time to share their memories and perspectives; details can be found in the Appendix. We are also grateful to the advisory board for the project: Jo Burns, Tom Campbell, Hilary Carty, Graham Hitchen, Andy Lovatt, Ruth MacKenzie and John Newbigin. Thanks, too, to the researchers who attended our *Cultural Policy under New Labour* symposium in September 2013 in Leeds, for their helpful comments and input, including Ele Belfiore, Franco Bianchini, Helen Graham, Clive Gray, Robert Hewison, Leila Jancovich, Jim McGuigan, Andy Pratt and Sara Selwood. Thanks, too, to Anna Upchurch for arranging the Cultural Policy seminar series at Leeds, which provided other opportunities to share ideas, and to Sylvia Harvey for comments on parts of our draft manuscript.

Some material in this book appeared in previously published journal articles:

- Sections of Chapter 3 appeared in Hesmondhalgh, D., Nisbett, M., Oakley, K. and Lee, D. (2015) 'Were New Labour's Cultural Policies Neo-Liberal?' *International Journal of Cultural Policy*, 21(1), 97–114 (published online January 2014), but have been substantially revised.
- Sections of Chapter 5 appeared in Lee, D., Hesmondhalgh, D., Oakley, K. and Nisbett, M. 'Regional Creative Industries Policy-Making under New Labour', *Cultural Trends*, 23(4), 217–231 (published online June 2014), but have been substantially revised.
- Some of Chapter 6 appeared in Oakley, K., Hesmondhalgh, D., Lee, D. and Nisbett, M. (2014) 'The National Trust for Talent? NESTA

and New Labour's Cultural Policy', *British Politics* 9(3), 297–317 (published online February 2014), but has been substantially revised.

David Hesmondhalgh would like to thank, as always, his friends and family for providing the context that makes the hard work of writing a book feel worthwhile, especially Helen, Rosa, Joe, Mum and Joolz; the northerners who live down south; and the Wharfedale posse. The School of Media and Communication at Leeds University is an excellent place to conduct research, and there are too many great colleagues there to thank individually in print. A big collective thank you.

Kate Oakley would like to thank Graham Hitchen and Rory Coonan for access to unpublished documentation, which was hugely useful. And to friends who worked with me on cultural policy in the New Labour years, but who don't feature in the interviewee thanks, namely Paul Owens, Jo Burns, Richard Naylor, Colin Kirkpatrick, Lucy Mantella, Tom Fleming, Andrew Erskine and John Knell.

David Lee would like to thank family and friends, in particular Rachel, Arina and Dylan who make it all worthwhile, and Mum and Dad for support and anecdotes from the front lines of the cultural industries. Thanks also to Calvin Taylor for insights into regional cultural policy and to the team at BOP Consulting (past and present) for introducing me to the strange, contradictory but always fascinating world of cultural policy, especially Richard Naylor, Paul Owens, Jo Burns, Chris Gibbon, Colin Kirkpatrick and Lucy Mantella.

Melissa Nisbett would like to thank family and friends for their support, in particular Robin, Helen and Claire. Thanks also go to friends and colleagues in the School of Media and Communication at the University of Leeds, and Bridget, Fidele and Christina in the Department of Culture, Media and Creative Industries at King's College London. Final thanks to cultural policy scholars Clive Gray and Dave O'Brien.

1
Culture, Politics and Equality: The Challenge for Social Democracy

1.1 What we are trying to do in this book

This book seeks to advance understanding of cultural policy, public policy and politics. It pays particular attention to the way in which cultural policy responded to, and sought to shape, changing relations between culture and economy. It does so via a case study of cultural policies in the UK between 1997 and 2010.

This was a period in which the Labour Party formed three successive national governments. The term commonly used for these Labour administrations is 'New Labour', because that was how the party presented itself to the public and the electorate. This was never the official name of the party, but it has stuck. New Labour's cultural policies are of particular interest, for at least two reasons. First, more than any other British government, and more than most modern national governments, New Labour placed great emphasis on culture and the arts in their political self-presentation and also to a certain degree in policy practice. Second, they did so by reconfiguring conventional understandings of cultural policy, by placing much greater stress on the economic role of commercial 'creative industries', while retaining and, indeed, raising subsidies for the arts.

We offer a sociological account which interprets, explains and evaluates cultural policy. We have conducted 45 interviews with many of the major players in UK cultural policy during the 1997–2010 period (including senior politicians and arts administrators), analysed many key documents and read a wide variety of secondary sources, academic, journalistic and others. We have used relevant social and political theory to interpret and evaluate what happened and what people told us.

This book isn't designed just for UK readers, or for students of British politics or of British cultural policy.[1] New Labour's cultural policies have been the object of considerable international attention (e.g., Flew, 2012; Prince, 2010a; Ross, 2009), as has New Labour's distinctive brand of politics (see Giddens, 2001). We endeavour to explain references to UK institutions and figures to non-UK readers, and we assume only a very low level of familiarity with British politics and society. British cultural policy serves here as a case study of events and processes that we think might be of wider interest: for those concerned with cultural policy, we aim to show the benefits of understanding politics and public policy as a means of analysing government action in the realm of culture; for those interested in government and politics, we seek to provide a detailed sociological account of cultural policy as a specific domain of public policy.

Our goal is to bring together public policy, politics and cultural policy in a new and distinctive way that we hope might enhance understanding of these domains. In a nutshell, we want to bring more politics and 'policy' to cultural policy studies, and more 'culture' to public policy and politics research. The best analysis of public policy suggests the need for a multidisciplinary approach that considers the role of ideas, institutions and the way in which groups pursue their interests, and achieves a balance between the messiness and contingency of policy making and its links to power and ideology. Surprisingly, very few studies have provided adequate accounts of the distinctive dynamics of cultural policy as public policy.[2] Equally, we hope to offer something distinctive to researchers and students of politics and public policy by paying careful heed to questions of culture. Public policy and political science have been weak in their understandings of the difficult concept of culture – both its influence on and its shaping by government. They have shown almost

---

[1] Many non-Britons are understandably confused by the relation between the various countries. The sovereign state of the United Kingdom of Great Britain and Northern Ireland comprises four nations: England, Scotland, Wales and Northern Ireland. Our primary concern is with policy under the UK New Labour government, and we do not have space to address policy developments in the various nations in any detail. Under New Labour, Scotland in particular gained significant devolved powers, including its own Parliament; Wales and Northern Ireland gained their own national assemblies.

[2] Academic analysis of cultural policy has boomed in recent years, and this is reflected in a growth of journals, books and master's degrees, and in the development of a field now called 'cultural policy studies'.

no interest whatsoever in cultural policy.[3] This both reflects and helps perpetuate cultural policy's low status in government, when compared with domains such as the economy, welfare, health, education, security and constitutional matters. Some of these areas may seem more crucial, more bound up with matters of life and death. But culture matters a great deal, not only for the flourishing of societies and individuals, but also, increasingly, for the economic role it plays. New Labour recognised this – though in problematic ways.

It's not just a matter of injecting some cultural studies into public policy, though.[4] A claim underlying the following study is that contemporary cultural policy cannot be understood without properly conceptualising changing relations between economy, culture and society – and, just as crucially, without understanding competing interpretations of these changes. Paying attention to these issues may also be of benefit for understanding other domains of policy, including education, science and technology, social policy and environment. In fact, vital to our task of explanation and evaluation in this book is the obvious but surprisingly neglected insight that cultural policy involves complex relations between cultural policy itself and other areas of policy (and society) – including education, welfare, health and even foreign affairs.

While our aim is to produce a book that has more general significance, we also want to explain and evaluate our particular case – New Labour's cultural policies. Bizarrely, the huge number of books and research papers on New Labour have paid almost no attention whatsoever to their policies on arts and culture.[5] This probably reflects the lack of communication between cultural policy researchers and researchers of public policy more generally, as well as a sense among

---

[3] Clive Gray is an exceptional example of a public policy researcher who has chosen to specialise in cultural policy (e.g., Gray, 2000). Other rare political science treatments of cultural policy include those of Mulcahy (2006) and Hetherington (2014). Gray (2009a) points out that in the six leading political and public administration journals, there were only four articles on museums and galleries in a collective 347 years of publication.

[4] Cultural studies is the interdisciplinary field that claims to be best able to provide an analysis of culture (a claim that anthropologists often bitterly dispute). Yet it has paid little attention to policy, whether cultural policy or public policy more generally. The main exceptions include Tony Bennett's mainly historical work (e.g., Bennett, 1998) and Miller and Yúdice (2002). Where cultural studies has addressed cultural policy, it has lacked sociology – partly, perhaps, because it has ignored the public policy literature.

[5] See, for example, the collections by Driver and Martell (2006) and Diamond and Kenny (2011). A rare exception is Chapter 4 in Toynbee and Walker (2010).

public policy researchers that the arts and culture are of marginal interest and importance – echoing the view of many politicians. So we are aiming to fill a gap, and to do so by considering the extent to which New Labour's cultural policies successfully balanced various goals that a democratic cultural policy might pursue: greater equality of access to cultural production and consumption, higher quality of cultural goods, contributing to democratic vitality, enhancing the flourishing of individuals, communities and groups.

Here the question of political ideology is fundamental. Cynics are wrong to suggest that there is no difference in policy between the political projects associated with the various types of modern conservatism and social democracy. Of course, there are areas in which the two have somewhat converged, and there are ways in which both social democracy and conservatism have moved to the left on some issues (e.g., to incorporate a greater recognition of the rights of ethnic minorities) and to the right on others (e.g., the rise of neo-liberal thinking in the realm of economic and industrial policy). Political fields are constantly mutating, and the last 30 years have seen the rise in many countries across the world of ultra-conservative populist movements, the decline of left governmental projects (except in Latin America) and the uneven emergence of green politics. So one way in which we frame our own analysis of New Labour's cultural policies is as an examination of the fate of cultural policy in an era when northern-world social democracy (and its Australasian equivalents) has had to reinvent itself in the face of neo-liberalism and conservative populism.

This book is not intended as a polemic against New Labour. Nor is it in any way a paean of praise to a government that is now remembered with little affection in the UK – as is, perhaps, the fate of most governments. Instead, we seek to capture the complexity of cultural policy and politics, to elucidate the ethical and political values of politicians, policy makers and commentators and to ask what they might have done better, taking into account the constraints they faced (or believed they faced) and the opportunities they had. Such scrutiny is surely an important part of any democratic debate.

In summary, then, this book seeks to draw upon, and contribute to, public policy studies, political studies and cultural policy studies. It does so by explaining and evaluating New Labour's cultural policies as examples of a social democratic political project.

In the rest of this chapter, we provide the foundations for the analysis in the rest of the book. In Section 1.2, we analyse cultural policy as a distinct sector of public policy, delineating its main sub-sectors, and providing an outline of the main elements of cultural policy as it has generally been practised over the last 100 years or so: nation branding and cohesion, heritage preservation, the shaping of cultural production, distribution and consumption and regulation. We discuss the importance of understanding cultural policy in relation to other areas of public policy, including the tendency of cultural policy makers to make links or attachments to other, more prestigious or 'heavyweight' domains. In Section 1.3, in line with our comments above, we suggest a number of ways in which themes and issues in public policy research might help us better understand cultural policy, in particular regarding questions of power, influence and democracy. Because our view is that public policy cannot be understood without reference to political beliefs and values, in Section 1.4, we provide an overview of social democracy, and its efforts to reinvent itself in response to erosion of its traditional sources of support and the rise of neo-liberalism from the 1970s onwards. Section 1.5 then addresses social democracy's relationship with culture, and with cultural policy, and we provide a brief account of the Labour Party's record on culture and arts during its periods of government up to the 1970s. We then, in Section 1.6, identify the main distinctive themes of New Labour's policies as a whole and introduce some of the controversies surrounding them, including whether they should be thought of as social democratic in any meaningful sense. Section 1.7 briefly discusses some of the main ways in which commentators and academics have evaluated New Labour's record on arts and culture. Section 1.8 explains the structure of the rest of the book, and lays out the main research questions that it seeks to answer.

1.2 Cultural policy as a distinct form of public policy

The years after the Second World War saw the beginnings of what we would recognise today as cultural policy, in terms of its distinctive mixture of funding, regulation, protection and promotion (Gray, 2000: 35–54). Most European countries, however, draw on a much longer legacy of religious and aristocratic patronage, government censorship and control of media, and commercial culture embracing popular entertainment and high art. In the case of the UK, public funding for culture, in the sense of establishing national institutions, really began in the mid-eighteenth century, and institutions such as the British Museum and the British Library date from that time. The nineteenth century saw the great expansion of education, including in the arts and design (Bird, 2000; Frayling, 1987), as well as agonised parliamentary discussion about the UK's loss of competiveness in manufacturing – a theme which in varying ways would echo throughout the next century. The Victorian era also witnessed the beginnings of what we might describe nowadays as urban cultural policy, with the growth of theatres and concert halls, art galleries and museums across British cities. As Hetherington (2014) points out, in the performing arts, theatres and concert halls were often commercially funded, while the development of museums, galleries and public libraries drew on philanthropic support, with some occasional state funding.

Thus, by the beginning of the twentieth century, what is sometimes described in a rather ungainly phrase as the cultural infrastructure of the nation – galleries, museums, libraries and concert halls – was widely developed. With the early twentieth-century surge in growth of the communications media and the cultural industries, 'picture houses' spread to almost every corner of the nation. What distinguished the post–Second World War period from earlier times was not only much greater amounts of public funding of culture, which allowed the arts to play a role in post-war reconstruction, but also the development of a series of rationales for state involvement in culture. Such rationales often carried within them echoes of earlier debates and ideologies: ideas about the civilising role of the high arts, and the economic benefits of aesthetic innovation (in the form of better design), for example. The post-war period would see these principles forming the basis of public policy, and the development of requisite institutions and agencies.

The complexities of cultural policy derive from tensions and contradictions between these different rationales, and the ways they are taken up or rejected by the key institutions. They also stem from the fact that cultural policy, like other forms of public policy, operates on a number of different scales. As one group of researchers puts it, '[c]ultural policy is now the province of all levels of government as well as suprastate bodies such as the European Union' (Stevenson et al., 2010: 159). Cultural policies do not involve a simple top-down hierarchy whereby central government cascades its agendas 'down' to regional and local scales (though there are examples of this, as we shall see); some ideas emerge 'below' local government – as is, arguably, the case with the importance of urban regeneration in culture (see chapters 4 and 5).

As the brief history above indicates, cultural institutions themselves play a part in the cultural policy-making process, not least because they pre-date the development of national government policy on culture. What is sometimes referred to as the 'arts establishment' – referring to those who work in the subsidised cultural sectors – has over the last 20 or 30 years been joined by the large-scale commercial cultural industries as key actors in the cultural policy arena. We will see that an absolutely central theme in New Labour's cultural policy – 'the creative industries' – derived from increasing activism on the part of lobbyists representing this commercially driven cultural sector.[6]

So, what do the state and other policy actors (see next section) do in the name of cultural policy?[7] More than in other areas of public policy, it is difficult to summarise the core aim of cultural policy. Health policy, however complex in its execution, has the overall aim of better health (of which longevity, infant mortality, morbidity rates and so on are components). Defence policy is fundamentally concerned with defence of the realm. But, given the diversity of aims for cultural policy, it is difficult to say whether its core purpose is more culture, better culture, more diverse culture, culture that helps solve social problems or culture that makes more money. This uncertainty means that not only is cultural policy attached to other policy areas, it is also directly shaped by them.

Nonetheless, there are certain types of activities that are frequently carried out under the remit of 'cultural policy' and which are described below.

Nation branding or promotion. This refers to the role of culture in telling the national story, bringing the nation together, and is one of the most common activities with which cultural policy is involved. 'Mega-events', including, in the UK, those associated with royalty (coronations and assorted royal weddings, christenings and funerals), are a key form of national cultural display, running alongside the hosting of various travelling shows such as the Olympics, World Cup and Expo. The fierce competition to host so-called mega-events suggests the importance that

---

[6] Throughout this book, we use the term 'cultural industries' to refer to the industries involved in cultural production, and 'creative industries' to refer to policies oriented towards those industries. For more on the difference between the terms, and on why the former term might be preferred for the industries themselves, see Hesmondhalgh (2008, 2013a).

[7] This section does not aim to be a comprehensive account of post-war cultural policy across the world (see Bell and Oakley, 2014; Miller and Yúdice, 2002; O'Brien, 2013; Throsby, 2010 for more general accounts of cultural policy). The focus is primarily on the UK, which has a particular cultural policy tradition and approach – influential in many Commonwealth countries, but in turn influenced by European cultural policies, and by the enormous cultural and economic power of the USA over the last 100 years – both the reality of that power, and anxieties about it.

national governments attach to this sort of self-promotion (García, 2004b). The building of major national cultural institutions – often called flagships – can also be seen as part of national self-promotion, as they were in the France of François Mitterrand (Looseley, 1995) as well as catalysts for urban regeneration via tourism and employment (see Chapter 4). Cultural 'institutes', such as the British Council, Alliance Française, Germany's Goethe Institute and China's Confucius Institute, also comprise key forms of national self-promotion (Paschalidis, 2009).

Protection of heritage and historical artefacts. Another aspect of cultural policy which many would see as part of its fundamental remit is the protection and promotion of national heritage or patrimony – often in the form of buildings or monuments (from stone circles to Gothic cathedrals) but increasingly in the form of intangible heritage: languages, customs, festivals, religious rites and so on can be classified as heritage, as can symbolically important non-cultural goods such as food.

Support for cultural production. In addition to protecting and preserving what the nation (or city, or community) already has, nearly all cultural policies assume some role for the state in supporting cultural production. The mechanism for this support may differ according to the societies' overall orientation to cultural policy, and Chartrand and McCaughey's (1989) four-fold typology of cultural policy approaches is useful here. In this typology, the USA exemplifies what they call a 'facilitator state' role, funding the arts via tax exemption or donation (often with matching funding as a lever); the UK is a 'patron state', devolving cultural policy implementation to so-called 'arm's-length' bodies such as the Arts Council and the BBC; the 'architect state', such as France, uses state bureaucracy directly to fund culture production; authoritarian 'engineer' states such as China directly control artistic production. Such a typology is a little crude, and many states would use a mix of these approaches. But it is a useful way to consider the different ways in which states provide support for cultural production. Arguments over what counts as culture and therefore worthy of public support (is it just the fine arts, or does it include popular cultural activities such as TV, videogames and stand-up comedy?) constitute one of the key battlegrounds of cultural policy. In the UK approach, 'arm's length' (quasi-independent) funding bodies such as the Arts Council fund the performing and visual arts and literature.[8] Parts of both the film and

---

[8] On the history of the Arts Council, see Hutchison (1982) and Witts (1998). The Arts Council of Great Britain (ACGB) was broken up into Arts Councils of

television industries have been supported via public funding from the earliest days in most European countries, and continue to receive tax breaks. In the UK, this comes via 'arm's length' bodies such as the UK Film Council or the British Film Institute, or via the hypothecated tax known as the licence fee in the case of the BBC, the UK public service broadcaster.

Distribution and cultural consumption. A vital issue in cultural policy concerns the potential tensions between the pursuit of excellence and access. The pursuit of excellence might be seen as the role of heritage, arts and media policies in supporting high-quality *production* that markets, with their emphasis on commercial reward, will under-produce in certain domains. Access, on the other hand, can be understood as the remit of policy concerned with *consumption* – the question of who gets access to culture and on what grounds (though there are also important issues regarding access to production). Although the term 'access' would not have been used until recently, promoting access to culture on the part of those with fewer resources is an old concern of cultural policy. Sir Henry Cole, founder of the Victoria and Albert Museum (V&A) in London, was said to have justified public expenditure on gas lighting within the museum to enable evening opening for the working class and thus provide a healthy alternative to the gin palaces of Victorian London (Gibson, 2008). The development of public libraries in the late nineteenth century was advocated on similar grounds. The idea that access to cultural activities has some educational or 'civilising' function has never entirely gone away (see discussion of New Labour's Creative Partnerships scheme in Chapter 7), though it has been joined over the years by a host of other benefits or 'values' said to accrue to both individuals and societies from cultural participation. Easily mocked, these can often be translated into shopping lists of values and benefits, from better health to less propensity to commit crime and greater well-being, the evidence for which is often weak (O'Brien, 2010). In fairness, however, any cultural policy must assume some benefits from watching plays or listening to music – otherwise it is difficult to see why one would support such activities in the first place.

As we shall see, New Labour placed strong emphasis on access and excellence in their cultural policies, implicitly claiming that they were combining the two. However, there are longstanding policy problems

---

England, Scotland, Wales and Northern Ireland in 1994. Unless otherwise stated, we use the term 'Arts Council' to refer to the ACGB when discussing the pre-1994 history, and the Arts Council of England (etc.) afterwards.

regarding cultural access and excellence, and the relations between them – in particular, if excellence is going to be a key criterion for public subsidy, the degree to which audience perceptions should or can be the measure of it (see chapters 2 and 3).

Control, censorship and regulation. In the 'engineer' model of national cultural policy, the state directly owns and controls the means of cultural production, and so can decide what counts as legitimate culture and what does not. Away from more obvious forms of censorship, subtle control of cultural production and consumption often takes place, for example through funnelling funds towards some types of culture and away from others (Alexander, 2008), what we might think of as 'soft censorship'. Critics of New Labour have accused it of promoting a 'politically correct' popular culture, under the guise of access, particularly when aimed at certain communities (see the discussion of Rich Mix in Chapter 3 and Mirza, 2012), and debates about what types of culture are favoured by state spending are a frequent part of cultural policy conversations. But the arm's length principle of cultural funding – via third party institutions – tends to protect governments from most rows about censorship and control, however 'short' the arm's length becomes. Regulation of culture tends to be rather piecemeal in a country like the UK, but it covers a wide range of areas, from gambling, to licensing laws, to use of the airwaves and content on public service broadcasting.

As we shall see, New Labour's key cultural policy concepts, the creative industries and, later, the creative economy (see chapters 2 and 4), attempted to change the prevailing relationships between these domains or sub-sectors of cultural policy. New Labour used these concepts to reduce the emphasis that had previously been placed on arts and heritage in post-war cultural policy. Paradoxically, they did so in order to legitimate extra funding for the arts (heritage, as we shall see, was a rather different case, though it did well under Labour despite Labour distancing themselves from it). This move was not unprecedented, and we discuss ideas and policies that New Labour drew upon in Chapter 2. But it had never been attempted so fully before, and it was inflected in particular ways under New Labour, drawing on their own distinctive attempt to remould (or abandon) social democratic politics.

There was a development in the latter decades of the twentieth century that provides vital context for New Labour's cultural policy innovations – and helps us to understand their precedents. In this period, cultural policy became aligned with other areas of public policy and/or became seen as important to the delivery of other public policy goals. Clive Gray (2002) developed the idea of 'policy attachment' to explain how culture can draw on the clout of other realms of public policy. According to Gray, cultural policy makers seek such attachment partly because of the *weakness* of culture as an area of public policy: national and local culture departments are often small, with constantly threatened budgets. Linking arts funding to education or welfare helps to legitimate cultural expenditure. Policy attachment is often linked to another concept, that of *instrumentalism*: a critical term, implying condemnation of situations in which culture is used to pursue non-cultural ends (economic or social) and in which the value attached to culture 'itself' is thereby diminished. Instrumental rationales that point to the social and economic benefits of investment in culture have been part of cultural policy discourse for centuries, and most writers agree that instrumentalism is not new in cultural policy (e.g., Belfiore and Bennett, 2008; Gibson, 2008). But some have argued that the New Labour era represents a step change in the use of culture as an instrument to pursue a wide range of policy aims (Belfiore, 2012; Gray, 2004; Hewison, 2014; Mirza, 2012). Indeed, Abigail Gilmore has recently argued that what characterises the New Labour period is how instrumentalism was institutionalised on every level from individual arts organisations upwards (Gilmore, 2014).

We discuss the problem of instrumentalism – and the problems surrounding its use as a critical concept – in more detail in Chapter 3 (and we return to it in Chapter 8). But there are other aspects of the integration of cultural policy into public policy that deserve attention, one of which is the degree to which we can understand other public policy in terms of its effects on culture. In other words, cultural policy is certainly not the only realm of policy that shapes culture. Jeremy Ahearne (2009) makes a distinction between what he labels 'explicit' and 'implicit' cultural policy. The latter includes a wide range of public policies, from education to immigration, which may have cultural consequences but which are not explicitly labelled as cultural policies. He argues that the most important forms of cultural policy are not always labelled as such. This certainly applies historically, for example in the case of the BBC, a hugely important element of the UK's cultural life, but one that would not conventionally be recognised in public discourse or academic analysis as cultural policy; it would tend to be bracketed under media policy.[9] It may well be a hallmark of contemporary cultural policy

---

[9] We do not address media policy in this book, for reasons of space, and following the convention that media policy and cultural policy describe different terrains,

that much of what affects the production and consumption of culture takes place under other policy remits, and it is central to the arguments of this book that the study of cultural policy needs to start from this premise, and needs to address the relations of cultural policy to other policy domains – and, indeed, the nature of cultural policy as public policy. This means considering public policy itself.

1.3 Politics, power and democracy

As we noted above, research on politics and public policy has often been neglected in cultural policy research (again, the work of Clive Gray is a major exception). Concepts that refer to the changing nature of the state, such as neo-liberalism, have been used, but sometimes in a rather reductive way. While we consider neo-liberalism to be an indispensable concept for analysing political-economic change since the 1970s and 1980s, and refer to it intermittently in what follows, it can often be used too loosely and broadly.[10] Cultural policy research needs to go beyond such simplifications.

We draw upon public policy analysis that shows how power is somewhat dispersed across an array of institutions and individuals, yet how the interests of powerful groups in wider society nevertheless often prevail. Central here are issues of influence, lobbying, agenda setting and the relationship between sub-sectors of policy. While we cannot claim to offer a comprehensive account of these issues, we can at least begin to correct their remarkable neglect in cultural policy studies so far.

One of the reasons that public policy research was shunned for many years was, perhaps, that it operated in a rather positivist way, and neglected questions of power that were of interest to critical cultural policy analysts. In recent years, public policy research has increasingly addressed questions of power. Assumptions in earlier research that policy makers translated their values into policy in a relatively straightforward way (according to what policy research calls 'comprehensive rationality') and that policy could be understood as a series of

---

even though media are obviously a key part of culture. See Hesmondhalgh (2005) for a call for the two to be integrated, in the context of an early discussion of New Labour's policies.

[10] See our earlier journal article (Hesmondhalgh et al., 2015) for further discussion of neo-liberalism, and a consideration of the degree to which New Labour's arts policies – and their policies in general – can usefully and validly be understood as neo-liberal.

discrete stages ('the policy cycle') have now been questioned for decades (see Cairney, 2012). Among the many strands of critical public policy research that have challenged the positivism that previously prevailed in policy research, we here identify two that are of particular relevance to our interests in this book, in relationships between power, democracy and control.

Governance and the modern state. One strand points to the fact that public policy now rarely operates in a centralised top-down kind of way. Instead, policy making is increasingly dispersed among a complex body of institutions and groups. One influential formulation, by Rhodes (1994), referred to 'the hollowing out of the state' and focused on the creation of policy networks that operate with a high degree of autonomy from the state, and are built out of interactions between network members, who exchange resources and negotiate shared interests. A key term is 'governance', which refers to the way a state is governed, but which is 'broader than government' and 'pays more attention to non-state actors', as Rhodes (1997: 53) put it. The term is intended to draw attention to the importance of interdependence between organisations, especially private, public and voluntary ones. Analysts such as Bevir and Rhodes (2006) emphasise the way in which a mixture of beliefs, traditions and dilemmas leads to a highly contingent set of practices which cannot be managed by a state. While this approach is valuable in drawing attention to the complex meanings at work in policy making, it may underestimate the degree to which the state continues to act as a powerful actor in an era marked by such intricate networks of policy actors. State theorist Bob Jessop (2002), for example, emphasised the continuing power of the state to exercise 'meta-governance' by setting the ground rules for how governance takes place, in a contemporary context of neo-liberalism. The nature of capitalist states had shifted in recent decades, Jessop argued, from centralised Keynesian systems to an emphasis on regulation of competition and private–public partnerships. Our empirical investigation of a particular domain (cultural policy), often far removed from the Hobbesian idea of the state as a force of power, examines not only the messy and dispersed nature of policy making, but also the way in which it draws upon coherent and consistent ideological views of how states might exercise authority.

Policy networks: sociologies of policy groups and interests. A second and sometimes overlapping strand of public policy research that we have found helpful is policy network analysis: PNA for short. As its name suggests, it shares with the governance school an interest in the (problematic) concept of the network, and some theorists (notably Rhodes) have made interventions in both strands. But our interest in these approaches does not stem from its employment of the concept of network, which has been over-used. More attractive is its programme of research on the pursuit of interests by particular groups, with varying characteristics and goals. PNA focuses on middle or meso-level issues concerning relations between different groups of policy actors, and relations within such groups.[11] For example, Marsh and Rhodes (1992) developed a model which established a continuum or scale with *policy communities* at one end, and *issue networks* at the other. Policy communities tend to be more limited in number of members, narrower in the range of interests that are represented and based on a strong degree of consensus. In Marsh and Rhodes' model, issue networks are at the opposite extreme, with more members, unstable interaction and lots of internal conflict. British government, according to Marsh and Rhodes at the time of their writing, was characterised by a limited number of tight policy communities dominated by economic/business interests, professional interests and central government actors. These policy communities exerted considerable power. As later empirical work (by Marsh, Rhodes and others) suggested, however, and in line with the governance approach, issue networks are on the rise, leading to greater complexity and fragmentation in policy making.

While we will keep things simple by referring to '*policy groups*' rather than making the policy communities/issue networks distinction, PNA points to the need for a sociology that registers the entangled nature of contemporary policy relationships. Policy rarely involves heroic or villainous politicians developing policy ideas with their advisers and then implementing them, or occasionally failing to. The reality is that ideas often come to policy makers from elsewhere – from think tanks, academics, or privileged and elite interest groups, many of them employing lobbyists. Politicians adapt such ideas to fit their values and their sense of what will gain them electoral success. We analyse efforts by policy groups to influence government policy, what interests they claimed to be representing, and the degree to which they succeeded and failed. The older question of interest groups (e.g., Grant, 2000) renewed by PNA (see Marsh et al., 2009) has been somewhat neglected in cultural policy research, so an engagement with PNA provides an opportunity to

---

[11] See Fawcett and Daugbjerg (2012) for a helpful discussion of the history of the two schools, and some of the disputes within and among them. There is no space to address these here.

correct this.[12] Put simply, we are trying to think seriously about how cultural policy came to take the form it did under New Labour.[13]

None of this assumes a simple relationship between groups of policy actors and outcomes. For example, 'inclusive' policy groups might still not achieve good policy outcomes, and groups acting on behalf of their own rather 'exclusive' interests might actually produce desirable democratic outcomes. Contingency has a role to play. We need a sociology of policy that recognises complexity, contingency and power. Such a sociology also needs normative underpinning, concerning what might be considered desirable and viable goals of cultural policy in a modern democratic society. Our aims in this book are to evaluate, as well as interpret and explain. This takes us to politics, and in particular to the question of how different governments, underpinned by different political ideologies (conservatism, social democracy and so on) orient their policies.

1.4   Social democratic politics and the British Labour Party

Much of the public and academic discussion of New Labour politics has concerned itself with the degree to which it represented a break with 'old' Labour, or traditional social democratic politics (e.g., Finlayson, 2003; Hay, 1999; Shaw, 2007). The crucial underlying issues are social justice, equality and freedom, and what might and should have been achieved by a party that claimed some link to the social democratic tradition of politics. For that reason, we outline our understanding of that tradition in this section. The next section addresses how social democratic parties have addressed culture, including 'the arts'.

Colin Crouch has provided one helpful definition of social democracy: 'political movements and parties that have as their historical mission the representation of [...] working people, including, prominently, trade unions, by seeking major changes in the operation of a capitalist economy and the inequalities and social damage that they

---

[12] Some studies of media policy and regulation have incorporated the question of *interests* much more successfully than cultural policy research. See, for example, Freedman (2008). Studies of copyright policy – which we would categorise as cultural policy, but many cultural policy researchers wouldn't – have been exemplary in this respect; e.g., Drahos and Braithwaite (2002) and Horten (2013).

[13] For an interesting application of policy networks to a different element of New Labour policy, see Ball and Exley (2010) on education.

perceive it to produce' (Crouch, 2013: 2). Social democratic parties such as the UK Labour Party have their roots in socialism – a political ideology and movement based on the aspiration to collective, social management of the economy. Early social democrats were committed to the overthrow of capitalism, but since the 1940s social democratic parties have sought to achieve socialism without supplanting capitalism, within existing liberal democratic institutions (Sassoon, 2014). Social democratic parties always had many aims and aspirations, including suffrage, better working conditions and an end to colonialism. In the second half of the twentieth century, as social democratic parties achieved positions in government across much of the world, the social democratic challenge was adjusted, with two particularly pronounced waves of 'revisionism', in the 1950s and the 1980s. Parties reinvented themselves as progressive pragmatists with programmes based on a 'mixed economy' of state-owned resources and markets, and as social liberals with commitments to civil rights and cultural freedoms. Rejecting communism fully in the Cold War, social democrats pursued general progressive goals of equality and solidarity, via principles of Keynesian state investment that had been developed in the 1930s to mitigate the global economic crisis. They drew support from an alliance of working-class and middle-class progressive voters.

In its own terms, the achievements of social democracy in its heyday from the 1920s to the 1980s were considerable. Across the world, social democratic parties, often formed initially by national trade union movements, as was the case in Britain, played an important part in achieving greater equality, universal suffrage and education, better working hours and labour conditions, and better health care and welfare support. Social democrats formed governments in Europe, Australasia, North America, and parts of Latin America and Asia, but their core territory was Northern Europe (Sassoon, 2014). In some places where fascism and authoritarianism prevailed, as in Spain from the 1930s to the 1970s, social democratic parties were in the forefront of efforts to resist – often in troubled alliance with the revolutionary left. Even where social democratic parties failed to achieve government, they had considerable influence on national policy through coalitions and alliances, and often achieved political domination within particular cities and regions. In many countries, centrist and even conservative governments increasingly took on social democratic policies themselves in response to the support of working-class people for social democratic agendas. All this was achieved in the face of great animosity from elements within media, state, organised religion and political rivals to the left and the right. Social democrats often suffered surveillance, violence, abuse and slander.

Social democracy's record is certainly not unblemished. It has been implicated in deeply illiberal forms of social and domestic security and foreign policy (see King, 1999). Many social democrats showed insufficient opposition to sexism, racism, homophobia, imperialism and stifling bureaucracy. Nevertheless, social democracy from the 1940s to the 1980s sought to manage economic affairs in the interests of social justice, sometimes limiting the growing powers of finance capitalism and major corporations. Social democrats made taxation more progressive, extended welfare benefits, and often played a major role in improving universal health and education provision. They played a major part in significant, though belated, decolonisation and the extension of fundamental rights and freedoms, eventually including greater recognition of the rights of women, ethnic groups and sexual minorities. They eased restrictions on cultural expression and relaxed censorship, often in the face of fierce conservative and religious opposition.

Politics is never static, and social democracy was constantly in a process of reinventing itself throughout the twentieth century. However, by the late 1970s, many social democratic parties were facing crisis. As inherent contradictions within the capitalist system unfolded in the form of a global economic crisis (Glyn, 2007), international consensus about the effectiveness of Keynesian techniques of public investment began to break down under pressure from a New Right, influenced by the neo-liberalism emerging from US university economics departments and think tanks. The traditional basis of social democratic support among the manufacturing working class was shrinking as increasingly mobile capital invested abroad to benefit from cheaper costs, and domestic labour forces withered. In the wake of a global economic downturn, New Right governments achieved power in the UK in 1979 and the USA in 1981, and, led by supposedly charismatic conservative figureheads (Margaret Thatcher and Ronald Reagan), they managed to persuade much of the media and a large number of citizens that the achievements of social democracy (including the centrist US version of the Democrats) were an aberration, and had helped to cause the economic crisis of the 1970s through profligacy and excessive government interference.

As a result, in the 1980s, social democrats across the world began to reinvent their politics for an era in which economic and other measures traditionally associated with the centre-left were considered to be impractical or unviable. When the Socialist Party finally achieved power in France in 1981, after decades of right-wing government, they tried out social democratic policies that had been widely adopted from the 1940s to the 1960s by parties in other countries, such as nationalisation and reflation (Sassoon, 2014: 534–71), and they also placed a great deal of emphasis on culture (Looseley, 1995). But they abandoned the 'French experiment' in the face of recession and major problems with inflation (Sassoon, 2014: 558–61), which was a huge blow for the 'old' model of social democracy. In the forefront of a new revisionism were governments in Australia and New Zealand, which accepted key tenets of a new neo-liberal economic orthodoxy now being pushed by newly influential international institutions such as the International Monetary Fund. In the USA, the Democratic Party, hardly social democratic but often seen as a 'sister party' by the international community of social democratic parties, shifted considerably to the right in order to capture votes lost by the shrinking of the US industrial working class. Bill Clinton was elected President in 1992 on a highly conservative and economically neo-liberal programme, with some elements of political liberalism.

It was in this context that New Labour emerged in the UK in 1994, but with particularly strong pressures forcing it to the centre and right, deriving not only from the decline of traditional sources of support for social democratic politics, but also from the electoral success of Thatcherism.[14]

1.5   Social democratic cultural policy

What goals have social democrats pursued in the realm of cultural policy? What has social democratic cultural policy looked like, and what has it achieved? A distinction is often made between two alternative tendencies or traditions that have existed among leftist and liberal critics of existing cultural arrangements, about what should be done to

---

[14] The Conservatives achieved large parliamentary majorities in the 1983 and 1987 elections over a Labour Party with social democratic agendas. The UK system sometimes allows governments considerable power and large parliamentary majorities even when they achieve a minority of the votes cast. Thatcher's two big election victories of 1983 and 1987 were achieved with around 42 per cent of the vote – less than in 1979, when her parliamentary majority was much smaller. New Labour benefited from the system, achieving huge parliamentary majorities with 43, 41 and 35 per cent, respectively, in 1997, 2001 and 2005. The system also places great emphasis on winning 'swing' constituencies – parliamentary districts where the margin of victory is relatively small.

reform culture in capitalist modernity, a distinction that we cautiously employ here. The first tradition or tendency is 'democratisation of culture' and the second 'cultural democracy' (Simpson, 1976). The former is based on an understanding of the potential of culture, understood as the highest achievements of civilisation, to enrich human experience. According to views categorised under this heading, politics, and by extension cultural policy, should aim to broaden access to that culture, to make the best available to the many, not the few, by extending the arts and heritage to those who have generally been excluded from them: notably the working class, and (in later revisions of social democratic politics) 'ethnic minorities' and the disabled. Views grouped under the 'cultural democracy' heading are based on a desire for a more thoroughgoing reform of culture and society, and on a more fundamental egalitarianism. They often include a critique of the paternalism that has underlain some formulations of cultural policy that might be categorised as 'democratisation of culture': for example, the narrow line between elevation and social control apparent in justifications for early library and museum funding. In particular, cultural democracy perspectives would see the arts as just one element in a broader definition of culture that includes everyday cultural activities. In certain versions, they pay serious attention to the working conditions of cultural producers under capitalism.

This division between two sets of ideas about cultural politics has parallels with a longstanding split in social democracy between two tendencies: what one might call its moderate and radical wings. The former is often described using terms such as 'reformist' and 'pragmatic', and has been strongly oriented towards the goals of achieving government, at national and local level; the latter has been more strongly oriented towards representing the interests and needs of working-class and other marginalised sections of society. However, the achievements of social democracy in the twentieth century in no small part rested on the always uneasy and often conflictual co-existence of these two tendencies. The same may well be true of 'democratisation of culture' and 'cultural democracy' tendencies, and it would certainly be glib to present these rival tendencies in such a way that one could simply choose one or the other. In the UK case, some would see the former 'democratisation of culture' tendency as grounded in the views of nineteenth-century poet, educationalist and commentator Matthew Arnold (1822–1888), with 'cultural democracy' deriving from the thought of the artist and campaigner William Morris (1834–1896). In such a portrayal, there is only one winner. It is easy to quote passages from Arnold that illustrate his

Victorian elitism, and to quote passages from Morris that highlight his inspiring visions of the need to integrate beauty into the everyday life of the masses. But cultural democracy perspectives have sometimes risked tipping over into a shallow populist philistinism, and, at their most well-meaning, they have sometimes neglected the contradictions in people's experiences of culture under capitalism.[15] There are important instances in many countries in which features of both tendencies or traditions have been brought together.[16] Nevertheless, the two tendencies can act as organising principles for understanding historical tensions in social democratic parties over the politics of culture.

For reasons of space, we must focus here on the British Labour Party, while making no claims that the Labour Party is typical of social democracy. We can provide only a brief historical overview. Bianchini (forthcoming, 2016) has provided the most comprehensive and authoritative treatment of Labour's relationship to cultural policy, and we draw on his account in what follows. Historians of socialism and social democracy have neglected the question of culture. Arts and culture are barely mentioned in Donald Sassoon's vast and impressive (2014) account, for example. We could find no comparative accounts of social democratic cultural policy – though Looseley (1995), Maas (2006), Duelund (2008) and others provide valuable case studies in particular countries or regions. Assessment of the degree to which the British Labour Party's cultural policies are 'typical' of social democratic cultural policies must await such a comparative account. But discussion of early engagements by socialists and social democrats with culture often point out that, compared with the Social Democrats in Germany (Waters, 1990: 2) or the Communists in Italy (Bianchini, 2016, forthcoming), British socialist parties, including the Labour Party, had very limited success in providing working-class people with an alternative to the commercial leisure and culture proliferating in the late nineteenth century and in the early twentieth century.[17]

---

[15] An example would be the community arts movement of the 1970s and 1980s, which, for all its achievements, took a view of people's engagement with commercially produced popular culture that risked reproducing the elitism that it sought to displace (see Lewis, 1990 for discussion).

[16] See, for example, Maas (2006) on the continuing influence of Emanuel Boekman on Dutch cultural policy, and the work of Jennie Lee and Hugh Jenkins as Labour arts figures in the 1960s and 1970s (see below).

[17] The historian Ross McKibbin argued in 1984 that, because of Britain's early industrialisation, its working class already had major leisure and cultural forms available before the rise of socialist and social democratic parties (as summarised by Waters, 1990: 4).

The main periods of Labour government of the UK before New Labour were from 1945 to 1951, under Clement Attlee; from 1964 to 1970 and 1974 to 1976, under Harold Wilson; and from 1976 to 1979, under James Callaghan. The Attlee government was the greatest government of egalitarian social reform in British history, yet it paid little attention to culture. The Arts Council gained its Royal Charter under Attlee, but it should not be seen as a welfare state institution, but, rather, as a product of early twentieth-century social liberalism, rooted at best in a 'democratisation of culture' model, and, particularly in the 1950s and early 1960s, acting as a deeply conservative institution that focused funding on the elite London institutions. Its predecessor institution, CEMA (Committee for the Encouragement of Music and the Arts) had supported local amateur activity as well as taking the work of elite national institutions to workplaces and leisure spaces in the regions, but these goals were abandoned in the newly established Arts Council (see Hutchison, 1982). The Attlee Labour government's only significant cultural project at the national level was the Festival of Britain of 1951, a broadly social democratic celebration of British science, engineering, design, culture, history and character, which was roundly attacked in the Conservative-dominated British press (as CEMA had been), but which was nationally very popular (Hewison, 1995: 57–65).

Any serious engagement with culture by the Labour Party in power had to wait until the appointment by Wilson of Jennie Lee as a junior minister with responsibility for the arts, within the Department of Education and Science, in 1964, and the consequent presentation by Prime Minister Wilson of a 'White Paper' consultation document to Parliament, *A Policy for the Arts: The First Steps* (1965). This reflected the increasing concern of the left in the 1960s with cultural issues, hard to ignore in the face of massive socio-cultural change. The White Paper laid the ground for a decentralisation of arts funding, based on the further development of the regional arts agencies that had started to spring up at local government level from the 1950s onwards, and an extension of definitions of the arts that included relatively 'new' media such as photography and genres such as jazz. It also laid the basis for a considerable increase in arts funding under the Labour government, and for closer links between arts policy and education – explicitly recognised as a vital battleground for greater equality in culture.[18]

---

[18] Jennie Lee's most famous contribution to British life was to establish the Open University, based on a fundamental commitment to the democratisation of education, in the face of huge opposition from the Conservative party and the Conservative press.

Labour Party cultural policy had important local dimensions as well as national ones. Although the Labour Party at the national level failed to enact legislation that would make local cultural provision mandatory, at the local government level, Labour-run councils maintained a strong commitment to cultural resources such as libraries and museums, as well as to organising public cultural events. And in the long period of Conservative national government from 1979 to 1997, significant social democratic cultural policy developments took place, particularly at the Greater London Council (GLC) controlled by Labour from 1981 until 1986, when it was abolished by the Conservative government. The GLC Labour administration was formed by those sympathetic to the socialist left, and their cultural policies represented a much more thoroughgoing engagement with inequalities in the realm of culture than anything that had been achieved by the national Labour Party. More than Jennie Lee's initiatives, they can be said to lean towards the 'cultural democracy' pole, and in doing so, they incorporated insights from the 'new social movements' of the 1960s and 1970s about the importance of cultural identity. The GLC's Arts Committee had been seen as a backwater, but with a new, young and dynamic chairman, Tony Banks, the arts and culture were given unprecedented prominence. Cultural expenditure increased considerably. There was a new emphasis on arranging and promoting cultural festivals, influenced by the European model of political festivals, and strongly linked to political campaigns for peace, jobs and racial equality. Arts funding shifted from supporting the big London arts organisations to pushing money into cultural activities of disadvantaged groups, including lesbian and gay groups, the Irish community and 'ethnic minorities'. There was a particular focus on supporting small, co-operative organisations, such as alternative bookshops, and encouraging film, video and photography. The separate Economic Policy Group at the GLC also developed a new and innovative approach to the cultural industries, emphasising the importance of distribution (though the announcement of the GLC's abolition in 1984 prevented the Cultural Industries Unit formed in that year from implementing its policies).

Many of the GLC's policies were popular but were ferociously criticised by the London and national press. The GLC and other Labour councils drawing on radical social democratic ideas were portrayed as 'the loony left'. Events at the GLC provide important context for understanding the New Labour cultural policies that are central to this book. In the wake of the 1987 general election, the Labour left were blamed by many inside and outside the party for causing defeat by tarnishing its media image. As the Labour leadership under Neil Kinnock (leader from 1983 to 1992) re-exerted the power of the party's 'moderate' and 'modernising' wing, they sought to distance themselves from the GLC's cultural democratic goals.

There are three main points to take from this very brief history of Labour's cultural policies. First, with one or two moments of exception, Labour, like most social democratic parties, generally treated culture and the arts as utterly marginal, in spite of the rich history of socialist and social democratic thought about culture and society. Second, social democratic cultural policy aimed to address inequality in the realm of culture and the arts, but there were conflicts about how this could and should be done, conflicts which might be initially summarised in terms of the 'democratisation of culture' and 'cultural democracy' poles, reflecting splits between the liberal and socialist wings of social democracy itself. Third, GLC arts policy represented a serious engagement with cultural democracy, but negative media coverage of the Labour left in general, and the defeat of the left within the Labour Party, meant that the party more than ever abandoned cultural democratic goals at the national level. As we shall see, New Labour represented a significant shift towards a much more serious engagement with culture, but on grounds that abandoned any 'cultural democracy' elements present in the Jennie Lee 'moment' of the 1960s or the 'municipal socialist' interventions of the 1980s.

1.6 New Labour and the 'Third Way': Economics, equality and governance

How might we characterise New Labour's policies in general, and their relation to previous forms of social democratic politics? Can New Labour be described as social democratic at all? New Labour's own presentation of itself was that it offered a 'Third Way', neither Old Left nor New Right, neither traditional social democracy nor conservative neo-liberalism. Even in its most intellectually respectable versions, such as those offered by leading sociologist Anthony Giddens, the Third Way concept ran the danger of setting up complex bodies of thought and practice as straw figures (see Giddens, 1999). Political scientists have generally rejected the Third Way as a piece of political PR. Instead, in Stephen Driver and Luke Martell's summary (2006: 24–7), three views of New Labour have found support among serious analysts:

- The first sees considerable continuities between New Labour and past Labour politics, in keeping with a long legacy of revisionism in the British Labour Party and among social democratic parties more generally. According to this view, social democrats have always been revisionists, and New Labour were just one example of this – a marked example, perhaps, but consistent with a longer social democratic history of readjustment.

- The second views New Labour as an 'accommodation' with the New Right and neo-liberalism, as Thatcherism mark 2.
- A third view holds the first two positions to be simplistic, and understands New Labour as a hybrid of social democratic and neo-liberal policies.

There are elements of truth in all three characterisations. New Labour represents the most pronounced decoupling of a major social democratic party from its political predecessors in recent decades, and this is one of the reasons why it is of more general interest than just the UK case, especially given that, in electoral terms at least, it was remarkably successful, achieving three considerable parliamentary majorities in consecutive national elections. New Labour could also be considered a success in other ways. They benefited from – and perhaps helped to foster – a sustained period of economic growth, which laid the basis for significant increases in public spending on certain sections of the economy, notably education and health. That economic performance turned out to be based, at least in part, on inflated land and property prices, and the under-regulated growth of a financial services sector that eventually played a major role in bringing that period of economic growth to a spectacular end with the bursting of the financial and property bubbles in 2007–2008. Nevertheless, New Labour presided over a remarkable decade of significantly rising prosperity. Box 1.1 provides an introduction to the main figures involved in New Labour, and a chronology of its electoral victories and final defeat; much of this will be familiar to British citizens who lived through the period, but we include the information mainly for non-British readers who might be hazy on the details.

Box 1.1   New Labour: The central characters and a chronology

After Margaret Thatcher – loved by some and loathed by many – resigned in 1990, Labour (under Neil Kinnock) lost a fourth successive election, in 1992, to Conservatives (under John Major) who sought to present themselves as moderate and 'compassionate', and Labour as economically and politically incompetent. The Labour leader elected in the wake of that defeat, John Smith, sought to continue Kinnock's project of moving the party towards the political centre, but when Smith died at the age of 55 in 1994, he was succeeded by Tony Blair (aged only 41), who immediately instituted a more radical rebranding (especially in terms of presentation, but also to some extent in terms of policy) of Labour as 'New Labour'. Working closely alongside him were two other key young stars of the Labour Party: Gordon Brown (aged 43 in 1994), who was essentially given charge of economic policy, continuing in his role as Shadow Chancellor of the Exchequer, and Peter Mandelson (aged 40 in 1994), who had already worked for many years with Neil Kinnock to make Labour more presentable to the voters of Britain. Blair, Brown and Mandelson were the remarkable triumvirate who shaped New Labour's radical revision of social democratic politics, and their names will appear frequently throughout this book.

The New Labour era of government began with the election of a Labour government led by Prime Minister Tony Blair in May 1997, following 18 years of Conservative rule under Margaret Thatcher (1979–1990) and John Major (1990–1997). Blair then led the Labour Party to two further election victories, in 2001 and 2005, before resigning as leader of the party and as Prime Minister in 2007. Gordon Brown, who had served as Chancellor of the Exchequer[19] since 1997, was elected by the Labour Party as its leader, and so he then became Prime Minister. The period from 1994 to 2007 had been a period of sustained economic growth and relative prosperity in the UK, but not long after Brown assumed his new role, a major economic crisis hit the UK and much of the world. Under Brown, Labour narrowly lost the 2010 general election to a coalition formed by the Conservative and Liberal Democrat parties, and he stood down as Labour leader shortly afterwards, marking the end of the New Labour project.

So New Labour represents a fascinating test case of thoroughgoing and, viewed from some angles, successful social democratic revisionism – including, as we shall see, in terms of cultural policy. What were

---

[19] The UK term for the position known in other countries as the Minister of Finance or Treasurer.

New Labour's policies, and in what ways have they been deemed controversial? For brevity's sake, we group their most distinctive policies into
three categories here: economics, equality and governance. We have no
space to address what became the most controversial and divisive element of New Labour, its foreign policy, and in particular Blair's and
others' support for the US-led invasion of Iraq, and for global restrictions
on civil liberties in the name of 'security'.[20]

1) *Economics*. New Labour rejected socialist state ownership and
embraced markets, but taking that path in itself did not represent a radical revision of social democracy. Social democratic parties had embraced
markets for decades, and most had rejected widespread state ownership
since at the least the 1970s.[21] Yet, in other respects there were significant
changes. A key element in New Labour's radical revision of social democratic politics was that it placed particularly strong emphasis on the
need for Britain to become more competitive in an increasingly global
economy, in order to maintain and nurture its prosperity and maintain
full employment (a key goal for nearly all social democratic parties).
Although terms such as 'post-industrial' and 'knowledge economy' were
used only intermittently, New Labour drew strongly on ideas that are
often characterised using those concepts: that Western economies were
changing irreversibly, and the only way they could compete in attracting capital investment was by investing in talent (or 'human capital'),
by making labour markets more 'flexible', and by encouraging greater
degrees of enterprise and innovation. According to its critics from the
social democratic left, all this meant that New Labour politicians were
too complacent about the way in which business, especially powerful
corporations, distorts markets (Hay, 1999), and about how labour market reform in the interests of competitiveness might damage people's
quality of working life (see Bunting, 2005).

2) *Equality*. Labour's articulation of its political values explicitly downplayed social democratic concerns with equality of wealth and income.
Instead, New Labour's stated aim was to combat 'social exclusion'

---

[20] New Labour's barely qualified support for US geopolitical ambitions is not out
of line with the chequered history of social democracy's foreign policies. The
government's decision to join the US-led alliance that invaded Iraq was a disaster
that permanently sullied many people's perceptions of New Labour.
[21] Although it was only in 1994 that Labour formally renounced its commitment to public ownership, articulated in Clause IV of its 1918 constitution, the
party's stated aim had long contradicted its practice. The rewritten Clause IV
was expressed in vaguer, more 'communitarian' terms: 'by the strength of our
common endeavour we achieve more than we achieve alone'.

and, in particular, exclusion from labour markets. Policy was oriented towards maximising people's life chances by increasing their assets. The higher levels of education and health spending that Labour introduced after an initial period of austerity were justified on the grounds that they allowed people to participate fully in the economy (Driver and Martell, 2006). Welfare policy was changed, in some respects in the direction of more coercive measures that would 'encourage' people back to work. Here the thinking derived not only from US neo-liberalism, but from suspicions about 'free riding' – or 'scrounging', in the parlance of the UK's deeply conservative tabloid press. In many respects, New Labour's policies were redistributive, in terms of tax and welfare policy – but the main effect was to close the gap not between the richest and the poorest, but between the poorest and middle income earners (Toynbee and Walker, 2010). The danger of this was that the wealthiest sections of society could exert a disproportionate influence on the rest, especially when their interests were embodied in the power of large corporations (see Crouch, 2013). New Labour, then, was at best ambivalent towards social democratic egalitarianism (typified by Tawney, 1931) and at worst hostile, famously exemplified by Peter Mandelson, who once told a group of US business people that he was 'intensely relaxed about people getting filthy rich', as long as they paid their taxes (Wighton, 1998).

3) *Governance.* Like all modern governments in 'Western' countries, New Labour declared itself opposed to bureaucracy, and committed to reform of the public sector. According to this model, government organisations were reconceptualised as service providers, rather than as guarantors of rights, security and other fundamental goods; and citizens were treated as consumers, or as a new hybrid: the citizen-consumer (see Needham, 2003). The model of service provision and consumption fitted with New Labour's strong and explicit embrace of markets. But, while New Labour accepted the need to regulate markets (and in this respect they were far closer to older forms of social democracy than they were to neo-liberal ideologues), they felt they could only defend sustained and higher levels of public expenditure within a mixed economy by exerting extremely tight controls over such spending, in the form of close monitoring. There had already been a nascent trend in many liberal democracies towards greater monitoring and audit of the public sector, and the Conservative administrations of Thatcher and Major were in the forefront of this and other aspects of the 'new public management' (see Chapter 3). New Labour embraced these trends with fervent enthusiasm. The result, in the words of Patrick Diamond (a former policy adviser to Gordon Brown) and political analyst Michael Kenny, was that New Labour

became associated with a style of governing, typically couched as centralist, statist and top down, which proved to be a major barrier to the fulfilment of social justice and the public interest...[T]he relentless rhetoric of political renovation became a substitute for concerted action.

(Diamond and Kenny, 2011: S5)

Meanwhile, the downplaying of people's identities as citizens in favour of consumers reflected an underlying assumption on the part of New Labour thinking that modern subjects are self-interested, with little interest in the common good (Marquand, 2004).

1.7   Assessments of New Labour, culture and the arts

As we shall see in the next chapter, all these characteristics of New Labour policy are directly relevant for understanding their cultural policies. We provide a long-overdue systematic assessment of these aspects of New Labour's approach in the realm of the arts and culture, in the context of considering what social democratic governments might and should achieve in the contemporary world (and incorporating a sociology of cultural policy as public policy, as we indicated above).

How, then, have commentators and analysts understood New Labour's record on arts and culture? Polly Toynbee, one of the UK's leading journalists and a critical supporter of New Labour, wrote in *The Guardian* newspaper in 2011 that 'Labour brought a golden era to the arts after two decades of drought' (Toynbee, 2011). She praised increases in arts funding, the introduction of free admissions to national museums and galleries, the Creative Partnerships initiative, the contribution of the creative industries to the economy, and a change in the ecology of the arts. Toynbee recognised that the class, ethnic and age composition for audiences of the arts remained white, middle class, and middle aged. But the obligations to widen participation, Toynbee claimed, had brought new energy. She contrasted the flourishing of arts and culture under New Labour with the problematic emphasis on sponsorship in the post-2010 Conservative-led coalition's approach to the arts.

Some academics have also been favourably disposed towards New Labour's cultural policies. Researchers associated with the Creative Industries Faculty at Queensland University of Technology (QUT) have seen the UK government's embrace of the creative industries concept as a breakthrough, which allowed cultural policy to incorporate recognition of the realities of globalisation and convergence, and to move beyond the elitism of old arts-centred models. For example, Terry Flew has written approvingly that the 'mapping of the UK creative industries played a critical formative role in establishing an international policy discourse for what the creative industries are, how to define them, and what their wider significance constitutes' (Flew, 2012: 10). His colleague Stuart Cunningham (2007) saw the gap between the remarkable enthusiasm with which the creative industries concept had been taken up across much of the world and academic criticism of the idea (see below) as evidence of a longstanding and deleterious fracture between policy and critique. Cunningham had little time for the critiques, and saw the international spread of the idea as a sign of policy dynamism and fecundity, with non-Anglophone countries bending the concept even further towards progressive ends.

Even conservative newspapers such as *The Economist* have provided favourable appraisals of New Labour's record on arts and culture. A February 2012 piece described 'a golden age of state subsidies' under New Labour. Such a phrase is usually intended negatively when coming from a right-wing source such as *The Economist*, but the paper praised the scrapping of entrance fees and the rejuvenation of regional theatres and orchestras, and the positive effects of such subsidy on the commercial creative industries.

Leading arts figures have also been very positive about New Labour's record on culture. Many were understandably quick to criticise funding reverses during Labour's reign, but National Theatre Director Nicholas Hytner was not untypical in a piece he wrote for *The Observer* in 2003: 'When I was appointed', wrote Hytner, 'I assumed that one of my jobs would be periodically to lay into the Government for its craven under-funding of the performing arts.... It is therefore with a twinge of disappointment that I am forced to break with tradition and recognise the seriousness with which the Department of Culture has been taking our cultural life' (Hytner, 2003).

However, Hytner (at times a strong critic of arts policy practice, especially later Arts Council strategy) was also not unusual in decrying 'a relentless and exclusive focus on the nature of our audience' and 'the target-driven culture' afflicting not only education but, increasingly, the arts. Such objections to New Labour's attempts to broaden and diversify audiences can be read in at least two ways: as a culturally conservative attempt to protect the privileges of the cultural elite; or as a genuine effort to protect artistic creativity against managerialism, bureaucracy and governmental interference. In some criticisms of

New Labour's record on arts and culture, there is some prevarication over the fundamental values underlying critique, and we aim to explore those underlying normative values more fully than in previous research. Central to this will be cultural policy dilemmas concerning excellence and access (see Section 1.2) that New Labour claimed to have transcended, and questions concerning the appropriate relationship between economic and cultural goals.

The most critical assessments of New Labour's cultural policies have come from academics on the Marxist and social democratic left. Jim McGuigan (2005), for example, saw New Labour's cultural policies as evidence of their capitulation to neo-liberalism and a reflection of how an all-pervasive 'market-oriented mentality' (229) in modern societies had put into question the role of cultural policy in providing even a 'modest counterweight' to commercial culture (235). McGuigan identified three main ways in which contemporary cultural policy, especially that of New Labour, might be characterised as neo-liberal. These were as follows:

- the increasing corporate sponsorship of culture that might previously have been funded by public subsidy;
- an increasing emphasis on running public sector cultural institutions as though they were private businesses;
- a shift in the prevailing rationale for cultural policy, away from culture, and towards economic and social goals: 'competitiveness and regeneration' (238) and 'an implausible palliative to exclusion and poverty' (238).

These will be prevailing themes in what follows.

Others have added their critical voices to McGuigan's, and we discuss their perspectives at various points in what follows (among others, see Belfiore, 2004; Gray, 2007; Newsinger, 2012). More recently, in his book *Cultural Capital*, Robert Hewison (2014) has written a sustained polemic against New Labour's cultural policies and the use of culture in their own self-presentation, accusing the party and its politicians of all manner of sins, including incompetence, inconsistency, wastefulness, philistine instrumentalism, and shortening the arm's length principle of autonomous funding of the arts. Yet, oddly, the third paragraph of Hewison's book contains a list of Labour's achievements that echoes those of sympathetic commentators such as Toynbee, and of Labour politicians (see next chapter). 'In 1997', writes Hewison, 'the British cultural world had been in a decayed and fractious state, stale and starved of public funding. By the time Blair's successor Gordon Brown left office, in May 2010, the scene was transformed.' Hewison's very readable insider narrative then seems to abandon any recognition of such achievements, and the overwhelming impression of the book is that there were no redeeming features in anything New Labour did. We think Labour's record is more complex than that, and we shall explain why in this book – while endorsing and elaborating upon Hewison's many entertaining and scathing verdicts.

1.8   Outline of the book and research questions

This book seeks to address four main questions. The first concerns continuity and change. Commentators have seen New Labour's cultural policies as marking a very strong break with preceding conservative and social democratic policies, while some have seen them as inheriting the neo-liberal conservatism of Thatcherism. *To what extent and in what ways did New Labour's cultural policies maintain continuity with previous cultural policy regimes, and to what extent and in what ways did they transform them?* This issue is tied to further questions involving explanation and evaluation. In terms of explanation, *how did the various policy groups articulate the interests of the institutions and ideologies they represented?* In terms of evaluation, our key question is simply *how should we assess New Labour's cultural policies?* As we have hopefully made clear, the key context for us in making such an assessment is social democracy's historical project of limiting the damaging effects of capitalism through state action. So a fourth research question is closely linked. *To what extent did New Labour abandon key values of social democratic cultural policy, and to what extent did it valuably reinvent them for new times?* These four key research questions are summarised in Box 1.2.

Box 1.2   The research questions

1. To what extent and in what ways did New Labour's cultural policies maintain continuity with previous cultural policy regimes, and to what extent and in what ways did they transform them? (Continuity and change)
2. How did the various policy groups articulate the interests of the institutions and ideologies they represented? (Explanation)

Box 1.2   (Continued)

3. How should we assess New Labour's cultural policies? (Evaluation)
4. To what extent did New Labour abandon key values of social democratic cultural policy, and to what extent did it valuably reinvent them for new times? (Evaluation)

Here is how we address these research questions in what follows. Chapter 2 begins by introducing New Labour's cultural policies and their place within New Labour's efforts to reform social democracy, as outlined above. It does so via analysis of a speech by Tony Blair, in which he made a series of claims about his government's record on arts and culture. Then, as a basis for our sociology of cultural policy formation, we lay out the main collective policy groups (sets of organisations and institutions) involved in cultural policy making in the UK during the period from 1994 to 2010. We claim that the main way in which New Labour's policies were substantially different from its predecessors was that it took much more seriously the interests of the cultural industries – and this was signalled in its sustained use of the 'creative industries' concept. So the next stage in our introduction of New Labour's policies is to show how that concept was developed by a small faction with close links to the Labour Party and the film industry. We go on to examine the intellectual roots of New Labour's cultural policies, emphasising the importance of information society/knowledge economy thinking, the notion of urban regeneration, and cultural postmodernism. As we show, however, actual cultural policies (rather than mere statements of intent) emerged only slowly during the first term of New Labour's first term in power, under Chris Smith, the Secretary of State for Culture, Media and Sport from 1997 to 2001.[22] We show that much of what happened – including a renaming of the department – was oriented towards

---

[22] 'Secretary of State' is the term used in the UK for some of the Cabinet ministers who head government departments. They share responsibility for those departments with 'junior ministers' who have particular remits – for example, in the case of the relevant UK department, the arts, or sport and tourism. We use the term 'Culture Secretary' as an abbreviation for the senior position – or 'Heritage Secretary' when referring to arrangements before the departmental name change of mid-1997 (see Chapter 2) – and 'minister' for the more junior role.

increasing the 'weight' of the Culture Department within government, in order to pursue a set of objectives, which we then analyse in some detail, showing how they were intended to appeal to different elements in government and different policy groups. We also discuss the early resistance that New Labour encountered from the powerful arts lobby and popular musicians.

By 2000, it was possible to speak meaningfully of a set of policies, and chapters 3–7 analyse what we consider to be the most important of these policies as they evolved over the next decade. Chapter 3 discusses New Labour's arts policies. We address increases in funding, including issues surrounding the use of lottery funding, sponsorship and philanthropy, and the problems surrounding so-called 'flagship' building projects. An important element of the discussion is New Labour's introduction of subsidies to support compulsory free admission to the permanent collections of national museums and galleries. This was the central plank of New Labour's avowed aim of opening up access to the arts to broader groups of people. This was by no means a novel goal of cultural policy, but New Labour pursued it assiduously. There were three problems surrounding New Labour's arts policies, however. One was that their efforts to shift access seem to have been only partially successful – and here we encounter, perhaps, the limits of what arts policy alone can achieve with regard to broadening audiences for the arts, at least in the short and medium term. The second – and here we return to our sociology of policy making – was that New Labour, as we explained above, was a political project that sought to reform the public sector on neo-liberal grounds, while providing greater levels of public funding. Many arts organisations and workers felt they paid a high price for greater funding by being subjected to sets of targets, audit and, in general, instruments of 'new public management', and this caused considerable resentment and conflict. The third was that many felt that New Labour over-emphasised the economic and social benefits of the arts over other 'cultural' values.

Chapter 4 addresses 'creative industries' policy at the national level. This is often viewed as the aspect of cultural policy most strongly associated with New Labour. We identify and analyse three aspects of national policy that might be labelled 'creative industries'. These are film policy, copyright policy and the increasing use of the term 'creative economy' rather than 'creative industries', which reflected the increasing importance of digitalisation and information technology in government cultural agendas. We argue that, in different ways, the first two of these aspects of cultural policy involve considerable novelty in relation to previous cultural policy, partly through the much greater emphasis on the interests of the cultural industries – though the copyright policy case provides some qualification to this, because of the influence of the newly powerful IT industries. The case of the Creative Economy programme, and the *Creative Britain* document that resulted from it, demonstrates the continuing emptiness of the creative industries concept in its rebranded form, and also its neglect of problematic working conditions in the sector. All of these developments represent a significant shift away from cultural policies in the social democratic tradition.

Chapter 5 turns its attention to New Labour's cultural policies at the regional or local level. The pursuit of greater levels of equality between different regions is a vital constituent of social democratic policy, and we examine how New Labour tried to pursue that goal in the realm of culture, paying particular attention to the marked use of 'policy attachment' here. A crucial context is New Labour's regional economic development policies, based on the problematic Regional Development Agencies, which quickly adopted 'creative industries' policies. But, following an early phase of autonomy, the focus of these policies and the associated agencies changed. There was an increasing focus on the neo-liberal concept of industry 'clusters'. There were also complex and shifting governance arrangements, and a shift from an, at least partially, social-driven set of goals to primarily economic ones, and these factors, along with the failure of New Labour's attempts to introduce regional assemblies, limited the effectiveness of regional creative industries strategies. Meanwhile, the regional strategies pursued by arts agencies achieved some significant regeneration, but did little to affect overall cultural inequalities.

Chapter 6 addresses two novel policy innovations, Creative Partnerships and the National Endowment of Science, Technology and Arts (Nesta), both of which allow further discussion of the relations between economic, cultural and social goals in contemporary cultural policy. These initiatives also permit us to consider relations between cultural policy and two other branches of public policy: education and science/technology. The two case studies demonstrate ways in which New Labour tried to combine policies that were social democratic in their efforts to increase equality of access with ones that were more economically focused.

Chapter 7 addresses the other core area of 'traditional' cultural policy besides the arts: heritage. New Labour downplayed their interest in this sector in order to emphasise their modernising intent and to differentiate themselves from the preceding Conservative government, which had made heritage central to its cultural policies. This led to criticisms of New Labour from the heritage sector, and accusations of underfunding. Nevertheless, there are reasons to think that heritage did well during the New Labour period, and certainly the sector took on issues of 'access' and 'diversity' based on criticisms of heritage and, indeed, paternalist cultural policy more generally. Yet there are reasons to think that this, too, arose for reasons somewhat independent of cultural policy, and in any case these policies met with limited success. A main theme is the limits of cultural policy, and the need to address other explanatory aspects of social change beyond politics.

Chapter 8 combines a brief account of what happened to UK cultural policy after New Labour lost power in 2010 with conclusions derived from the study as a whole. Some critics of New Labour from the left came to view them a little more favourably once the succeeding Conservative–Liberal Democrat government had been in power for a few years. Drawing on that context, the chapter provides an overall assessment of New Labour and summarises the implications of the book for understanding New Labour, social democratic politics, public policy and cultural policy.

2
New Labour, Culture and Creativity

2.1 New Labour's cultural policies introduced: Blair's retrospect

In 2007, towards the end of his time as UK Prime Minister, Tony Blair gave a speech at the Tate Modern gallery in London to representatives of the UK arts world – senior creative personnel and administrators in the main UK arts institutions, and those involved in the various bodies that support and lobby on behalf of them. His speech was also, of course, aimed beyond these figures, to those interested in the arts and culture who would hear about the speech via the media. Blair was self-consciously seeking to shape future histories of New Labour's record on the arts and culture. The speech offers a helpful summary of what Blair and others in government (including at the Department for Culture, Media and Sport (DCMS), the ministry with responsibility for culture) saw as the central arts and culture achievements of New Labour.[1]

The Tate Modern setting symbolised aspects of contemporary British culture with which Blair and his government wished to associate themselves: the rising popularity of the arts, and the rising status of London and Britain in the international arts world. Blair skilfully anticipated potential charges of claiming the credit for the artistic and cultural success of others. He was there, he said, to express gratitude rather than 'to advertise the success of government'. He heaped praise on his listeners, thanking them for their 'creativity'. Nevertheless, the then Prime

---

[1] The speech as released to the press in advance of its delivery (there is no recording or transcript of the actual spoken version, as far as we are aware) is too long to quote in full here, but at the time of this writing it is available via the *Guardian's* website: see Blair (2007).

Minister declared, 'I don't think you could have done it, or at least not so easily without a change in government policy.' Crucially, Blair claimed that New Labour had resolved the supposedly false dilemma between 'access' and 'excellence' that had haunted cultural policy since the origins of significant state arts funding in the mid-twentieth century (see Chapter 1). For Blair, the US model of cultural policy had prioritised access, seeing culture as 'a private activity' but one that should reach as many people as possible via the market. The European model of cultural policy, by contrast, pursued excellence by acting as though 'high art can only be protected by insulation from the market'. New Labour's 'distinctively British' model was one of a mixed economy, and this had enabled the UK to get the best of both worlds: 'We have deepened our culture, extended its reach, with at the same time no compromise on quality, indeed rather the opposite.'[2]

Blair's list of policies and achievements was a long one, and he began with questions of access to the arts and culture.

- The government had introduced policies that kept ticket prices down and in the case of nationally funded museums, had ensured free admissions.
- This had resulted in a huge surge in popularity for the arts and culture, manifest in the *History Matters* heritage campaign of 2006, huge increases in attendance at the seven major regional theatres, and a rise of 30 million in visits to national museums.
- This surge in arts consumption, according to Blair, was not confined to the educated middle class, however – free admissions had increased museum visits by lower socio-economic groups by 30 per cent between 2002–2003 and 2004–2005, and funding had brought about a boom in attendance in regional theatres. The Creative Partnerships initiative had brought arts to schools in deprived areas.
- The government-funded People's Network had connected thousands of libraries to the internet via broadband, and museums had made their collections accessible online.

Blair then turned to the *economic* contribution of the arts and creative industries – the latter a key term in New Labour cultural policy, as we saw in Chapter 1. The creative industries had grown rapidly, Blair

---

[2] The 'we' is ambiguous here: it is not clear whether it refers to the UK, the arts world and government, or the government alone. See Fairclough (2000) on this and other aspects of New Labour's use of language.

claimed, faster than the economy as a whole, and now employed almost 2 million people. Exports from the arts sector contributed £13 billion to the balance of trade in 2004. The music, advertising, publishing and broadcasting industries had all provided economic benefits, and were world-renowned. There were enormous economic gains, too, in tourism – seven of the ten most popular tourist attractions in the UK were government-sponsored museums and galleries, and 28 per cent of visitors to the London theatre came from overseas.

Blair's speech provides a good initial way of understanding how New Labour's arts and culture policies fitted more generally with its underlying policies and philosophies, as we outlined them in Chapter 1, because it shows how central a particular understanding of economic life was to New Labour's cultural policies. In Blair's Third Way account, New Labour had implemented cultural policies that were neither neo-liberal (the US) nor outmodedly social democratic (Europe), but based on a successful 'mixed economy' of public and private. In fact, as we discussed in Chapter 1, social democrats had long been thorough believers in a mixed economy (although left social democrats favoured large-scale nationalisation). But domains such as education and health were seen by social democrats as primarily a matter of state management and government, in the face of conservative opposition. New Labour were much less ambivalent than their Labour and social democratic forebears about the effects of markets on such domains, and sought, as policy makers were increasingly tending to do in an era of neo-liberalism, to justify public expenditure on them in terms of their potential contribution to a more internationally competitive and therefore prosperous Britain. Blair's speech shows this thinking being applied to the arts and culture, apparent in the way in which the second half of its case for policy success is built entirely on the economic contribution of the arts and culture to the UK. This was in line with something that New Labour had inherited not only from Thatcherite Conservative cultural policy, but also from international trends: an increasing tendency to justify public expenditure on arts and culture in terms of economic rewards. This is a key theme in the history of New Labour's cultural policies, and Blair's list of the contributions to the economy of industries such as music, publishing, advertising and so on reflects the centrality of the creative industries idea in New Labour's cultural policy – an issue we explore later in this chapter and in Chapter 4.

But the speech also provides an important indication of why New Labour revised cultural policy to include the creative industries, and, indeed, of why they felt it necessary to support the arts. Blair opened his speech by claiming that from the beginning of his time as Labour leader, he had made the arts and culture part of the 'core script' of New Labour, more than just 'an add on, a valued bit of fun when the serious business of government was done' (see also Box 2.1 on 'Cool Britannia'). The arts and culture, he said, were central to 'a modern nation like Britain'. The 'utterly critical' reason Blair gave is worth quoting in full:

> My argument is this. A country like Britain today survives and prospers by the talent and ability of its people. Human capital is key. The more it is developed, the better we are. Modern goods and services require high value added input. Some of it comes from technology or financial capital – both instantly transferable. Much of it comes from people – their ability to innovate, to think anew, to be creative. Such people are broad-minded: they thrive on curiosity about the next idea; they welcome the challenge of an open world. Such breadth of mind is enormously enhanced by interaction with art and culture. The whole process of stimulation through plays, books, films, works of art; the delight in design, in architecture, in crafts: all of this enlarges a country's capacity to be reflective, interested and bold. Dynamism in arts and culture creates dynamism in a nation. So when more children get access to the joy of art, it is not the art alone that they learn; it is the art of living, thinking and creating. They may never be, probably won't ever be, an artist or a dancer or a designer, but in whatever job, in whichever walk of life, they will carry an idea that is not just about the buying and selling, but about what makes the ordinary special. When people on low incomes can visit museums free of charge, and see great works of art, they take something of the inspiration with them. A nation that cares about art will not just be a better nation. In the early 21st Century it will be a more successful one.
>
> (Blair, 2007)

There is a concern here with the way in which arts and culture can enhance lives; an emphasis on 'people' and how they can be stimulated and made more open-minded and curious; and an acknowledgment that the value of arts and culture transcends 'buying and selling'. In all this, Blair and his speechwriter(s) were adeptly showing his sympathy with the humanist values of the audience, and with any concerns they had that New Labour might be in danger of abandoning such values for those of commerce and the market. Yet this 'soft' language was framed by a much stronger emphasis on the role that arts and culture can play in a nation's prosperity and success. And underpinning Blair's (and New Labour's) understanding of that role is the idea, apparent here in the reference to 'human capital', that governments, especially of 'post-industrial' countries where labour costs are higher, can most effectively invest public expenditure by developing knowledge and talent that generate 'high-value' input.

In fact, 'human capital' was only one of a number of concepts and theoretical traditions that New Labour drew upon in order to provide intellectual underpinning for its revision of cultural policy, and related areas of policy such as education. A useful, though not quite adequate, general term for this set of ideas is 'knowledge economy' (or 'information society') thinking, and we shall come back to this idea later in this chapter, and at various points throughout our account. We shall also see that an emphasis on 'creativity' was an important element in New Labour's use of knowledge economy thinking in the realm of cultural policy.

Box 2.1   Cool Britannia

Blair's Tate Modern speech referred to the arts and culture as 'more than an add on, a valued bit of fun when the serious business of government was done'. In the use of the word 'fun' here, there is a subtle allusion to political and cultural histories with which his entire audience would have been familiar: 'the Ministry of Fun' was a supposedly humorous and dismissive term for the UK's first Culture Ministry (revealingly titled the Department of National Heritage (DNH) until New Labour came to power), set up under the previous UK Conservative government in 1992. Blair's speech, instead, stressed the seriousness of New Labour's approach to the arts and culture. Early in its period of government, New Labour had been subjected to criticisms, from the political left and right, that its engagement with arts and culture was frivolous. New Labour, and Blair in particular, were accused of chasing the superficial glamour of celebrity, rather than pursuing the earnest business of statehood. For many critics, this was symbolised by pictures of Tony Blair interacting with the guitarist and songwriter Noel Gallagher, then of the rock band Oasis, at a reception hosted by Blair at the Prime Minister's official residence (10 Downing Street, London) in July 1997 (see Figure 2.1). Show this image to British people who were politically and culturally conscious in the late

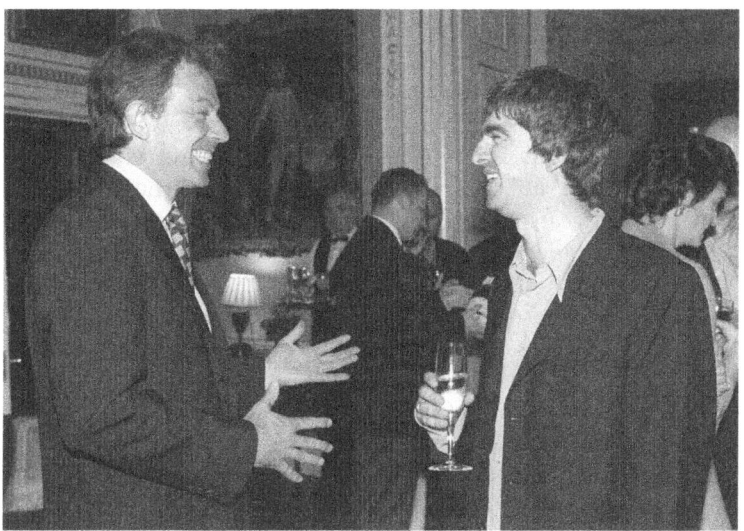

Figure 2.1   Tony Blair and Noel Gallagher at 10 Downing Street

1990s, and many of them will utter the words 'Cool Britannia'. This term was a pun on 'Rule, Britannia!', a patriotic song from the eighteenth century of which more or less every British person is aware.

'Cool Britannia' was initially used by the UK media to refer to a recovery by the UK of its formerly prominent place in global popular culture, manifested in the international success of British art, British rock and pop, film and fashion, and its post-rave club scene. A key moment was a *Newsweek* magazine cover of November 1996 ('London Rules – Inside the World's Coolest City'). In the wake of this, the term 'Cool Britannia' began to be widely used by the media.[3] The term came to be associated with New Labour, but actually it was the DNH under the Conservatives that issued a series of press releases using the phrase in 1996–1997, and

---

[3] Among hundreds of examples, see the *Independent* newspaper, 12 November 1996: 'Cool Britannia: Major Claims the Credit' (Bevins, 1996). The phrase may have been inspired by a new flavour of Ben and Jerry's ice cream that had appeared with that name early in 1996.

Box 2.1 (Continued)

both Labour and the Conservatives were keen to rebrand British national identity (see Leonard, 1997).[4] In fact, New Labour seemed to do everything possible to dissociate themselves from the term 'Cool Britannia' after taking office. Nevertheless, the term stuck to them for years, a piece of banal and lazy journalism, often repeated by academics.

There are many things to criticise about New Labour's cultural policies, and one of them might be their creation of pseudo-consultative bodies such as the Creative Industries Task Force – which included Alan McGee, the head of Oasis's record label. But the term 'Cool Britannia' is largely irrelevant to any meaningful consideration of New Labour's achievements and failures, other than helping to explain why, after their initial trumpeting of their support for arts and culture, New Labour began to be much quieter about this aspect of their policies. Blair's speech at Tate Modern was his first about the arts and culture as Prime Minister, and he was rarely pictured with entertainment celebrities after the backlash against his and other New Labour figures' early engagement with that world. New Labour was actually much more interested in courting executives and senior managers of creative industry businesses and older, established individuals, rather than younger musicians, who tended to say the wrong things, such as Damon Albarn, who was highly critical of Labour's education and welfare policies. In this respect, as we shall see, Sir David Puttnam (later Lord Puttnam), a film producer and former head of a major Hollywood studio, was far more representative of New Labour's arts and culture networks than Noel Gallagher.

---

[4] These were witheringly listed by Culture Secretary Chris Smith in a debate on culture, media and sport in the House of Commons on 29 July 1998. Robert Hewison (2014: 36) claims in his polemical attack on New Labour's relationship to arts and culture (Chapter 2 is entitled 'Cool Britannia') that Smith 'declared that "Cool Britannia is here to stay"', in a piece Smith wrote for *The Times* on the day that New Labour renamed the Department of National Heritage the Department for Culture, Media and Sport (Smith,1997). But that phrase appears to be a sub-heading inserted by a *Times* sub-editor, rather than anything Smith wrote.

A second way in which Blair's speech shows how arts and culture fitted with New Labour's general policy agenda is apparent in Blair's discussion of audiences for the arts and heritage, where he places much emphasis on inclusion and access. Post-war social democratic governments had shown themselves to be more willing to subsidise the arts than centrist and conservative parties.[5] But this had always presented a problem: how could social democracy, committed as it was to reducing inequality, justify the subsidy of practices primarily associated with the better-off and more educated sections of society? This led to highly ambivalent relationships between the left and arts funding in Britain and elsewhere (Lewis, 1990). There were two key responses from the left, deriving from some of the cultural policy themes that we delineated in Section 1.2. One response was to tie funding to policies aimed at democratising access to the arts, beyond the relatively privileged groups that tended to produce and consume it (*greater equality in access to the arts*). Another, rather different, response was to encourage artistic activity that might be argued to have an effect on social inequalities in general (*arts as a means to promote greater social equality*). New Labour embedded such concerns in its cultural policies. But it departed from previous social democratic policy by introducing systems of targets and monitoring that derived from a post-Thatcherite suspicion of – indeed, antagonism towards – the public sector. What's more, as we shall see, key New Labour thinkers were influenced by cultural postmodernism: systems of thought in which the cultural hierarchies associated with modernist and other supposedly elitist notions of cultural value, where classical and modernist culture were seen as superior to popular or mass culture, were outmoded and/or undemocratic.

One consequence of this New Labour mixture of postmodern scepticism about the cultural value of the arts with suspicion of the public sector is apparent in the many statistics that Blair littered throughout his speech. There's nothing unusual in politicians using statistics to vaunt their performance, but the level of detail here reflected New Labour's concern with the kind of performance measurement we referred to in

---

[5] In the British case, arts expenditure increased in real terms under all governments from 1945 to the 1990s. But, as Robert Hewison (1995: 242–65) showed, the increases of the 1980s were insufficient to keep pace with the increasing demand for arts and heritage, and there were regular crises of funding in the sector. What's more, prominent English Conservatives often spoke out against there being any arts funding at all, and even senior politicians such as Richard Luce, Arts Minister from 1985 to 1990, regularly warned of the need to adjust to new economic and political realities, and of the need to get rid of a 'welfare state mentality' in the arts.

Chapter 1. Professionals in the health, education and welfare sectors were vexed by such mechanisms, and saw them as threats to their professional autonomy. As we shall see in Chapter 3, arts and cultural workers (whether creative practitioners or administrators) were also concerned, and saw such interventions as potentially infringing limits on state interference in arts and culture. The distinctive way in which the UK has managed the problem of state interference in culture is via 'the arm's length principle', by which key organisations such as the Arts Council(s) and the BBC operate semi-autonomously under mechanisms such as Royal Charters, with control only indirectly imposed via state appointments to their boards; similar mechanisms also operate in the fields of education, science and so on. New public management techniques of targets, monitoring and audit of arts and culture potentially shortened the 'arm's length'.[6] Cultural organisations and workers often felt that such mechanisms created bureaucratic requirements that distracted them from pursuing core cultural goals regarding artistic innovation, stimulation and enrichment.

A third and final element in Blair's speech is worth noting briefly here, concerning urban regeneration and social inclusion. In laying out the economic success of New Labour's cultural policies, Blair spoke of how cultural regeneration had created thousands of jobs and huge investment in various cities, which had been regenerated by a newly thriving cultural life, achieved by the 'interaction of public and private finance'. We return below to regeneration and to the way New Labour saw the relations between public and private.

2.2   Cultural policy: The key policy groups and their interests

Although his speech helps locate New Labour's cultural policies within the strategy and language of New Labour more generally, Tony Blair did not invent New Labour's cultural policies. He did not even provide much input into their development. Beyond discussions of the general direction of travel, he would have had little time for such an electorally insignificant area of policy. New Labour's cultural policies emerged, as most policy ideas do, from a mixture of existing policies

---

[6] For the then Arts Council Chairman Christopher Frayling (2005: 18), by the time New Labour had been in office for a few years, the arm was becoming very short, 'almost Venus de Milo length'. On the 'arm's length' principle, first articulated for the arts in the 1970s, but a longstanding feature of British government, see Gray (2000) and Hewison (1995, 2014), among many others.

(custom and tradition play a significant role) and networks of specialists concerned with the generation and dissemination of new thinking. In the remainder of this chapter, we outline the early formation of New Labour's cultural policies, and their early strategy on entering into government, using an approach consistent with the policy networks literature in political science that we introduced in Chapter 1 (Fawcett and Daugbjerg, 2012; Marsh, 2011; Marsh and Rhodes, 1992; Rhodes, 2007). We explained that this research often focuses on the relationship between interest groups and government departments, often emphasising a historical shift in policy making in the late twentieth century from a strong central state to a wider range of partnerships, networks and para-state bodies.[7] This complexity is an important part of our story, but our concern is more with the question of whose interests were being represented by whom, and the constraints under which New Labour politicians felt they were acting. A key issue here is New Labour's attempts to remould social democracy, and how their 'Third Way' approach made them more accommodating than previous administrations to a rethinking of cultural policy that brought economic growth benefits to the fore. Insofar as New Labour's cultural policies were innovative, this is where the principal innovation lay (Figure 2.2).

Figure 2.2 introduces the key policy groups – institutions and organisations – involved in cultural policy in the UK between the early 1990s and 2010. The key political groups are in the middle, and there are five other categories of groups around them representing different and often competing sets of interests. The set of key political actors comprises government, opposition parties and parliament, with the government broken down into the main departments that shape or enact cultural policy.[8] The departments involve the work of ministers, and increasingly of special political advisers (SPADs for short) tied to the party of government, but also, of course, civil servants whose role is to implement government policies.

---

[7] Less work has been done on policy networks informing political parties when they are in opposition, when resources are smaller. Our analysis examines this moment – particularly relevant in cases such as those of New Labour, where there was a very strong sense that New Labour were likely to win the 1997 general election and form the next government.

[8] In this section, where the aim is to establish a more general picture of cultural policy groups, we have called these departments Culture, Education, Business and the Treasury for short. In fact, in the UK, the names of the relevant departments, apart from the Treasury, changed during the 1994–2010 period that we are mainly concerned with, and in the remainder of the book we have tried to use whichever term was current at the time of any events being described.

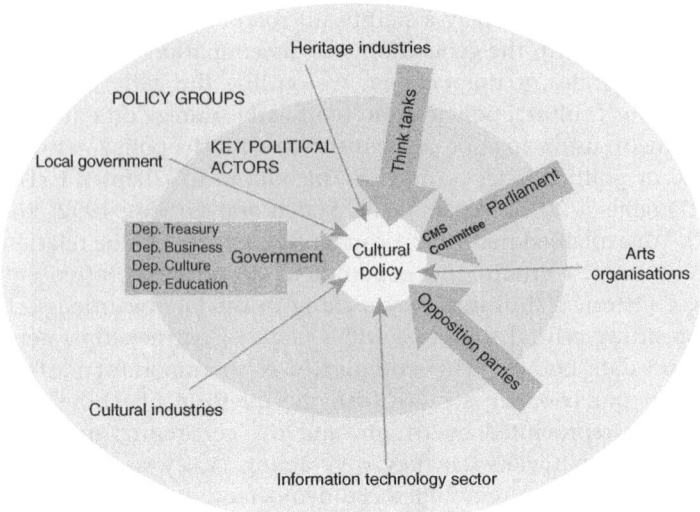

Figure 2.2   Policy groups and political actors in cultural policy

In seeking to differentiate its policies from those of rivals, each political party in a modern democracy draws on advice from various actors who represent the interests of relevant groups with sufficient power to cause trouble for the politicians if their voices are not heeded. In many respects, those involved in any policy actor grouping may well have rather divergent interests. What matters is that they come together sufficiently on matters of shared interest, so that they will represent themselves in a coherent or convincing way to politicians and policy makers. Some of these interest groups provide funding for parties, if those parties are deemed to be sufficiently supportive. In return for incorporating the interests of these actors into policy, parties and government gain legitimation from their contact with them, or they save time and energy as a result of winning compliance and/or media silence. In all this, the media are an absolutely vital forum in which these groups represent their interests in situations where there is conflict and dissensus, if negotiations break down, or as a way of strengthening their hands in such negotiations (see Koch-Baumgarten and Voltmer, 2010).[9]

---

[9] In some areas of policy – including copyright, but also in media policy – the media, or sections of them, powerfully advocate their own interests. This is why media policy is such a difficult and controversial terrain of government.

The five main policy groups seeking the eyes and ears of government and opposition parties during the period under discussion were as follows.

Arts organisations seek greater amounts of subsidy, or to be released from obligations attached to subsidy that raise their administrative and other costs. The main recipients of funding in England are the big national institutions, which receive their money direct from the DCMS (in the case of the big, mainly London-based museums and galleries) or via the Arts Council of England (in the case of performing arts institutions such as the Royal Opera House, the National Theatre, the major orchestras and so on), on the basis of the 'arm's length' principle.[10] Such organisations lobby collectively for greater arts funding, and, individually and in packs, for slices of the cake. The heads of these institutions become minor media arts celebrities, joining prominent artists as significant players in drawing more money to the arts, and often more money to the big institutions. Lobbying organisations, such as the National Campaign for the Arts (which was particularly active in the late 1990s), provide a forum. The arts funding bodies of the four constituent nations of the UK (currently the Arts Councils of England, Wales and Northern Ireland, plus Creative Scotland) also make representations to government about the level of arts funding.

Similarly, *heritage organisations* compete with each other, but also share an interest in increasing the overall pot. A non-departmental public body, English Heritage, both distributes funding and acts as an advocate for greater funding, and for heritage policy that fits with the sector's general needs. Meanwhile, the Heritage Alliance (formerly Heritage Link) is the biggest coalition of 'independent' or private heritage interests in England.

The cultural industries, based on the creation and circulation of cultural products, seek to work with government to gain subsidies of various kinds, and to ensure forms of legislation and regulation that do not damage their efforts to make profit. They are represented most powerfully by associations that bring together the businesses within a particular industry, such as recording, film and television. Sometimes there are separate groupings of large corporations and small companies, reflecting the fact that there are different interests at work within the sector. Nearly all cultural industries want longer, stronger, stricter copyright regulations, as

---

[10] In Scotland, the Scottish government funds some major national organisations directly, while others were funded through the Scottish Arts Council (now renamed Creative Scotland after a merger with Scottish Screen).

ownership of copyright is the core of their business, because it constitutes the main means to provide artificial scarcity (see Hesmondhalgh, 2013a: 26–33). In this book, we use the term 'cultural industries' to differentiate this policy group more clearly from the concept of creative industries *policy* as developed by the New Labour government.

A fourth policy group comprises sub-national or *local government*. In the UK case, this refers to representatives of the nations and regions beyond London, who, through the Local Government Association, pursue the need for funding from central government to maintain local services and, increasingly important from the 1980s on, to provide the means to achieve 'regeneration' via culture. Prominent city council executives provide an important media voice.

A fifth and powerful policy group entered the cultural policy field from the late 1990s on: *the information technology sector*, especially computer software companies, some of which have formidable lobbying capabilities in themselves (such as Google and Facebook), but which are also represented through trade bodies, such as the UK IT Association (UKITA). This policy group has tended to be much more concerned with other dimensions of policy that normally fall under business departments. It is important for our story because copyright is ultimately a matter of cultural policy. The most vital issue affecting cultural industries concerns copyright legislation and practice. In the UK, New Labour included 'creative industries' in the remit of the Culture Department, but copyright policy was determined elsewhere, notably in the Treasury and Business Departments.

Two other institutions have a significant role in national policy generally, and in cultural policy more specifically. The first is parliament or its equivalent, and, in the UK, the parliamentary committee that scrutinises the DCMS on behalf of the House of Commons is important. We have placed Select Committees 'inside' the political field; they take representations from policy groups. A second key institution is think tanks, which act as sources of political ideas for the parties and for government. These bodies are nearly always attached to a particular party, in the UK mainly to the Labour or Conservative Party. The main leftist think tanks in the UK during the period under consideration were the Institute for Public Policy Research (IPPR) and Demos, both of which made contributions relevant to cultural policy – though, as we shall see, only once New Labour had achieved power.[11]

---

[11] Although Demos founder Geoff Mulgan had a background in cultural industries policy dating back to the 1980s, Demos played very little part in informing New Labour's cultural policies when in opposition.

The picture of policy making we have presented above is overly static, in that it does not capture the changing relations among the actors over time. Nor does it indicate the degree of power and prestige held by particular actors, and the complex relations between cultural policy making and other fields of policy making. The rest of the book provides detail on these issues; our initial picture, at least, gives some indication of the main actors involved in shaping cultural policies. In this chapter, we will begin to see how some of these various policy actors interacted, and which tended to prevail, during the early years of New Labour: the years in opposition from 1994 to 1997, and Blair's first term, from 1997 to 2001. Here we remind readers of two of our central questions (see Box 1.2), concerning change and continuity in New Labour's policies: which interests were represented by which policy groups, and to what effect?

2.3 New Labour's cultural policies: Formation, early character and the creative industries concept

The main way in which New Labour's cultural policies differed from those of its predecessors was that it took the interests of the cultural industries much more seriously. New Labour signalled this through its use of the term 'the creative industries', and made this the basis of efforts to get various departments of government to work together to develop these industries. On the part of politicians, advisers and civil servants, this was an attempt to raise the status of culture and cultural policy in government, by bringing commercial cultural activity into the cultural policy fold, and by making stronger connections or attachments between cultural policy and other more 'heavyweight' areas of policy, such as regional economic development and education. However, early on in New Labour's time in government, when extra money did not seem to be forthcoming, this was interpreted by arts and heritage organisations as an attempt to displace them from the centre of cultural policy, and by critics from right and left as a pandering to commercialism, entertainment and triviality (as we saw in Box 2.1).

New Labour sought to temper the 'economism' of the creative industries concept by appealing to values concerning access, social inclusion and the value of education. There was little that was novel about these aspects of Labour policy. The mobilisation of such ideas often represented an extension of initiatives and techniques that had been adopted in the UK under the Conservatives of 1979 to 1997, and in many other places too. These values had a social democratic veneer, but they had become a standard part of cultural policy discourse even in the neo-liberalising 1980s, across most political parties. Sometimes, as we shall see, seemingly social democratic concepts were in fact underpinned by forms of thinking (particularly 'knowledge economy' ideas) that emphasised the need for economic and social transformation in ways that were at odds with social democratic goals. The only real resistance to this move came from representatives of arts and heritage, anxious about being displaced from the central position in cultural policy that they had previously occupied,[12] and, as we shall see, from artists and civil society groups that made links between New Labour's cultural policies and the perceived conservatism in, for example, their welfare and economic policies.

In line with our aim to build a sociology of New Labour's cultural policies, we show how the ideas and initiatives covered by the term 'creative industries' were formulated, and what precedents they drew upon. We examine the formulation of Labour's policies in the period from 1994 to the end of New Labour's first term in 2001, and what some key policy actors were trying to achieve.

One particularly significant person in the early formation of New Labour's cultural policies was the film producer David Puttnam. After major success in the 1970s and 1980s, and a difficult stint in Hollywood as Head of Columbia Pictures, Puttnam was in the 1990s still making films at his Enigma Productions company, but from the early 1980s onwards had become increasingly interested in education and in policy. Puttnam was part of a network of industry activists who were seeking to exert influence on government by persuading them of the economic importance of industries such as film, music recording and so on.[13] In the 1990s, Puttnam assembled at his company a group of people working on public policy issues, notably John Newbigin, a former speechwriter for Neil Kinnock with strong connections inside

---

[12] A notable case was former BBC journalist, and Managing Director of London's Barbican Arts Centre, John Tusa – see Tusa (1999) for a collection of some of his interventions early in the New Labour period.

[13] In interview, David Puttnam recalled a gathering in the late 1980s where representatives of the music industry (according to Puttnam, the then President of EMI Records, Rupert Perry, hosted the meeting) made a presentation concerning the economic contribution of their industry to an audience including Gordon Brown, then a junior shadow minister for trade and industry, who was struck by how few jobs were created by the industry compared with its financial contribution. Puttnam took this as a sign of how much Labour's thinking needed to adjust to the specific nature of industries such as film – at that stage, yet to be named 'creative industries' – with their unusual employment profile.

the Labour Party, and Ben Evans, who had previously worked as an adviser to the Labour Shadow Arts Minister Mark Fisher. Puttnam and his young advisers became part of a working group set up by Jack Cunningham, who was Shadow Heritage (i.e., Culture) Minister from October 1995 until the election in 1997, to help construct a Labour policy with regard to the National Lottery, introduced by the Conservatives in 1994.[14]

Puttnam provided legitimation for New Labour's emergent cultural policies. His role as a producer of 'quality' films such as *Local Hero* made him attractive to a party leadership alive to the fusion of creativity and business in high-quality commercial popular culture. Producers are, after all, the key mediators of creative and business inputs in the film industry. Puttnam had no formal role, but was highly influential and respected in Labour circles, as Estelle Morris, Minister for the Arts from 2003 to 2005 (and Secretary of State for Education from 2001 to 2002) comments:

> Sometimes you realise he's never had a formal title but he's everywhere. He was never appointed to *anything* under Labour, he was never anyone's adviser. He got a pass to come into the Department for Education because he was so valuable but you'll not find a job role for him throughout the whole of the Labour years but he was there, he was everywhere, very trusted.
>
> (Estelle Morris, interview)

For Puttnam, there were three main themes to Labour's distinctive version of cultural policy as it emerged in opposition and was put into practice in government – and here, it seems, Puttnam is as much talking about what he wanted New Labour cultural policy to do as characterising their policies. The first theme was film policy (see Chapter 4), where the aim was

> to take the film industry seriously, which was a sort of win win, and there was never any question about that, there was never any

---

[14] Other members of the working group included Peter Hewitt and Andrew Dixon, both involved in regional arts initiatives linked to regeneration in the north of England, and both later to be very senior arts organisation executives. Their inclusion reflected New Labour's interest in culture-led regeneration, which we address in Chapter 5.

question that film wouldn't be a strand, it suited Gordon [Brown], it suited Tony [Blair] for different reasons and it suited Chris [Smith].

(David Puttnam, interview)

The second was the coining of the term 'creative industries' – as we shall see, a fundamental part of New Labour's early presentation of its cultural policies. The third was copyright, the financial core of the sector. This trio of themes reveals the importance Puttnam placed on economic aspects of cultural policy. But, although Puttnam played a very important role in New Labour's cultural policy, drawing on his work on the Arts Council board and in various educational settings, he was also channelling the growing lobbying sophistication of the cultural industries, honed in Hollywood and elsewhere, in the face of threats to copyright on the part of new technologies such as the video recorder and the audio cassette, and the 'piracy' they enabled. Essentially, New Labour politicians worked with cultural industry 'stakeholders', led per-suasively by Puttnam and figures from other industries such as music, to reshape cultural policy so that the interests of the cultural industries were incorporated more fully into government. The 'creative industries' idea was used to mobilise government support for business (for both economic and cultural reasons), and for culture-led regeneration, and thereby legitimate public expenditure on the arts. This was very 'Third Way'. It seemed to counter conservative neo-liberalism by legitimating public expenditure, yet it did so on the basis of contribution to eco-nomic growth rather than social or cultural provision. The danger was that such an attitude would actually serve to endorse conservative sus-picion of public expenditure on the arts for any reasons other than economic ones.

2.4   Intellectual roots of New Labour's cultural policies

This new turn towards economic pragmatism fitted well with the new accommodation with business characteristic of New Labour (see Chapter 1). But it had a set of (mainly international) intellectual and policy roots, which are important for understanding New Labour's ideas on cultural policy and their presentation of those ideas. Three can be identified here.

The first was the knowledge economy/information society thinking already introduced via Blair's speech quoted above. For some time, there had been an increasingly shared view among governments of 'advanced industrial' countries that information and knowledge were of unprecedented importance in contemporary economic life. Discussions of the 'information society' and 'the knowledge economy' had their roots in the work of writers such as Peter Drucker, Daniel Bell and Marc Porat in the 1960s and 1970s. By the 1990s, these ideas had been translated into mainstream policy terms, for example in the report on *Europe and the Global Information Society* delivered to the European Commission in 1994 by a group of experts led by then Trade Commissioner Martin Bangemann MEP. That report crystallised the international neo-liberal economic common sense that the future of Europe's prosperity lay in its ability to respond *entrepreneurially* to the challenges and opportunities afforded by online and digital communication – as the USA demonstrated in its information technology-led recovery from its 1980s doldrums (the massive role of the US government in laying the basis for this boom was ignored in the report). Although the Bangemann Report would not have been treated as gospel by those forging New Labour cultural policy in opposition in the mid-1990s, it represents the intellectual environment in which the idea of the 'creative industries' was shaped.

In parallel, centrist and centre-left thinkers were developing analyses that sought to understand the role of education and knowledge in economic prosperity. Particularly notable was endogenous growth theory, which stressed how growth could be produced by investment in innovation and 'human capital' (Romer, 1994), and which, in 1994, Gordon Brown had announced was central to New Labour's economic strategy (White, 1994). Associated concepts were those of human capital (mentioned by Blair in the speech analysed above) and social capital.

A second source for New Labour's development of a cultural policy that emphasised the concept of creative industries was the increasing importance of 'culture-led regeneration' since the 1970s.[15] This term refers to a number of interlinked international developments, including: the redevelopment of former industrial (especially dockland and waterfront) areas to include arts, entertainment, sport and food facilities that might attract tourists; investment in 'landmark' buildings such as galleries (the Guggenheim in Bilbao) to attract tourists and to increase the city's global reputation; and the development of bohemian neighbourhoods into 'quarters' of cultural production. There had been major developments in the UK in this respect, such as 'cultural quarters' in

---

[15] See Bianchini and Parkinson (1993) for a useful survey for the early years of this trend.

Manchester and Sheffield, and the redevelopment of disused cotton mills in Halifax (Dean Clough) by a local entrepreneur.

This is a key context in which to understand the decision to adopt the term 'creative industries' and variants such as 'creative economy' rather than 'cultural industries'. The latter term had prevailed in urban regeneration policy following the development of 'cultural industries' strategies at the left-dominated Greater London Council in the 1983–1985 period (never implemented because the GLC was abolished by the Conservatives). New Labour was happy to draw upon the positive achievements of some of its local councils in achieving culture-led regeneration.[16] But the term 'cultural industries' carried associations with a period of intense conflict between the then Labour leadership and the left-wing 'municipal socialist' councils of the 1980s. The 'creative industries' was a term greatly to be preferred, at least in the early years of New Labour. It drew on the idea of 'creativity' as an economic motor, already apparent in 'the creative city' notion that had emerged in urban policy think tanks in the early 1990s, in particular via the work of the policy consultant Charles Landry at the UK think tank Comedia. It also invoked an emerging celebration of 'creative management' led by business gurus and advocated by consultants.

A third intellectual source for New Labour's cultural policy thinking was, as we alluded to in discussing Blair's speech above, cultural postmodernism. By the 1980s, British social democrats were turning against the traditional arts and heritage subsidy model and its association with 'high culture' elitism.[17] The then fashionable academic movement called 'cultural studies' provided some intellectual legitimation for this move – but the cultural democracy vision of writers such as Raymond Williams was often lost amidst populist rhetoric.[18] One of

---

[16] A notable case was Glasgow, which had been named European Capital of Culture by the European Commission in 1990, following Florence, Berlin, Amsterdam and Paris.
[17] See *Saturday Night or Sunday Morning?* written by Geoff Mulgan and Ken Worpole (1986), Labour figures associated not only with the Greater London Council (see Section 1.6) but also with the Comedia think tank and *Marxism Today* magazine, for one influential statement of such a position. See also Justin Lewis's thoughtful *Art, Culture and Enterprise* (1990).
[18] Colin MacCabe, Head of Production and later Research at the British Film Institute (1985–1998), once remarked: 'I never felt in any way threatened by my Tory political masters as I did by New Labour from day one. I mean these people have done Cultural Studies courses so they know that art is a bourgeois con-trick' (quoted by Newsinger, 2009: 91).

the most important revisionist journals for young leftist thinkers in
the 1980s was the former journal of the Communist Party, *Marxism
Today*. Under its editor Martin Jacques, it gradually moved from moderate euro-communism towards an early form of 'Third Way' thinking
that rejected not only Marxism, but also many aspects of traditional
social democracy. It featured writers who would play a major part in New
Labour thinking, such as Geoff Mulgan, Charles Leadbeater and Andrew
Adonis.[19] Tony Blair was a subscriber, and the magazine included a
lengthy interview with him in 1991, when he was largely unknown
outside the Labour Party. When New Labour began to forge its cultural
policies after 1994, it did not take much to translate the cultural postmodernist rejection of traditional arts and heritage subsidy into a focus
on creative industries – though, as we shall see, New Labour embraced
the arts in many respects.

2.5 Creativity

New Labour was not alone in drawing on such sources. One important
international forerunner of New Labour's cultural policies was the policy vision encapsulated in a document called *Creative Nation*, published
in 1994 by the then Labour-led Australian government of Paul Keating
(Government of the Commonwealth of Australia, 1994). The cultural
policy put forward for Australia by that document was also, it declared,
'an economic policy'. 'Culture creates wealth', it continued. 'Broadly
defined, our cultural industries generate 13 billion dollars a year.' It also
provided employment: 'Around 336,000 Australians are employed in
culture-related industries.' In addition, *Creative Nation* called for an
embrace of the 'information revolution' and 'new media'. This mixture
of economic pragmatism and modernisation was highly attractive to
New Labour, and, according to Puttnam's adviser John Newbigin (later
a special adviser to Chris Smith, the first New Labour Culture Secretary),
Tony Blair was impressed by the document.

> I knew that Blair had liked that, and *Creative Nation* is quite an
> interesting... it's very interesting to read it now because its basic
> assertion was every aspect of government policy has a cultural dimen-
> sion to it. Because all these things are a statement of our national

---

[19] Stuart Hall and Martin Jacques' 1989 collection, *New Times*, provides a good
flavour, consisting mainly of pieces from the journal. *Marxism Today* was revived
for one issue in 1998 to launch a critique of New Labour.

culture and the way we project ourselves abroad. So, tourism, the economy, the film industry, and this is from an Australian perspective, all that is part of our cultural agenda. And the way forward in the world is going to be increasingly that creativity is the thing that differentiates countries and therefore we need to think about creativity in government policy.

(John Newbigin, interview)

That focus on creativity was to be particularly important in the first term of New Labour's power. In fact, *Creative Nation* had hardly used the words 'creative' and 'creativity' at all outside its title, but it suggested a way in which a number of policy themes attractive to New Labour's modernising Third Way thinking might be brought together under the 'creativity banner'. John Newbigin suggests the attractiveness of the concept of creativity to New Labour in a policy context influenced by the sources outlined in the previous section:

And really it was picking up that idea and the whole idea of creativity, not just defined in arts terms, but creativity as a driving fuel for the future of the British economy, that was something that was very much in the air already and it was trying to give a bit of focus and shape to that. That's what really got us going on the creative industry agenda.

(John Newbigin, interview)

Creativity featured as a term both in the 'creative industries' notion and also in a more general concept of 'the creative economy'. Use of the latter term often reflected a deeper commitment to knowledge economy goals of instilling creativity in the economy as a whole, via government cultivation of skills, talent and entrepreneurship, rather than just a particular group of industries rather problematically delineated as creative.[20] Later, as we shall see in Chapter 4, the 'creative economy' idea seemed to come more into vogue. The terms were often used interchangeably, but the creative economy concept was more 'imperialistic',

---

[20] Entrepreneurship, like 'creativity', was a term used relentlessly by early New Labour. See, for example, the Labour Party's document on its strategy for business, published before the 1997 election, 'New Labour: a Government for Entrepreneurs' (Labour Party, 1997b). Its 'five ways to a more enterprising Britain' included greater links between schools and businesses, 'lifelong learning' and Nesta (see Chapter 7).

in that it supposedly delineated a desirable feature of entire economies. For example, in a speech to the Confederation of British Industry (the main representatives of British capital) in November 1997, Blair laid out six principles behind New Labour's economic policy, all resting on 'one belief' that 'to succeed, today, Britain must be the world's No 1 creative economy. We will win by brains or not at all. We will compete on enterprise and talent or fail' (Blair, 1997). Not surprisingly, the think tanks and policy intellectuals intensified their focus on creativity in response to such cues. By 1999, a 100-page pamphlet for the Demos think tank laid out for centre-left modernisers a programme of how to understand 'the creative age' that drew on the management and psychology approaches mentioned above (Seltzer and Bentley, 1999). Around the same time, former *Marxism Today* contributor and policy consultant Charles Leadbeater published a book on creativity and the knowledge economy – including its potential pitfalls. It was called *Living on Thin Air: The New Economy* (Leadbeater, 1999)and carried a front cover blurb by Tony Blair praising this 'extraordinarily interesting thinker' for raising 'critical questions for Britain's future'.

So New Labour's reshaping of cultural policy around 'creativity' emerged from an agenda led by knowledge economy/information society thinking – and also by a profound reaction against the cultural democracy aspirations of the GLC's arts and culture policies of the 1980s. An interesting insight into the way these themes worked together comes from a memo[21] sent by then Arts Council staffer Graham Hitchen to Mary Allen, Secretary General of the Arts Council, in February 1996. It followed a meeting between Hitchen and David Miliband, then Head of Policy in Tony Blair's office. Hitchen reported that Miliband had highlighted two aspects of arts policy which he felt could fit the 'New Labour' agenda: populism and branding. Populism he saw as 'promoting the arts to ordinary people', a fairly standard democratisation of culture aim, but inflected with ideas about how to encourage participation, including 'pay as you can' schemes and 'Punters' Panels', where local residents rather than artists would decide how funding should be allocated. The second, branding element aimed to use the cultural industries ('new music, fashion, design, etc.') to build a new image of Britain. The cultural industries in this understanding were both commercially viable and able to represent the UK's national interests overseas. The understanding that had shaped GLC policy, concerning the embedded nature

---

[21] Arts Council internal memo dated 2 February 1996 and entitled 'Labour Party'.

of local popular culture, was missing here. The state's role in popular culture was seen as an economic one.

However, it would be wrong to say that New Labour cultural policy operated entirely in the interests of the cultural industries, or of a neo-liberal notion of the knowledge economy. For, as we saw in Section 2.3, there were other interests at work in the cultural policy landscape. There was the heritage sector, anxious about the attitude towards them that the modernising Labour Party would take. And there were 'the arts', the subsidised institutions and the artists working with them, many of whom had great prestige, considerable media access and close links with the Labour Party. And New Labour did not abandon its long-standing social democratic democratisation of culture commitments to access and the contribution of culture to combating inequalities – though, as we shall see, it reconfigured them. The challenge for New Labour, marked at least superficially by a consensual political style at odds with that of Margaret Thatcher's combative Conservatism, was to try to keep these various interests satisfied sufficiently that they would not disrupt policy implementation. But what all this would actually mean in terms of policies on the arts and culture was not at all clear as Labour approached the 1997 election.

2.6 New Labour's early days: Creative industries mapping and not much else?

As we saw in Chapter 1, some have seen the advent of New Labour as marking a decisive and welcome shift to a new set of cultural policies based on 'creative industries' rather than traditional arts subsidy (Cunningham, 2007; Flew, 2012). In retrospect, what is striking is how long it took for actual policies to emerge – partly because of New Labour's commitment to stick to the spending plans of the previous government – and how continuous many of the policies and practices were with earlier ones. As some public policy analysts have emphasised (such as a widely cited discussion by Hall, 1993), there are few clean breaks in modern policy making. Change tends to emerge gradually, and it takes time for policy makers (politicians, civil servants and advisers) to establish a set of policies – perhaps especially in 'weak' departments such as cultural ones.

New Labour's cultural policies only really emerged in the second and third terms of government (2001–2005 and 2005–2010), and it is only in that later context that they can really be assessed – the work of later chapters in this book. The rest of this chapter concerns the rather slow emergence of New Labour's cultural policies during its first term. We focus on the way in which Smith's DCMS presented its main cultural policy goals, and unpack the language used and values invoked. We also discuss the problems that New Labour encountered as it slowly edged towards an actual set of policies, particularly from the arts policy group discussed above.

New Labour's election manifesto of 1997 was based around a 'contract' consisting of ten pledges, each given a section. Buried in the eighth, on environment and transport (a section headed 'we will help you get more out of life'), were three paragraphs on 'arts and culture', which included sport and tourism – the areas covered by the then DNH. The first paragraph spoke of the contribution of arts, culture and sport to creating a sense of community, identity and civic pride. The second focused on the much more measurable business of economic achievement. Arts, sports and culture, echoing *Creative Nation*, were 'significant earners for Britain', employed 'hundreds of thousands of people' and brought millions of tourists each year, who would be 'helped by Labour's plans for new quality assurance in hotel accommodation'.[22] The third was the promise to introduce a 'national trust' for talent – a National Endowment for Science, Technology and the Arts (Nesta, see Chapter 7), partly funded out of the Lottery. So much for all the meetings about cultural policy in opposition: here were just three paragraphs emphasising the economic contribution of culture (including sport and tourism), and making two relatively minor commitments. This reflected the marginal status of cultural policy. However, Labour had produced a separate cultural manifesto, *Create the Future* (Labour Party, 1997a), written by Shadow Culture Secretary Jack Cunningham and Shadow Arts Minister Mark Fisher. Aware of the views of arts organisations, this claimed that the arts 'should be supported by government for their intrinsic merits' but also promised to refocus the department to 'play a major part in the economic regeneration of our country'. New Labour were making clear from the start their focus on the economic benefits of culture.

When New Labour achieved their landslide victory in May 1997, Chris Smith was appointed as Secretary of State for National Heritage, rather than Jack Cunningham (who apparently had fallen out with Gordon Brown, according to David Puttnam, interview). Smith had served as

---

[22] The Visitor Attraction Quality Assurance Scheme was trialled in 1998 and was then operated by VisitEngland – one of the non-departmental public bodies funded by the DCMS.

Shadow Heritage Minister for a year from October 1994 to 1995, and was determined to give the Heritage Department greater weight within government in order to increase the chances that he, his advisers and senior civil servants would be able to realise their ambitions for the department (see below). This, in particular, meant being taken seriously by other departments, especially the two all-powerful ones: the Prime Minister's Office and the Treasury, the latter of which in 1997–1998 would conduct a Comprehensive Spending Review to decide upon departmental budgets and targets for 1999 to 2002.

Smith made two moves in his efforts to give his department greater weight. First, he had the name of the ministry changed from 'National Heritage' to 'Culture, Media and Sport'.[23] He explained to the Parliamentary Select Committee for Culture, Media and Sport in 1998 that the new name was more suited to a 'department of the future' which was 'about creativity, innovation and excitement' (Parliamentary Select Committee on Culture, Media and Sport, 1998: viii). Second, he placed considerable emphasis on the economic and social contribution of the elements in his department. His mechanism for doing so was the concept of 'the creative industries', based on the pre-election input of Puttnam and others, but now embodied in the form of a 'Creative Industries Task Force', which brought legitimation in the form of not only big cultural businesses, but also ministers and staff from other departments, in a process of 'policy attachment' (see Chapter 1).

The name change was significant, but some history helps to contextualise it. The UK only gained a culture department in 1992, when John Major's Conservative government established the DNH.[24] This had brought together a number of disparate elements previously located in other departments of state. So the DNH took over responsibility for:

- arts and libraries: previously, the 'Office of Arts and Libraries' had been located in the Department of Education and Science (DES –

---

[23] Smith revealed to Stephen Hetherington that he wanted it to be 'the Department for Culture full stop. The Prime Minister wasn't having that, he thought that sounded too arty farty, insisted on including sport in the title. I thought, well, if we've got culture and we've got sport we might as well just make sure that we hang on very firmly to media, which is how the name emerged' (Chris Smith, quoted in Hetherington 2014: 97).

[24] There had been cabinet positions for arts ministers since Labour Prime Minister Harold Wilson appointed Jennie Lee to that role in 1964, but responsibility for the arts was moved around various government departments.

and before that the Treasury); the new department also took over responsibility for sport from Education;

- built heritage, transferred to DNH from the Department of the Environment;
- the National Lottery, plus broadcasting and press regulation, transferred from the Home Office;
- various issues regarding film and export licensing of works of art, transferred from the Department of Trade and Industry;
- tourism, from the Department of Employment.

This earlier 1992 event, the creation of a culture department, was a much greater step in cultural policy's rising significance than the name change of 1997. It reflected the increasing importance of culture in contemporary life, and the greater (though still marginal) significance attached to cultural policy by government. Even in 1981, Margaret Thatcher had said she was convinced of 'the need for the arts to have its own independent voice in government' (Hewison, 1995: 244). By the early 1990s, all parties were committed to the creation of a culture department, and if they had won the 1992 election under Neil Kinnock, Labour would have created such a ministry. However, National Heritage was still the least powerful and prestigious of all government departments, known dismissively in the media as the 'Ministry of Fun' (see Box 2.1).[25] Even more than in other countries, culture and the arts in the UK, at both national and local levels, are 'policy areas that are normally considered to be of little real importance or significance' (Gray, 2004: 41), as we explained in Chapter 1. Smith's two moves were a canny way of trying to change this.

But the emphasis on the importance of creativity, the creative industries and the creative economy that had been developed in opposition provided a further, equally significant way for Smith to raise the profile of his department. On coming to power, New Labour had set up a whole host of 'task forces', intended to bring people from different departments together with other 'stakeholders' to achieve 'joined up government' (see Barker et al., 1999; Pollitt, 2003), a light-hearted reference to children learning 'joined-up writing'. Smith and his advisers

---

[25] See, for example, Hewison's (1993) article in the *Sunday Times* – the first mention of the term we can find. The same piece may also have coined another put-down – that the Ministry became the Department of Nothing Happening after its first minister's departure.

set up a Creative Industries Task Force, comprising prominent characters from the world of entertainment, fashion, media and so on.

> It was me trying to shift it up the importance scale for government. It was also an attempt to bring other departments to the table to talk and think about it and it was also a way of bringing in people from the outside world who knew what they were talking about – so bringing in people like David Puttnam and Gail Rebuck and Paul Smith and so on. Robert Devereux from Virgin.
>
> (Chris Smith, interview)[26]

Smith also launched initiatives to define and 'map' the creative industries – which, crucially, meant coming up with methodologically respectable estimates for the share of the economy for which the 'creative industries' were responsible, to support the fundamental claim that art and culture were growing in economic significance. The 'economic importance of the arts' had been of increasing interest since the 1980s.[27] However, this trend was not merely a product of Thatcherism, nor, indeed, of Conservative governments. Governments and arts administrators in many countries were beginning to emphasise such economic value at the time, even in the Nordic countries (Duelund, 2008: 16–17). What explained this international shift? One possibility is that culture, including the expressive symbol making upon which the 'arts' are based, was becoming a larger part of economic life as leisure time and facilities grew (Hesmondhalgh, 2013a: 111). A second was that culture was increasingly perceived as an opportunity for economic development, by businesses, governments and politicians. A third is that other rationales, based on the 'intrinsic' value of the arts and culture, or on their ability to cultivate human attributes, or on their contribution to quality of life, were being eroded by conservative postmodernist and other anti-elitist views. Probably all these factors were involved. New Labour did not invent economic rationales for funding the arts, but they embraced them whole-heartedly. And while a complete rejection of economic

---

[26] Rebuck was a senior figure in publishing, married to a key New Labour figure, Philip Gould (who managed their strategy and polling, in close alliance with Mandelson). Smith was a major international fashion designer. Devereux was a partner in the Virgin business empire, and a significant art collector.

[27] The 1980s saw a new emphasis on the economic contribution of the arts. The Arts Council's *A Great British Success Story* report (Arts Council of Great Britain, 1985) represented an important moment, as did Myerscough's research in *The Economic Importance of the Arts* (1988). See Hewison (1995: 251–94).

rationales seems naïve and unnecessary, a case for arts funding and the value of culture based too much on economic grounds has significant limitations – as we shall see.

The idea of 'the new economy', particularly popular in the heady days of the 1990s, held the promise that the arts and culture could stand alongside other rising sectors such as biotechnologies, financial services and so on. But many were sceptical about such claims, and some of them worked at the powerful Treasury, including the Chancellor himself.

> I remember being so frustrated because every time that Gordon [Brown], as Chancellor, made a speech about where the new sources of wealth of the British economy were going to come from, it was all about biotechnology, about pharmaceuticals, about financial services, about science, not a mention of the creative industries.
>
> (Chris Smith, interview)[28]

What gave Smith and his colleagues sufficient political credibility to make claims about the economic importance of the creative industries, without being altogether dismissed, was the backing of the copyright-holding cultural industries, who wanted to establish this importance in order to gain stronger protection for copyright and other government support such as tax incentives. David Puttnam found Smith to be a valuable ally in his focus on the contribution of the creative industries to the economy.

> Chris was the first person with whom we worked in a kind of coherent way with the objective of driving forward the percentage of GDP that could be achieved through the arts and creative industries.... I think the very first number we ever coined for the value of the creative industries was about 2.2 per cent. I can't remember who came up with it – one of the universities, actually, came up with the notion that the creative industries, roughly, represented 2.2 per cent of GDP. In conversations with Chris Smith and you need to talk to him, my memory is saying to me, he said we could drive that to 3.5 per cent,

---

[28] Eventually Brown came round. 'It was after I stopped being Secretary of State, some time in the early 2000s [...]. I remember listening to the *Today* programme and they were interviewing Gordon. And he was launching into his usual list of the new sources of wealth for the British economy and suddenly, there were the creative industries. And I remember, leaping out of bed saying, "yahoo, he's got it!" ' (Chris Smith, interview).

you know, we certainly could drive it to 3.5 per cent and maybe beyond that. We then started getting very excited talking about 5 per cent. I think the figure at the moment, not many people will argue [with the view] that it's probably a tad under 6 per cent.

(David Puttnam, interview)

In order to achieve this, the Creative Industries Task Force and the DCMS statisticians had to take a very inclusive definition of the creative industries that brought in the very large sectors of software and architecture, alongside those that would normally have fallen under previous definitions of the 'cultural industries'. Table 2.1 lists the industries included in the original DCMS definition. This definition has been the object of some criticism over the years, with some commentators claiming that the inclusion of the software category included forms of information technology activity which had little to do with cultural production, in a way that artificially inflated the size and scale of the sector (Garnham, 2005; O'Brien, 2013).[29]

However problematic the definition, and however much the creative industries agenda was driven by economic ends, it would be wrong to understand the DCMS' and Smith's motivations for emphasising the economic importance of the arts and culture as merely a means to accumulate political capital for the sake of power and reputation. Such motives may well have been involved, as they are in so much of what people do. But this emphasis was also a means to secure higher levels of funding so that the arts and heritage would flourish. As we shall see,

Table 2.1 Creative industries, as defined by New Labour

Advertising	Leisure software
Antiques	Music
Architecture	Performing arts
Crafts	Publishing
Design	Software
Designer fashion	TV and radio
Film	

Source: DCMS (1998).

---

[29] More recently, the DCMS has revised its mapping methodology completely, drawing on recent work by Nesta and QUT, in an attempt to measure the numbers of employees engaged in creative occupations in sectors outside of the creative industries, including IT, advanced manufacturing and the digital economy (Bakhshi et al., 2013; DCMS, 2011).

the term used to signal this goal in New Labour's presentation of its cultural policies was *excellence*. However, the DCMS was also clear that the price for supporting the arts and heritage better was that organisations would be required to attract audiences beyond the traditional white, middle-class, middle-aged profile of audiences for theatres, museums and heritage sites – a democratising goal that fitted with New Labour's Third Way aspirations, in that it sought to please both left-wing advocates of greater equality and right-wing sceptics about public subsidies for elite taste. The term used for this goal was *access*. We have already seen, in Chapter 1, that tensions between access and excellence are at the heart of modern cultural policy. But what was the relationship of these goals to the creative industries idea?

2.7 Four aims: Access, excellence, education and creative industries

Government and departmental documents about the DCMS from the first term of the New Labour government nearly always specified four main aims for the department. One example is the *New Cultural Framework* document published by DCMS in 1999, with a foreword by Chris Smith, listing the following themes:

- the promotion of access for the many, not just the few;
- the pursuit of excellence and innovation;
- the nurturing of educational opportunity;
- the fostering of the creative industries.

The language of the first three aims hardly varied over the period from 1997 to 2001. However, it's revealing that Treasury documents tended to sideline the concept of creative industries in favour of more directly economistic notions such as *growth*. In the vital White Paper detailing the outcomes of the Comprehensive Spending Review of 1998 (see below), the first three aims are expressed in almost exactly the same language as that quoted above, whereas the fourth is converted into 'promoting economic growth and employment'.

Whether the fourth aim was expressed as 'creative industries' or in terms of promoting growth and employment via culture and creativity, note how the first three themes came before the economic orientation of that final goal for cultural policy – at least in presentational terms. These other themes, on the surface, suggest a rather different set of values than the economic orientation of the fourth goal. They also embody a desire to appeal to rather different sets of actors than those who would be attracted by reference to the economic contribution of art and culture, and/or the importance of creative industries in a 'new economy' – such as 'the business community' or a hostile Conservative press ready to accuse Labour of being wasteful of public funds. Excellence invokes high-quality cultural production – pleasing to the arts and heritage lobbies. Access and education would appeal to the Labour Party's own social democratic elements. Yet the emphasis on access fitted with the government's 'Third Way' rewriting of social democracy in terms of a more centrist focus on social inclusion (Levitas, 2005), in a way that would enhance the department's prestige in government. Similarly, the stress on education fitted with New Labour's relentless focus on the economic rewards of education in a knowledge economy. So, in this respect, the access and education goals are not so far removed from the economic concerns of the fourth aim as may at first appear.

The list of aims, then, represented skilful politics on the part of Smith and his colleagues. It made clear a desire to push an economically driven agenda but was also the basis for rhetoric and strategy that would keep those potentially dissatisfied with such an agenda sufficiently contented that they would not disrupt policy (or vote for another party at the next election). But there were two sets of problems with this list of aspirations. The first was that, as we shall see in the chapters that follow, there were significant obfuscations and confusions in how the goals were presented and embodied in policy. The second set of problems derived from New Labour's commitment to match Conservative spending plans for the first two years after they took office – which had effectively frozen expenditure in the DCMS. Local government budgets had been frozen too, which meant that local government support for the arts and culture was also suffering. The DCMS could do little to pacify the arts and heritage lobbies in terms of their demands for funding, resulting in a considerable degree of criticism of New Labour, Smith and his department. These criticisms are revealing of the views and tactics of the arts policy group. There were also criticisms from other, more leftist cultural sources.

2.8   Early criticisms, a surge in funding, and strings attached

The first wave of criticisms came quickly. Arts Council cuts to allocations in January 1998 occasioned a storm of fury, following what was perceived to be years of underinvestment. Perhaps the most vocal critics came from the world of theatre. The theatre directors Peter Hall and

Michael Bogdanov condemned Labour's arts record. Bogdanov painted the following picture of the UK's cultural world in an article in the *New Statesman*:

> Museums are charging, contracting, shutting for whole days of the week. Orchestras are merging. Theatres are closing. Courses and facilities at all levels have disappeared.... Bureaucracy and Mammon rule. The various devolved Arts Councils have degenerated into bungling, bureaucratic, hands-on governmental lackeys. Funding for the arts is on a level with a car boot sale.
>
> (Bogdanov, 1998)

Another set of criticisms came from certain elements within the cultural industries – not the executives courted by New Labour, but leftist musicians who denounced New Labour's emerging welfare and educational policies as they bore on music and young people. The focus of growing discontent was a *New Musical Express* cover story (dated 14 March 1998) in which numerous popular music figures attacked the introduction of tuition fees for higher education, and the compulsion involved in new welfare provisions (based on the US 'workfare' model).

New Labour responded to the arts lobby and, to some extent, the criticisms of the alternative rock world. They squeezed £5 million out of existing resources in March 1998 to support a 'New Audiences' initiative intended to promote the access and education goals.[30] This involved cut-price theatre tickets for school leavers, more touring funds, voucher schemes, support for orchestras' work with young people, and funding for the arts in deprived areas (*The Herald*, 1998). And in June, Labour announced the introduction of a 'New Deal for Musicians', a variant of its New Deal welfare policies which provided the same terms, but with greater access to training and advice (Cloonan, 2002, 2007). While the introduction of this Department for Education and Employment measure was broadly welcomed, it did not arise directly from interactions with musicians,[31] but from negotiations with creative industry executives who welcomed what was effectively a subsidy for training – for example, in the 'Music Industry Forum' chaired by Chris Smith. When

---

[30] The funding was made available because of savings derived from the strength of the pound, which made European Development Funds stretch further.

[31] An impression that could easily be gained from reading accounts such as those of John Harris (2003) with its highly entertaining reliance on anecdotes about contacts between stars and politicians.

Peter Hall renewed his attacks on Labour following new Arts Council allocations in 1999, and claimed to be setting up an 'alternative Arts Council' (Glaister, 1999), Labour supporters such as the broadcaster and novelist Melvyn Bragg were able to defend Labour and Chris Smith (see Bragg, 1999), pointing to considerable increases in allocations to a number of theatres. Nevertheless, Hall blamed his decision to move to the USA in 1999 on New Labour's philistinism and attitude to funding, and the great conductor Simon Rattle did much the same on leaving Birmingham for Berlin (Hughes, 1998).

There was, then, simmering discontent with New Labour on the part of creative practitioners during New Labour's first years in power. New Labour's response suggested the power of that lobby in relation to the Labour Party, but also the growing power of creative industry interests.

After the Comprehensive Spending Review, the DCMS was finally able to articulate a set of policies that it could defend both to the Treasury and to the arts and heritage lobbies that dominated media coverage of its remit. In its Annual Report of 1999, the DCMS laid out policies for each of its main areas of activity. Those most directly relevant to cultural policy were a new £15 million fund for improving the infrastructure of museums and galleries; the already announced New Audiences Fund, run by the Arts Council, and intended to 'broaden access to the arts to the widest possible audience'; the creation of a new body bringing together different film agencies – this would become the UK Film Council (see Chapter 4) – which was presented as a way of rationalising, and eliminating bureaucracy; and the launch of a Creative Partnerships scheme, involving 'creative professionals' working in schools (see Chapter 7).

But the most important element in the spending review was that it provided the DCMS with what it was able to announce as 290 million pounds of extra money. That signalled to the various arts and heritage worlds the possibility that more resources would be made available. A key moment was when Smith introduced a new scheme to mandate museums and galleries to allow free admission, justified in the name of access. In 2000, the policy stalled because of tax regulations, but these were eventually overcome. In addition, lottery funds were beginning to have an effect on arts and cultural infrastructure in the regions – and we discuss this aspect of funding in the next chapter.

As the 2001 general election approached, the DCMS was in a position to lay out, in a 'Green Paper' consultation document, a summary of what it had done over the previous four years, and what it wanted to do in the next ten years (DCMS, 2001). The proposals were structured around

education, excellence and access, with most of the business proposals that might be categorised as 'creative industries' policies appearing
in the excellence section. While many of the proposals were rather
vague (and many seemed to be taken from the Education Department's
portfolio), the 50-page document was a striking sign of a department
with a significant agenda.

However, the document made little reference to something that had
featured quite strongly in the Comprehensive Spending Review. That
earlier document explicitly warned that the extra money allocated to the
DCMS came with 'strings attached'. 'In return for this increased investment', the review cautioned, 'DCMS will introduce reforms to ensure
that these funds are used efficiently and effectively' (HM Treasury, 1999).
This took the form of new methods of monitoring and audit, notably,
in the DCMS, the creation of an agency called QUEST (the Quality,
Efficiency and Standards Team), which aimed to assess how sponsored
bodies were delivering government objectives (see Hetherington, 2014:
136–7). But there were also to be many other measures by which the
New Labour government sought to ensure that its money was spent in
pursuing the goals above. In the next chapter, we look at these various
issues – arts funding, the free admissions scheme, lottery funding and
bureaucracy – and we examine how they played out over the full period
of New Labour's time in power.

3
The Arts: Access, Excellence and Instrumentalism

3.1 A golden age for the arts?

In his speech at Tate Modern, with which we opened Chapter 2, Tony Blair claimed that the previous ten years, since Labour came to power, had seen 'a renaissance of British culture' and that one contributor to a Downing Street seminar had said that the period would come to be remembered as a 'golden age'.[1] What happens in the arts and culture in a nation is only ever partially a matter of government action, and we have no intention of systematically assessing the overall cultural vitality of the UK during the period under discussion. That is a worthwhile project, but our main brief is cultural policy, and we have two main aims in this chapter. The first is to examine the degree to which Labour's cultural policies added to or hindered the thriving of the arts. The second is to assess what, if anything, they did to shift fundamental inequalities regarding access to the arts and culture.

We begin by discussing the important question of how much money the New Labour government provided for the arts and 'cultural infrastructure', and where the money went. This includes discussion of the practicalities and ethics of lottery funding, from where a great deal of the money came.[2] Sponsorship and philanthropy provide an important source of money for arts and culture, and we discuss the degree to which New Labour encouraged this problematic form of funding. Perhaps the

---

[1] The Conservatives had referred to a 'renaissance of British culture' in their general election manifesto of 1997.
[2] We remind readers that we deal with other funding issues elsewhere: film policy and tax incentives in Chapter 4, Regional Development Agencies in Chapter 5, Creative Partnerships and Nesta in Chapter 6 and heritage in Chapter 7.

most celebrated arts policy of the Labour years was the introduction of free admission to government-sponsored museums and galleries, and we discuss this in Section 3.5, arguing that the effects of the policy were somewhat more mixed than Labour politicians have tended to recognise. Furthermore, as we began to see in the last chapter, while there can be no doubt that Labour provided significant increases in arts funding, these came with strings attached – strings that were characteristic of New Labour. Arts and culture institutions were expected to set targets, which were increasingly audited and monitored, and the principles of New Public Management (NPM) were applied to the sector with fervent rigour. We assess this aspect of New Labour policy and discuss the concerns expressed by the arts community in response. One way in which this issue was discussed was via the concept of 'instrumentalism' – and we examine the degree to which this is a useful way of characterising the benefits and downsides of Labour's cultural policies. We then discuss another response made by New Labour to the concerns of the arts community: a shift towards a greater focus on excellence.

3.2 Funding and the lottery

Labour politicians have tended to claim that they considerably increased funding for the arts and culture. For example, in a speech in 2010, the then Labour Minister for Culture and Tourism Margaret Hodge claimed that investment in the arts had gone up by 83 per cent in real terms since 1997. Labour's so-called 'cultural manifesto' (one of a number of documents that have been called *Creative Britain* over the years), prepared for the 2010 general election, stated a real-terms expenditure increase of 90 per cent.

How accurate are these figures? It's not clear how either of these percentages were arrived at. Changes in accounting procedures make comparisons using Department for Culture, Media and Sport (DCMS) data very difficult, but Arts Council funding provides at least one measure, and this increased from £186.6 million in 1998–1999 to £452.9 million in 2009–2010 (see Table 3.1). This represents a real increase of something like 35 per cent, assuming the Bank of England's average inflation rate of 2.7 per cent per year between 1999 and 2010. That is a very significant increase, even in an era of relative economic prosperity.

However, Arts Council expenditure also significantly increased between 1980 and 1994 under a series of Conservative administrations in the UK – by some 49 per cent (Gray, 2000: 109). In this case, though, as Gray notes, much of this increase occurred as a result of the

Table 3.1   Government grant-in-aid to Arts
Council England, 1997–2011

Year	Funding (£ million)
1997–1998	186.60
1998–1999	189.95
1999–2000	228.25
2000–2001	237.155
2001–2002	251.455
2002–2003	289.405
2003–2004	324.955
2004–2005	368.859
2005–2006	408.678
2006–2007	426.531
2007–2008	423.601
2008–2009	437.631
2009–2010	452.964
2010–2011	438.523

abolition of the Greater London Council and the six metropolitan councils (Greater Manchester, West Yorkshire, etc.) in 1986, and the removal
of their arts budgets into Arts Council funding – to be distributed via the
then Regional Arts Boards. There can be little doubt that Labour showed
considerably more commitment to funding the arts from general taxation than their Conservative predecessors. But, as we shall see, it was
lottery funding that was to provide much of the overall increase.

On top of that increase were considerable extra cultural subsidies from
three further sources. One was the BBC, a vital form of cultural funding
in the UK. Lunt and Livingstone (2012: 116) cite a 63 per cent increase
in BBC funding between 1997 and 2010, which would equate to about
14 per cent in real terms.

The second avenue of extra expenditure was local government spending on arts and culture, funded from a mixture of central government grants and local revenue sources.[3] Local government funding is
extremely important in cultural policy, but is rarely examined (though
see Holden, 2006, 2007). A report by the Local Government Association
(England) in 2012 claimed that local councils contributed £800 million
to the arts and culture in England at that time – as much as Arts Council

---

[3] The most notable local government revenue source in the UK is the 'council
tax', which is linked to the value of land and buildings. Another is charges made
by local governments for services such as parking.

England – and that they co-funded 60 per cent of the organisations funded by ACE. It is very difficult to find composite figures regarding local government expenditure on arts, culture and heritage. But New Labour increased central government grants to local government from £82 billion in 1999 to £173 billion in 2010 (UK Public Spending website). This enabled local government to invest, particularly in 'cultural infrastructure' such as refurbished or completely new galleries and concert halls. Much of the money came from EU 'Structural Funds', though of course European Union money derives from the contributions of its member states.

Another source of extra arts funding was lottery revenue, and this is vital to understanding New Labour's interventions in the arts and culture. The National Lottery was introduced by the Conservative government of John Major in a 1993 Act and was launched in 1994. Between 1997 and 2010, some £3 billion of funds were distributed to the arts and heritage. It should be emphasised that these funds were *in addition* to the increases in the Arts Council, local arts and culture, and BBC budgets already discussed above. There are problems with the lottery as a means of funding the arts and culture (see Box 3.1). Nevertheless, the lottery enabled unprecedented expenditure on the arts and culture in the UK.

Given that the policy was introduced by the Conservatives, how much credit can be given to New Labour for their management of the lottery? Over the first two franchises, covering 1994–2007, 28 per cent of revenues were provided to what were called the 'Good Causes' via a distribution fund. A major development was that New Labour's 1998 Lottery Act allowed 13.3 per cent of the distribution fund to be spent on health, education and the environment, leading to a reduction in funding to 'arts, sport and charitable causes' from 20 per cent to 16.6 per cent. From 2005, 50 per cent of Good Cause lottery money went to the Big Lottery Fund, combining health, education and environment with funding for the voluntary and community sectors. The remaining 50 per cent was divided equally between arts, heritage and sport.[4]

Much of this money went on big building projects – which also drew on central and local government funds raised through tax. These were controversial, and we examine them in the next section.

---

[4] By 2010, there were 14 lottery distribution bodies, including the four national Arts Councils, the UK Film Council, Scottish Screen and the Heritage Lottery Fund.

Box 3.1   Lottery funding of arts and culture: The downsides

There are some significant problems with lottery funding of the arts and culture. A first is that, when it is considered as a form of 'implicit taxation', there is considerable evidence that lottery funding tends to be regressive in social distribution (Clotfelter and Cook, 1989: 221–30). Lower-income groups spend a much higher proportion of their income on lottery tickets (Clotfelter and Cook, 1989: 229; see also Clotfelter, 2000). When used to fund the arts and culture, there is a danger that the regressive element becomes worse, given that they often seem to be used to fund activities undertaken and products consumed primarily by higher socio-economic groups (this argument is made polemically by Wisman, 2006).[5]

A second objection to lotteries is that they prey on people's mis-understandings of their chances of winning, which are extremely small. Against this has to be set the possibility that, if the state were not administering such lotteries, people would still gamble against significant odds, but private companies (such as football 'pools' businesses) would be the main beneficiaries. Nevertheless, we should remember that state lotteries are aggressively marketed and are often targeted to those who are most likely to use them – a sub-section of groups with low levels of education and income, who invest in them out of misplaced hope and a propensity for gambling. Scholars across various academic disciplines have explored this issue. For example, Beckert and Lutter (2009: 477) state that empirical studies of lottery customers have shown a 'correlation between lower education levels and an overly positive perception of winning the jackpot'. They argue that the purchase of lottery tickets increases when people experience 'desperate financial circumstances' (477), in a vain attempt to escape these conditions.

A third downside of lottery funding is that policy makers inevitably come to see the lottery as a potential substitution

---

[5] Many of the most cited lottery studies concern state lotteries conducted in the USA and Canada (see Clotfelter et al., 1999). Pickernell et al. (2004) argue that the UK National Lottery substitutes for taxation raised elsewhere, and is doubly regressive, taking disproportionately from lower income groups and giving to the better off. However, they base this claim on a comparison of the wealth and lottery expenditure of regions, rather than individuals.

for other (usually more progressive) forms of taxation. Although this is impossible to prove, it seems unfeasible that policy makers would somehow eradicate the knowledge of lottery funding from their minds when considering other funding. (Ironically, this was a charge made against New Labour by their Conservative opponents during the early years.)

The above factors may not collectively mean that social democratic and left-liberal thinking should argue against lotteries altogether. They cannot be used to support an argument that New Labour's use of lottery funding represented an attempt to move away from subsidy. But they suggest that praise for increased funding for arts and culture, where that funding derives significantly from lottery sources, needs to be qualified.

3.3 Flagship projects and other initiatives

Even critical commentators have pointed to the success of various prestige projects associated with New Labour, many of them funded in part by the lottery. London's Tate Modern is often mentioned in regard to both lottery funding and the boom in arts and culture under Labour. In fact, the refurbishment of Millbank Power Station as Tate Modern was initiated under the Conservative administration (led by then UK building regeneration agency, English Partnerships, drawing on lottery and other funds). It opened in 2000, and Labour got much of the credit for its high visitor numbers and popularity. Another project widely seen as a success (e.g., by Millard, 2010), the British Museum's Great Court, a huge covered square at the museum's main entrance, opened in 2000, and *was* funded by lottery money (£46 million out of the £100 million total) – and also by considerable corporate sponsorship. Outside London, facilities such as the Lowry in Salford, and the Sage-Baltic complex in Gateshead, have often been praised (e.g., Frayling, 2005; Toynbee, 2011). Labour politicians and defenders point to the large numbers of visitors at these and other sites and the popularity of some attractions with local visitors. Academic researchers have been much more cautious about such projects, but in some cases have recognised how more successful projects might enhance (some) residents' perceptions of their own city or town (such as Miles, 2005 on the Sage-Baltic complex).

However, critics, especially journalists, have claimed that under New Labour too much money was spent on expensive, and in some cases unsustainable, prestige building projects. The most notorious instance of such a failed flagship project was the Millennium Dome near Greenwich, London, which was built to provide a home for a vast exhibition marking the end of the second 'Christian' millennium. The idea was to reproduce the nation-cohering effects of the Festival of Britain of 1951 and the Royal Exhibition of 1851, and to regenerate a dismal former dockland area of south-east London. The project was initiated under the Conservative government, but Blair and Mandelson pursued it with enthusiasm, in spite of serious reservations on the part of many members of the Cabinet. Estimated spending was based on extremely high projected visitor numbers during the exhibition planned for 2000 – a total of 12 million. Only 5.5 million visitors paid. The costs to the lottery-funded Millennium Commission soared. The UK National Audit Office reckoned in 2002 that the net contribution rose to £628 million from an original estimate of £399 million (National Audit Office, 2002). In addition, there were high costs associated with winding down the original project and selling it on. And what did the Dome achieve in cultural terms? The exhibition was enjoyed by many visitors, but is unlikely to be remembered as contributing anything lasting to knowledge or national identity (see Gray, 2003; McGuigan and Gilmore, 2002). The Dome has since become home to the highly profitable O2 entertainment complex, owned by an American private equity company. The structure is widely used – generating profit for its owners and landowners (Trinity College Cambridge) on the back of what was effectively a massive public subsidy. In the words of McGuigan and Gilmore, this was 'a cultural disaster'.

There were numerous other lottery-funded failures too: Sheffield's National Centre for Popular Music (which closed in 2000, and cost £11 million of lottery money); the National Centre for Visual Arts in Cardiff (closed in 2000, £3 million of lottery money); and Life Force, a museum in Bradford about the history of religious belief (£2.2 million lottery grant, closed in 2001). The House of Commons Committee of Public Accounts reported in 2000 on projects funded through Arts Council England's lottery-funded capital programme, focusing on 15 of the 28 projects that had secured more than £5 million of money in the capital round of 1995–2000, and expressed serious concerns about their management (House of Commons Public Accounts Select Committee, 2000). A follow-up report found that of the 13 such projects by then completed, four were more than a year behind schedule, and 13 of the 15 were over budget, by between 1.7 and 58 per cent (National Audit Office, 2002). These had been projects initiated under the previous

Conservative government, and the Arts Council claimed to be learning from earlier mistakes, but there continued to be problematic or failed projects.

Many of the most controversial large capital projects fitted with New Labour's emphasis on access, even if they were not directly managed by the DCMS. The Public, in West Bromwich (West Midlands), was one example, absorbing around £31.8 million of Arts Council money, plus around £25 million more of local government grants. The building, which combined art, retail and leisure facilities, opened in 2008, many years behind schedule. It required considerable subsidy from local government (Sandwell District Council). Although by 2012–2013 managers of the Public claimed that the building was receiving considerable visitor numbers (380,000 in that year), it was closed in November 2013 (see Blackstock, 2011 for one assessment of what went wrong) and it has been taken over by a local college.

Some London-based projects have suffered a similar fate. Ocean in Hackney, East London, which was centred on popular music training and production, closed in 2004 (it is now an arts cinema). Others, such as Tottenham's Bernie Grant Arts Centre and Deptford's Stephen Lawrence Centre, have survived by changing their mission somewhat (though the latter has, distressingly, been vandalised on several occasions and is now surrounded by security gates and barbed wire). In many of these cases, the shadow of racism and the problems of multiculturalism in a complex modern society loom large.[6] See Box 3.2 on 'Rich Mix'.

Box 3.2   Rich Mix

Perhaps the best known example of a regeneration-based arts flagship project in London is Rich Mix in Tower Hamlets, East London. This is still a functioning arts centre, and so is not a failed project as such. But, in its early years at least, it was perhaps more famous for the criticism it attracted than for any artistic success it may have had (Hewison, 2014; Mirza, 2012). Dogged by delays, cost over-runs and questions about its management,

---

[6] Bernie Grant was a prominent black Labour MP, subject to numerous attacks in the conservative UK tabloid press; Stephen Lawrence was a young man murdered by racist youths in 1993.

Box 3.2   (Continued)

it finally opened in April 2006 with a three-screen cinema, café, artist-in-residence workspace and a mix of eating spaces, to which performance and exhibition spaces were later added. Its genesis had been in the 1990s politics of Tower Hamlets, a part of London characterised by extreme poverty and high levels of ethnic diversity and, situated cheek by jowl with London's financial district, being subject to gentrification and displacement. It was also, both in historical terms and currently, a key site of far-right politics and of anti-fascist resistance movements.

As Mirza (2012) and others have commented, Rich Mix was plagued by mixed motivations from its earliest days. The original hope for the centre was that it would be a celebration of the area's ethnic diversity, a centre for the 'arts that Britain ignores' (Khan, 1976) or 'the ICA of East London', and there was talk of a Museum of Immigration, alongside the rather more basic need to provide a cinema in an area that didn't have one. An article in the *Times* newspaper put it rather more crudely: 'a meeting point for City boy, Bangladeshi grandmothers and dungaree-clad students' (Bartlett, 2008). Appealing to both a London arts establishment and an enormously heterogeneous local community was always going to be difficult, but the project became particularly high-profile because of its association with two key New Labour figures: Oona King, then local MP and a member of the Cabinet; and a Labour member of the House of Lords and prominent media figure, Waheed Ali. It was also championed by London Mayor Ken Livingstone and his Office, and it received one of the largest single grants from the Greater London Authority for any cultural project.[7]

Such was the burden of expectations on Rich Mix that it could hardly meet them all. It was blighted by its New Labour connections (via Oona King) and its association with the fractious politics

---

[7] Livingstone was a prominent critic of New Labour. He was also the leader of the Greater London Council from 1981 to 1986 during the cultural policy innovations discussed in Section 1.6. He was elected Mayor of London as an independent in 2000, before switching back to Labour for the election in 2004, which he also won. He lost the 2008 and 2012 mayoral elections to Conservative Boris Johnson.

of Tower Hamlets.[8] As a result, it suffered unfair criticism (e.g., Bartlett, 2008). Yet Mirza's argument that Rich Mix failed to set out an artistic vision that could in some way protect it from its warring supporters and opponents has some merit. An 'ICA of the East' would need a cultural story about the kind of arts or artistic vision to which it was committed, a story that, as Mirza points out, the Whitechapel Art Gallery, just down in the road in the same area, has had throughout the twentieth century. The Whitechapel was established at a more culturally confident moment, in 1901, when bringing great art to the impoverished communities of London's East End was a justification for its existence. But if the primary purpose of an arts organisation is defined exclusively in social or economic terms – in this case, in terms of relationship to its communities – it can obviously fail on those terms. Nowadays, and somewhat ironically, Rich Mix probably fits its local 'hipsterised' community better than it did when it was launched, with its mix of cinema and live music, popular culture exhibitions and lots of space for 'hanging out'. At the same time, it's hard to say what sets it apart from other leisure facilities in what is now a very gentrified area. There are 'communities' around it from which it remains remote. Its strong identification with the black communities of the East End is becoming less apparent all the time.

Some criticisms of some projects seem heavily imbued by a metropolitan snobbery that portrays any difficulties in luring substantial crowds as a sign of outright failure and waste (such as Millard's comments on Walsall's New Art Gallery and the Baltic). Nevertheless, a major issue, especially in the early days of New Labour, seems to have been optimistic, sometimes even absurd, projections of visitor numbers – as with the Dome. Cultural policy researcher Linda Moss (2000) attributed these inflated projections to the 'huge moral and political pressures' on policy makers and consultants to support large regional visitor attractions, especially when making comparisons with other attractions. How much New Labour can be blamed for such developments is a difficult question. The UK media were not slow to attack Labour for problems. However,

---

[8] In the 2005 election, King lost her local parliamentary seat to former Labour MP George Galloway, who had formed a new party called Respect. King's support for the Iraq war and Galloway's opposition to it were major factors.

the failure to abandon the most misguided projects suggests that New Labour politicians and policy makers often failed to exercise proper scepticism about these initiatives.

The considerable expenditure involved may seem to refute the suggestion that New Labour's cultural policies were 'Thatcherite' or 'neo-liberal' or 'privatising'. But there is a connection to neo-liberalisation nevertheless. These projects were nearly all justified on the grounds of urban regeneration, a concept that spread across the developed world during the era of neo-liberalism (see chapters 2 and 5). Some urban regeneration schemes have, according to their critics, appropriated art and culture for the purposes of economic development, as a means of addressing post-industrial decline in Western cities. Although dependent on huge amounts of public subsidy, such projects were often – though not always – based on partnership projects. In the British case, flagship urban regeneration projects were frequently linked to the idea that the creative industries were a growing and dynamic part of modern economies and so could provide employment opportunities. The fact that such opportunities are increasingly the preserve of the highly educated and socially advantaged means that such regeneration projects have generally been implicated in increasing inequality rather than combatting it (see Oakley, 2011).

Internationally, such flagship projects have been condemned as 'isolated and exclusive spaces that are designed to serve visitors over residents and that are divorced from any public planning process' (Grodach, 2010: 354). A case study approach to such flagship projects shows that there are many variations among them, and some projects are much more effective than others in achieving a meaningful revitalisation of cities (Grodach's fine study of three Californian cases demonstrates this). The best projects take into account local lived experience and histories, including the nature of local cultural and artistic production. Even in such cases, however, the exclusions and displacements of gentrification are never far away. What's the alternative? Evans (2009: 22) contrasts such 'new-build cultural facilities' and other flagship projects – whether relatively successful, failed or struggling – with the more 'organic' and 'community-oriented' arts centres that, in his view, thrived in an earlier generation. Perhaps sometimes a previous generation's practices are romanticised by later commentators; and a critique of gentrification should not lead to a dismissal of any and all attempts to construct new 'official' art spaces. Yet some of the problems surrounding major flagship projects built in the 2000s should be a serious concern for supporters of public subsidy of the arts and culture. These projects derived from political and cultural trends that were considerably larger than New

Labour, but they fitted well with New Labour's desire to show the UK to be a leader in a new, highly competitive globalised economy, and with its focus on private–public partnerships and on justifications of the arts based on their contribution to economic growth and social amelioration. These often grandiose projects left little space for grassroots initiatives in an era where the bohemianism that had sustained previous generations of artistic innovation was increasingly under threat (see Lloyd, 2006).

3.4 Sponsorship and philanthropy

Philanthropy has long been a source of funding for the arts, even when government arts funding rose dramatically between the 1950s and the 1970s. But the increasing use of private sponsorship and philanthropy to support the arts has undoubtedly been one of the major developments in cultural policy over the last 30 or 40 years. What was New Labour's relationship to these means of funding?[9]

The UK has seen significant increases in sponsorship and philanthropy, and in the resources devoted by arts and heritage institutions to raising money. A key organisation involved in arts sponsorship claims that business sponsorship of the arts in the UK increased between 1976 and 2009 from £600,000 per year to £686 million per year (Arts and Business, 2015). In her major book on the subject, Chin-tao Wu (2002: 47–82) argued that the increasing presence of corporate intervention in the arts in the USA and the UK, including sponsorship, was intimately connected to attempts by the Reagan and Thatcher governments to reduce the public sector and radically expand the power of big business – what many would call neo-liberalism, or neo-liberalisation. By the late 1970s, the UK Conservative Party was embracing the ascendant ideology of neo-liberalism after a period of 'one nation' moderate or paternalist conservatism in the 1950s and 1960s. As we saw in Chapter 2, some prominent Conservatives had argued from the late 1970s that there should be serious cuts in public funding of the arts (and some even argued that the Arts Council should be abolished) on the grounds that they would be better supported by the spending, philanthropic

---

[9] Corporate sponsorship and philanthropy are traditionally distinguished from one another. In the former case, the corporation seeks a marketing opportunity via public association with an arts institution; in the latter case, no such association is presumed. Sponsorship will generally come from the marketing department of a company; philanthropy is more likely to come from an individual, or a company concerned with corporate social responsibility. Phillips and Whannel (2013) argue the two are merging.

and otherwise, of private individuals who would be enriched by lower taxes (Phillips and Whannel, 2013). The mid-1980s saw the introduction by Thatcher's Conservative government of the Business Sponsorship Incentive Scheme, based on matching funding and administered by the Association for Business Sponsorship of the Arts (ABSA), founded in 1976 and itself a product as well as a prime mover of the shift towards sponsorship from the 1970s onwards (see Gray, 2000: 118–19). A key figure in that organisation later remarked that arts sponsorship was 'one of the cornerstones of Thatcherism' (Colin Tweedy, quoted by Wu, 2002: 3). This is hyperbole, but the strong connections seem evident.

Increasing arts sponsorship and corporate intervention, and reliance on philanthropy, has been a long-term trend in cultural policy across much of the world – see Box 3.3 for discussion of the problems surrounding it. However, the key question in the present context is: to what extent can New Labour be seen as actively promoting that trend in the UK – or at least failing to inhibit it? New Labour continued the Conservatives' close relationship with the aforementioned arts and business sponsorship organisation (ABSA), renamed Arts and Business in 1999, in order to 'emphasise the widening and deepening of the partnership between arts and business', in the words of its then Director (quoted by Philips and Whannel, 2013: 109). From 1999, Arts and Business were provided with core funding directly from the DCMS, later channelled via Arts Council England (ACE).[10]

Box 3.3   Sponsorship and philanthropy: What's the problem?

Arts sponsorship and philanthropy have obvious benefits for arts organisations that can access them. But there are many reasons to be concerned about the increasing emphasis on sponsorship and philanthropy of the last 30 years. First, research suggests that sponsors tend to direct their money towards the most prestigious and powerful arts organisations (Dight, 2007; Gerolymbos et al., 2013; Stanziola, 2007). In the UK, such institutions are overwhelmingly based in London, and to a lesser extent in the other three national capitals (Edinburgh, Cardiff, Belfast). As a result, sponsorship and philanthropy potentially undermine the

---

[10] The Conservative–Liberal Democrat coalition cut Arts and Business's funding on coming to power in 2010 – though this by no means meant that they reversed Labour's sympathetic view of sponsorship; in fact, quite the opposite (see Chapter 8). See Stanziola (2007, 2012) for more discussion of Arts and Business.

way in which public subsidy might be used to equalise resources between different parts of the country. They also tend to privilege metropolitan notions of 'excellence' over local and grassroots ideas of quality. Second, Wu's (2002: 9–12) claim is that such sponsorship potentially strengthens class inequalities as a whole, by favouring the tastes and inclinations of a managerial elite. Cultural spending in general tends to favour the tastes and practices of 'higher' classes (Bennett et al., 2009; Bunting et al., 2008), but arguably sponsorship and philanthropy especially favour privileged sections of the upper middle class, with high levels of both economic and cultural capital.

Third, although in the British context there is little evidence of direct interference in content by sponsors and philanthropic donors, major galleries, theatres and so on are nevertheless likely to consider their reactions as one of a number of issues in choosing exhibitions and performances. This is often evident in considering which exhibitions and performances gain no sponsorship versus those which do. Blockbusters that would already be likely to gain a large audience tend to attract sponsorship, whereas exhibitions and performances that attempt to innovate, challenge or explore new perspectives may struggle. One controversial example of sponsorship during the New Labour period was the leading UK gallery Tate Modern's deal with Swiss bank UBS, which supported the Tate's 2006 rehang; as part of the deal, a special exhibition was mounted of photographs from UBS's own collection.[11] This collection could, of course, be expected to grow in value as a result of such exposure. As with other sponsorship deals, there seems to have been little transparency about the size of the donation and its conditions.

Fourth, sponsorship deals serve to make corporations appear altruistic, masking the way in which their imperatives to maximise profit and/or shareholder returns can militate against the well-being of societies, communities and individuals not associated with the corporations. Moir and Taffler (2004) concluded that

---

[11] The Tate was itself founded by a philanthropist, the sugar baron and collector Henry Tate (1821–1899), but now receives funding from the DCMS. A number of writers have commented on how sponsorship represents a return to Victorian notions of patronage. The UBS sponsorship deal ended in 2010 following the bank's catastrophic losses in the financial crisis.

Box 3.3   (Continued)

altruism is overwhelmingly *not* the motivation for corporate giving to the arts and culture in the UK, based on a statistical analysis
of 95 case studies of business support for the arts.

Fifth, we should not underestimate how more direct effects on
content may come to be a feature of the sponsorship landscape. As
even the economically liberal and politically conservative newspaper *The Economist* pointed out in 2001, 'what was off limits
yesterday can become tomorrow's norm' (*The Economist*, 2001:
90). As an example of encroaching commercialism linked to
sponsorship and philanthropy, its writer discussed the New York
Guggenheim's aggressive marketing and its exhibitions of dresses
by Armani (linked to a $15 million donation) and of BMW motor-
bikes. In this respect, corporate intervention is part of a broader
problem of commercialisation and commodification in the arts,
including the increasing presence of business people on boards,
and an increasing reliance on revenue from cafés, museum shops
and so on to supplement other sources of income (Alexander,
2008; MacPherson, 2002; Strom, 2003).

New Labour also extended tax exemptions for charitable 'giving' (via
the Gift Aid scheme), and New Labour made some play of this as a
measure to encourage corporate and personal giving. But, arguably,
they placed relatively little emphasis on sponsorship and philanthropy,
certainly in comparison with the succeeding Coalition government.
Neglecting to make improvements to arrangements for philanthropic
giving should not be treated as a positive, however (Brown, 2011). The
Treasury-commissioned Goodison Review made recommendations in
2004 to make philanthropy to the arts and museums sector easier. But
New Labour did not follow them up. Only with the Coalition's Cultural Gift scheme (see Chapter 8) were Goodison's recommendations
implemented.[12]

New Labour's general 'pro-business' orientation – manifest in
its 'Third Way' commitment to public–private partnerships (see

---

[12] 'Only the other day, one of the senior DCMS officials admitted in a public
conference, "well, actually what we're doing in the cultural gift scheme now are
only the things that Nicholas Goodison wrote however many years ago" – which
he did' (Sandy Nairne, interview).

Chapter 2) – was quite in keeping with the move on the part of arts and cultural organisations towards greater 'partnerships' with the private sector. However, a truly 'privatising' cultural policy would presumably seek strongly to substitute such private income for public expenditure. As we have seen, this was not the case with New Labour. Rather, they saw encouragement of sponsorship as a supplement to increased public investment. One significant example of such investment was New Labour's policy of free admission to government-sponsored museums, which we consider in the next section.

3.5 An access success? Free admission to museums and galleries

The free admission policy was the central plank of New Labour's cultural policy access agenda, and is frequently cited as one of the greatest achievements of its period in office. Unlike other elements of New Labour cultural policy, the subsequent government has felt unable to remove it (see Chapter 8), and while steep charges for special exhibitions may be said to be eroding the principle, free admission to permanent national collections seems now to have attained the status of cross-party consensus.[13]

While it did not feature in Labour's 1997 election manifesto, the Labour Party in opposition had consistently opposed admission charges (Falconer and Blair, 2003) and it committed itself to a 'review' of such charges during the 1997 election campaign (Labour Party, 1997a). The issue had been a party political one since the early 1970s, when the Conservative administration of Edward 'Ted' Heath (1970–1974) had removed the statutory impediments to charging that existed in the legislation governing some museums, and allowed government-sponsored museums to introduce charges as they deemed necessary.[14] The 1974 Labour government again abolished charges, and it was not until the Thatcher government of the 1980s that some museums, under pressure to reduce dependence on public funding, reintroduced them. These included many of the more high-profile London museums, such as the Science Museum and Natural History Museum, while others, including the British Museum, the Tate galleries and the National Gallery, held out

---

[13] Though one Labour Shadow Cabinet member, Tristram Hunt, expressed a different view in a piece for the *Observer* in 2011 (Hunt, 2011).
[14] A number of Britain's national museums, the British Museum and National Gallery included, have a history of free admission, dating back to their foundation.

against charging for entrance, though they generally charged for special exhibitions, as they continue to do.

For the incoming New Labour government, the process of abolishing museum charges was lengthy and relatively contentious, with even museum directors who were sympathetic to the idea expressing concern about loss of revenues (Mark Jones, interview). Free admission was introduced gradually, with charges abolished for children in 1999, for the over-60s in 2000, and for all visitors in 2001. A major concern was value-added tax (VAT), for which museums would cease to be liable when they ceased, by virtue of not charging, to be 'businesses' under the existing VAT legislation. This meant they were unable to reclaim VAT paid on the supplies and services they bought, which was crucial for those undertaking large capital expenditure, as many museums were doing in the wake of increased lottery funding. In 2001, after lengthy and complex negotiations over VAT with the Treasury and the European Commission, and with a new Finance Bill in place, the DCMS increased the subsidy to the national museums to compensate for the loss of income, and free admission was introduced.[15]

While chiming perfectly with New Labour's core cultural policy theme of increasing access, the specific aim of abolishing museum charges was not articulated at the time. Chris Smith described it to us as 'much more of a personal crusade than a bit of preformed policy' and linked it to his own long-time opposition to entry charges (Smith, interview). Christopher Frayling (Chair of Arts Council England, 2005–2009) described it as 'part of the policy of access' and described the 'extraordinary combination of circumstances', leading to 'free admission . . . to buildings that had been enhanced by the lottery' (interview). A stronger sense of New Labour's aim in this respect can perhaps be gleaned from then Minister of Culture Tessa Jowell's statement in January 2002 responding to the rise in admissions that followed the scrapping of charges:

figures show what a spectacular success the scrapping of admission charges at our great national collections has been. Clearly, charges were acting as a restraint to many people, particularly families . . . Free

---

[15] Detailed histories of the implementation of free admission and the complexities around the VAT issue can be found in Babbidge (2000), Falconer and Blair (2003) and Cowell (2007).

admission has democratised the nation's treasures, making them accessible to all.

(DCMS, 2002)

The degree to which free admission 'democratised' the nation's cultural assets has been the source of much debate (Jancovich, 2011; O'Neill, 2008; Ross, 2004; Sandell, 2002, 2003). Simply providing free access to existing collections, without any discussion of 'what culture' and 'whose culture' constitutes 'the nation's treasures', is a rather thin notion of a democratic culture. Labour's notion of 'access' was concerned with extending and diversifying audiences, not diversifying collections (O'Neill, 2008; Ross, 2004). As Stewart Wood, adviser on culture to Prime Minister Gordon Brown from 2007 onwards, put it, 'it was definitely an expanding access to culture imperative, rather than a democratising the substance of culture imperative – definitely' (Stewart Wood, interview).

In terms of 'expanding access to culture', however, it is difficult to dispute the fact that the decade or more since the abolition of charges has seen a huge rise in the number of both visits and visitors to museums and galleries in the UK. The figures vary somewhat depending on when they were calculated, but the majority of sources agree that visits to museums and galleries have increased significantly. The DCMS claimed that visits to 'those institutions that used to charge an entrance fee' increased by 158 per cent between December 2001 and 2012 (DCMS, 2013). Cowell's earlier analysis (2007) of research on free admission calculated an increase in museum visits of over 60 per cent or 24 million visits in 1998/9 compared with 39 million in 2006/7 (Cowell, 2007). Selwood and Davies (2005) claimed that in the first year of free admissions alone, there was an increase of 69 per cent in visits to government-sponsored museums across the country.

The figures for individual institutions are even more impressive. For example, both the Victoria and Albert Museum and National Museums Liverpool saw their visitor figures increase by 139 per cent between 2001 and 2006. And this, it should be remembered, was in the context of a museums sector that was, according to a report of 1999, experiencing a 'levelling off in volume of visitor demand despite a growing number of museums generating greater capacity' (Babbidge, 2000: 3).

Yet the degree to which this is an unalloyed policy success continues to be debated. Selwood and Davies (2005) have argued that it is difficult to separate the effects of increased lottery spending – the opening of new galleries and enhanced facilities – from the effects of free admissions in

encouraging visitors. They argue that free museums that did not introduce significant new facilities or collections failed to see similar increases
in visitor numbers. Falconer and Blair (2003), writing not long after the
policy was introduced, questioned the degree to which cost was ever
a barrier to entry in the first place. And even those more sympathetic
to the policy (Cowell, 2007) argue that evaluating its 'impact' would
require a clearer sense of what government had intended from the policy in the first place. In particular, was the aim to diversify the museum
audience – as Jowell's reference to democracy and accessibility to all
might be taken to suggest? Was it to increase the appeal to overseas
tourists? Or was it simply to encourage more visits, even if it meant the
same people (in terms of demographics) visiting more often? Cowell,
in his assessment of the impact of free admission, assumes that an aim
of abolishing charges 'was to encourage more visitors to the sponsored
museums, especially by those visitors who may not have been willing to
pay an entrance fee' (Cowell 2007: 208).

There is some legitimate dispute about the degree to which cost was
or is a barrier to people's willingness to visit museums and galleries.
A public opinion survey of 2003 purported to show that a lack of attendance was largely due to a combination of limited time (43 per cent)
and lack of interest, with almost a quarter saying they had never considered visiting a museum and 40 per cent saying they were unaware
of the free admission policy (Ipsos Mori, 2003). But an even more
significant question concerns the degree to which different audiences
have been brought into museums by the abolition of charges. The
National Museums Directors Conference, which represents the majority of government-sponsored museums, argues that 'audiences have
become more diverse since the introduction of free museums' (NMDC,
2013), but the evidence on this is rather mixed. Cowell (2007) analysed the first five years of free admission, examining the data collected
from various sources, including the research undertaken by Mori and the
DCMS's quarterly *Taking Part* surveys. He found increases in the number
of visits by both working-class and ethnic minority people. The number
of visits by working-class people increased from 15 per cent to 16.7 per
cent of total visits. Visits by ethnic minorities increased from 3.2 per
cent of all visits in 2000/1 to 4.9 per cent in 2005/6, though it should be
borne in mind that in London (home to many of these museums) the
ethnic minority population is close to 40 per cent, so the rise needs to
be considered in that context.

While diversifying museum visitors was not an explicit aim for
the overall policy of free admissions, once Public Service Agreement
performance targets were introduced (see below for more discussion of

this), one of the main targets for museum performance was 'number of visits by UK adults aged 16 and over from lower socio-economic groups' (DCMS, 2008). A further DCMS target (PSA3) stated that it would

> increase the take up of cultural and sporting opportunities by adults and young people aged 16 and above from priority groups ... [by] increasing the number accessing museums and galleries collections by 2%.
>
> (DCMS, 2005: 20)

When more detailed national data became available, following the introduction of the *Taking Part* survey in 2005 the figures look less impressive.[16] Visits by people in lower socio-economic groups had declined by 11 per cent between 2006/7 and 2010/11, while growth in ethnic minority visitors appears to have stalled and members of ethnic minority groups remain less likely to visit a museum than those who define themselves as white (DCMS, 2013). It is difficult to know what accounts for the change between the first five years after abolition of charges, which seemed to witness an increase of visits by so-called 'target groups', and the following five years, when this increase declined or went into reverse. But there may be some support for Selwood and Davies' argument that the large increase in capital spending on 'flagship' projects around the turn of the century attracted an increase in visitors across all groups that in some cases was not sustained in later years.

It therefore seems legitimate to question New Labour's record on this issue. There was an overall growth in museum visitors as a result of free admission, but less change in the representation of particular groups within that overall number. But, as Cowell argues (2007), free admission was not intended to be the government's only policy for attracting new audiences; under New Labour there was also an attempt to reposition museums as, in the words of one DCMS report of 2000, 'centres of social change' (DCMS, 2000a). In considering this, it is useful to draw

---

[16] Introduced in 2005 and funded by the DCMS as well as the major sports, arts and heritage agencies, *Taking Part* is a quarterly national survey of arts, sport and other cultural participation. The survey was designed to show not only participation in these activities, but also the benefits derived from them, for example in terms of well-being, and thus to serve as a legitimating device for public spending in these areas. The survey has been criticised for, among other things, only measuring participation in publicly funded cultural activities, rather than looking at the whole range of cultural activities that people undertake. See Miles and Sullivan (2012) for a useful critique.

on Gibson's (2013) distinction between the museum as an institution or building, and the activities or programmes that take place inside museums and through their external engagement. While the 'spectacularisation' of the museum as an element of urban regeneration projects has been rightly criticised (Evans, 2003; Garcia, 2004a; Ponzini, 2012), Gibson contends that this concentration on the symbolic character of the museum as building ignores its activities as a cultural and educational space. And New Labour's policy, while undoubtedly conforming to the cultural regeneration 'script' of new buildings and capital improvements, did not stop there. It also pressed such institutions into greater engagement, particularly in the educational sphere. Such activities were numerous, but, to give a flavour, included the following: the establishment of regional cultural diversity networks to promote awareness among staff of the need to serve diverse communities; specific projects on themes such as migration, identity and refugees; archive projects such as *Celebrating the Black Presence in Westminster 1500–2000*, which aimed to dispel the myth that black people were new arrivals in the capital; and specific work with schools, for example on the Holocaust or the links between slavery and contemporary racism (MLA, 2004). Such initiatives should not be dismissed.

3.6 Targets, audit and the New Public Management

Although their record shows a commitment to considerable public expenditure on arts and culture, New Labour were also keen to show themselves to be friendly towards business, and adopted a longstanding conservative suspicion of the public sector. A dubious view of the private sector as more efficient and effective than the public sector was undoubtedly given a major boost by the international rise of neo-liberalism, and New Labour did little or nothing to question that growing attitude. In a number of its policies, New Labour successfully completed the implementation of neo-liberalising policies that the Conservatives had struggled to realise – notably Private Finance Initiatives and the centralisation of local control over the delivery of services (see Shaw, 2007; Wilks-Heeg, 2009).

One important way in which New Labour's ambivalent attitude towards the public realm was manifested across Labour's policies in general, including its cultural policies, was its adoption of NPM mechanisms, especially top-down performance management tools. Two influential articles by Christopher Hood (1991, 1995) crystallised the term 'new public management' to describe a series of developments in public administration in the 1980s, especially in the UK. The main characteristics Hood identified have been summarised by Lapsley (2009: 3) as follows:

- unbundling public sector into corporatized units organized by product;
- more contract-based competitive provision, with internal markets and term contracts;
- stress on private sector management styles;
- more stress on discipline and frugality in resource use;
- visible hands-on top management;
- explicit formal measurable standards and measurement of performance and success;
- greater emphasis on output controls.

Intended to achieve accountability and transparency, these techniques embodied a lack of trust in public service workers and managers, who were implicitly (and sometimes explicitly) understood as being in need of constant vigilance and monitoring. New Labour adopted these techniques with new vigour. From 1998, all government departments under Labour were required to adhere to Public Service Agreements (PSAs), with lists of objectives which were known as Delivery Service Objectives (DSOs), addressing (slippery) targets such as 'excellence' and 'economic impact'. As one later document produced by the DCMS helpfully explained,

> In October 2007, 30 new PSAs were announced as part of the Comprehensive Spending Review 2007 and set out the priority outcomes for the CSR2007 period, 2008–09 to 2010–11 .... Each department also agreed with HM Treasury a set of DSOs, which are designed to complement and sometimes underpin related PSAs. DCMS leads on one PSA (PSA22), and has four DSOs.
>
> (DCMS, no date)

The PSA targets for culture included increasing visitor numbers to national museums, diversifying audiences in terms of class and ethnicity, increasing the number of internet connections in libraries, and increasing the amount of educational work undertaken by arts organisations. While none of these seems an unworthy goal for cultural policy, the stress on *measuring* was resisted by arts organisations, largely because of the administrative burden it placed upon them. Measuring visitor numbers was at least simple, if costly, but in other cases targets were essentially qualitative, and sought to capture the impact of cultural funding in terms of wider goals such as urban regeneration. Providing evidence of achieving these wider aims presents serious methodological challenges, not least in terms of causality, and the cultural sector often lacked the skills and resources to provide the kind of evidence that was being required of them.

The problems surrounding targets and NPM were also very much evident in local government. New Labour's scheme for bringing about the 'modernisation' of local government, which they called Best Value, was introduced in the Local Government Act of 1999 (see Miller, 2008). Local government analyst Gerry Stoker reported in 2004 that there was a 'widespread sense that the processes associated with Best Value have presented a major challenge but that they have largely been adopted, and led to small-scale incremental improvements in services in a wide range of cases' (Stoker, 2004: 94). The price paid, however, was time-consuming and expensive performance management. Best Value, among other elements, required local councils to undertake a quinquennial performance review measuring the degree to which they achieved the three 'E's of economy, efficiency and effectiveness, assessed via the four 'C's criteria: challenge, comparison, consultation and competitiveness. The result was that by 2004, as cultural policy researcher Clive Gray (2004: 39–40) outlined, local, sub-national cultural strategies needed to take into account,

> at least five different central government departments, four separate task forces, and ten arm's-length 'sponsored agencies', as well as at least ten statutory plans and five nonstatutory ones, alongside the local authority's own corporate strategy, Best Value plan, [and] individual service strategies and plans, and more or less anything else up to and including the planning kitchen sink.

Eleonora Belfiore (2004) drew on critical studies of the 'audit society' (Power, 1997) to consider the implications of these techniques for cultural policy. She argued that they represented an intensified form of top-down control that made arts and cultural policy vulnerable to changes in political direction, including funding. More broadly, as Belfiore pointed out, drawing on critical analysts such as John Clarke and Alan Finlayson, these methods served to remove political discussion and debate from the process of government, or at least to diminish its role. They also represented an attack on the public domain. As David Marquand (2004) argued, New Labour evinced a populist scorn for intermediate institutions and professionalism – which, like Conservatives, Labour tended to see in terms of the protection of vested interests. In crime, education and migration policy, the Labour leadership was often antagonistic towards the social liberalism and/or libertarianism at large among professionals working in these sectors, and the same was true in cultural policy (see Hesmondhalgh, 2005).

In fact, as Bowerman et al. (2000) usefully point out, the term 'audit society', developed by Power (1997), is useful but insufficient. They offer, instead, the idea of a 'performance management society' to describe the permeation of such techniques throughout most modern organisations. Performance management includes not just audit itself, but also techniques of inspection, benchmarking, self-assessment, strategic planning, target setting, key performance indicators and service agreements. Researchers of public administration, such as Irvine Lapsley (2009), have discussed how NPM techniques constantly *disappoint* policy makers, because of their reliance on (often ineffective) management consultants, unrealistic expectations of the contribution of IT systems, the creation of tick box cultures of compliance, and the stifling of innovation through stultifying forms of so-called 'risk management'. This perspective, we should add, comes not from a radical critic of management, but from a figure committed to making public administration more effective (see also James, 2004).

One does not have to be a neo-liberal to recognise the importance of efficiency and accountability in government, and it would be absurd to portray social democratic parties (of the 'Old Labour' kind) as inherently hostile towards them. Nevertheless, in its adoption of 'Third Way' policies, New Labour significantly distanced itself from social democratic views of the way in which the pursuit of profit by businesses might damage the well-being of workers and citizens, and pursued techniques of governance that fitted with a suspicion of public sector professionals. Here, then, the accusation that New Labour were essentially 'neo-liberal' inheritors of Thatcher's legacy (see Chapter 1) has some purchase.

3.7   The arts backlash, cultural value and the 'instrumentalism' debate

Few professionals working in the arts and heritage objected to New Labour's seemingly benign goals of opening up access and providing educational opportunities in culture. But the use of targets and auditing to monitor access and education and other aspects of their work were deeply disliked within the arts and heritage communities, in ways that directly parallel the resentments of teachers, medical professionals and university academics towards similar infringements on their autonomy in their own respective fields. From the early 2000s onwards, senior arts figures began to make public statements to this effect. For example, an article in *The Observer* by incoming National Theatre Director Nicholas Hytner in 2003 praised increased arts expenditure by Labour, but castigated the monitoring of audiences in order to ensure the broadening of access to new constituencies (Hytner, 2003). Arts institutions, wrote Hytner, have 'learnt to speak the language of access, diversity and inclusion' and 'share aspirations with our political masters'.

> We all of us want to play to as wide a public as we can find. But there is a real danger in a relentless and exclusive focus on the nature of our audience. Performing artists, once under attack for apparently not paying their way, are now in the dock for attracting the wrong kind of people. And it doesn't seem to matter whether what we do is any good or not. The orchestras were attacked not for the quality of their playing but for the unacceptably low proportion of young people in their audiences.

A different but related set of concerns were also being expressed by many in the arts and heritage worlds. The term 'instrumentalism' came to be employed widely.[17] It referred to the idea that culture was being used too much as an instrument to achieve non-cultural ends such as economic and social outcomes. Much criticism of New Labour's instrumentalism focuses either on concerns about protecting the autonomy of the arts from such direct policy control (Mirza, 2012) or on the fact that such interventions do not 'work', as the claims made for them can rarely be substantiated (Belfiore, 2002).

In response to both sets of concerns (the 'access' focus on audiences rather than quality, and the drift towards 'instrumentalist' rationales), the issue of 'the value of culture' was explored at a seminar hosted by the influential Labour think tank Demos. The seminar was attended by the then Culture Secretary, Tessa Jowell, who responded by writing a highly unusual personal reflection on cultural value.[18] Predictably,

---

[17] An early use of the term with regard to cultural policy is Vestheim (1994).
[18] Jowell replaced Chris Smith after the 2001 election, and was Culture Secretary from 2001 to 2007, during which time she was very much involved with the successful London bid to host the 2012 Olympic Games.

this was greeted in many policy and media quarters as unacceptably wishy-washy, because it supposedly failed to make hard choices between cultural spending and other needs, such as prison officers (see the response by think tank IPPR cited by Holden, 2004). John Holden, writing for Demos, went further than Jowell in trying to outline a conception of 'intrinsic value' that drew on anthropological and other thought, while maintaining the need for accountability.[19] Yet the framing of the debates in terms of 'instrumentalism' – especially when opposed to 'intrinsic' value – ultimately led to intellectual dead ends (*Cultural Trends*, 2011). Rationales based on 'intrinsic' cultural value have proven elusive. And it is perfectly legitimate to value culture for reasons that are secondary to its fundamental nature – what matters is how those 'non-cultural' or 'less cultural' ends are conceived, and to what purpose. While it is to Jowell's credit that she made an effort to engage reflectively with cultural value, her essay, as O-Kyung Yoon (2010) has pointed out, mixes invocations of such intrinsic value with a different set of instrumentalist rationales, involving 'aspiration'.

In the interviews conducted for this project, the term 'instrumentalism' was generally associated with the debate on 'targets', and for those who had worked in government there was a certain amount of defensiveness about that. Few people were willing to defend instrumentalism per se. However, Mark Jones, Director of London's Victoria and Albert Museum from 2001 to 2011, maintained that it is 'absolutely right to understand that organisations can, often surprisingly, achieve policy objectives which are not their core policy objective', and that other people working in museums do welcome 'the opportunity to show what they could do in terms of education or inclusion' (Mark Jones, interview). Hilary Carty, former Director of the Arts Council-funded Cultural Leadership programme, commented on the fact that, for many of those who had been working in community arts or education programmes in cultural organisations in the past, the explicit 'social' agenda of New Labour's cultural policies was welcome.

> You now had societal permission to tackle social issues using the arts and culture. You no longer had to feel like an outsider, siphoning off precious resources from a mainline programme in order to do this activity. You could bring it right into the fold. So that was very,

---

[19] Holden resorted to the then fashionable, but later somewhat discredited, concept of public value to articulate policy pragmatics. See Lee et al. (2011) for critical discussion of the concept of public value.

very rewarding, I think, for individuals who'd been working on the inclusion agenda for a while.

(Hilary Carty, interview)

Social exclusion – a key New Labour theme – was firmly within the remit of the DCMS, almost from its creation, and certainly after the Policy Action Team 10 report (DCMS, 1999). Policy Action Teams were set up by the Social Exclusion Unit (SEU) in Labour's first term to report on particular issues relating to social exclusion. PAT 10 was the arts team, charged with 'using arts to engage people in poor neighbourhoods, particularly those who may feel most excluded, such as disaffected young people and people from ethnic minorities' (DCMS, 1999: 5).

This set the tone for much of New Labour's social instrumentalism in culture. Cultural organisations and activities were seen to have the ability to 'engage' people, to bring people together and to 'include' people or communities that are in some sense excluded. Under the influence of US thinkers such as Robert Putnam, this engagement was often referred to in terms of 'social capital' (Putnam, 2000) and was influential in policy on children and young people (Department for Education and Skills, 2003), citizenship (Cabinet Office, 1999), volunteering (Department for Education and Employment, 1999) and neighbourhood renewal (ODPM, 2001), as well as cultural policy.

A problem for arts and culture, however, was that the New Labour period was marked by frequent changes in social policy objectives or priorities. A report for the Museums, Libraries and Archives Council (MLA) (MLA, 2005) found at least six areas of social policy that cultural agencies were being asked to address in some way: social exclusion, neighbourhood renewal, community cohesion, cultural diversity, health (particularly mental health) and regeneration. This was further complicated in the newly devolved nations. Scotland and Wales had their own responsibilities for social policy and their own definitions of notions such as social exclusion. An example of a priority change was the shift away from 'social exclusion', which had been a favoured term of the first New Labour administration, symbolised by its establishment of the aforementioned SEU. By the time of the second New Labour administration, particularly following the Cantle Report on the Bradford and Oldham riots (Home Office, 2001), social or community *cohesion* was the favoured term. In this case, the shift was not merely terminological, but represented a concern that Britain's communities were fragmenting along ethnic or religious lines (Donohue, 2013; Mirza, 2012). The reality that they were fragmenting along socio-economic lines seemed to provoke less anxiety.

What was distinctive about the New Labour approach, therefore, was not the idea that the arts might have wider social benefits, but the degree to which these social benefits needed to be demonstrated (Levitt, 2008; Selwood, 2010). As Will Davies (2014) has argued, neo-liberalism is typically less concerned with expanding markets as such than it is with expanding the reach of market-based techniques of evaluation. Yet evaluation of the degree to which cultural institutions can be successful in meeting social policy objectives is hugely complex, made more so by the variety of social policy aims to which they are articulated, the lack of agreed and robust indicators of impact, and weaknesses in the evidence base, particularly the lack of longitudinal studies that could show changes over time.[20]

3.8 The return to excellence

In his reflections on 'the value of culture' following the Demos seminar of 2003, think tank analyst John Holden had written the following:

> A growing sense of unease pervades the cultural sector as it sets about justifying its consumption of public money. Instead of talking about what they do – displaying pictures or putting on dance performances – organisations will need to demonstrate how they have contributed to wider policy agendas such as social inclusion, crime prevention and learning.... Even where targets refer to cultural activities, they are often expressed in terms of efficiency, cost-per-user and audience diversity, rather than discussed in terms of cultural achievement.
>
> (Holden, 2004: 13–14)

This picked up on the concerns of national arts leaders such as Nicholas Hytner (see the previous section); but the problem, Holden noted, was 'particularly acute in the relationship between local authorities and the cultural organisations that they fund'.

The third New Labour Culture Secretary, James Purnell, who occupied the office in 2007–2008, made some efforts to distance the party's cultural policies from NPM techniques when, in 2007, he signalled a shift away from targets. In a speech, he coined the word 'targetolatry' – a version of idolatry, but with numbers and spreadsheets as the

---

[20] Such evaluations include Belfiore (2002); Cowling and Keaney (2003); Evans and Shaw (2004); Hooper-Greenhill et al. (2004); Jermyn (2001); Newman and McLean (2004); Ruiz (2004).

false gods.[21] Purnell's response was based on a renewed emphasis on 'excellence' as a basis for funding the arts. This was very much what the powerful UK arts establishment wanted to hear. He commissioned a report from the former Director of the prestigious Edinburgh International Festival, Brian McMaster, which was delivered in 2008. Its sub-title was indicative: 'from measurement to excellence'. McMaster was asked to come up with a 'light touch and non-bureaucratic' means of judging performance (McMaster 2008: 6, 21) – and to lay out how to encourage 'risk taking' and artistic innovation through public money. Access and a concern with audiences were part of the brief – but there was emphasis on the 'depth' as well as the 'width' of engagement. Among the recommendations contained in the report were the suggestions that ten organisations 'with the most innovative ambition' (which, like 'excellence' itself, the report struggled to define) should be provided with ten-year funding, that there should be more touring, and that boards should contain at least two artists.

What effects did this have on DCMS practice and on cultural institutions? Some flavour is provided by museums scholar Helen Graham's (2009) critical analysis of a 'pilot' conducted by the DCMS that sought to test how the monitoring of museums might be modified in the light of McMaster's recommendations. Three 'peer review' audit panels visited three institutions funded by the DCMS: the Natural History Museum, the National Portrait Gallery, and Tyne and Wear Museums (which consisted of 12 museums in the Newcastle-Gateshead area). But, rather than basing their assessments primarily on numerical indicators, the peer reviewers were charged with assessing the museums via six criteria derived from McMaster's report. Access ('open to everyone') was still included, and there was reference to 'international reputation', but the other four criteria emphasised aesthetic 'excellence':

- provides a life-changing experience;
- shows creativity and innovation;
- is willing to take risks;
- presents relevant and challenging concepts to the public.

---

[21] Purnell's attack on 'targetolatry' is discussed by Belfiore as an example of what Brandenberg calls 'political bullshit', in the sense of the term developed by philosopher Harry Frankfurt: 'a proactive strategic communication, meant not to hide a truth or reality or to divert from a particular responsibility, but to create or manage an impression' (Belfiore, 2009: 351).

On the basis of a reading of the panels' comments, and responses from the museums, Graham found that the criterion of providing 'life-changing experience' simply could not be judged on the basis of a three-day visit by a panel. She also found that review by a peer group (mainly consisting of senior museum professionals from other national and international institutions) based on such criteria could not adequately engage with the complexity and subtlety of museum experiences. How to assess 'life-changing' on the basis of a tour and meetings with managers? Nor were the panels able to engage adequately with the local pressures facing museums with a responsibility to serve diverse local publics – and with all the pressures that derive from mediating between local government and publics, as well as national funding bodies.

Democratic institutions need to be able to assess whether public money has been spent well. Purnell and McMaster's renewed focus on aesthetic criteria was in many ways a welcome departure from the NPM obsession with measurability. Yet institutions subject to auditing need to feel that they have been judged fairly, and Graham's study shows that the focus on excellence made transparency and fairness harder to achieve. Pressures to achieve accountability and fairness will tend to push in the direction of more measurability and more audit, rather than less.[22] An end to audit madness can only be achieved by accepting the inevitable limits of fairness and accountability – and, in spite of Purnell's efforts, New Labour did not provide a hospitable climate for such acceptance. Quite the opposite.

Moreover, the shift described here reveals that there are intractable tensions between the two first goals of New Labour cultural policy: access and excellence (see Chapter 2).[23] The 'arm's length' principle of accountability adopted in post-war British cultural policy assumed that producers were the people best positioned to judge what was 'excellent' enough to be worthy of support. But the extension of what constituted fundable artistic endeavour from the 1940s to the 1990s called into question the criterion of 'excellence' as a basis for judgement. Who could judge across the vast panoply of forms, genres and aesthetic

---

[22] An example of this phenomenon in a different context is the Higher Education Funding Council of England and Wales' audits of UK research universities, based on laborious and yet inadequate 'expert review'. See Sayer (2014) for a scathing and insightful account.

[23] In an important, though overly compressed, discussion from 2000, Nicholas Garnham addressed this question, and our discussion draws upon, but reworks, his ideas, especially pages 456–7.

communities? Both neo-liberals and leftists increasingly took the view from the 1980s that cultural policy should be reconfigured towards audiences. The compromise that emerged emphasised the imperative to broaden access: for the right, to ensure taxpayer value for money, and for the left, in order to avoid subsidising the preferences of the educationally and financially better off. The problem is that policies genuinely based on broadening audiences (access) require a redistribution of funds. For example, access might be pursued by promoting excellence in under-supported regions or by supporting the artistic efforts of under-supported groups. But that would raise the possibility, given the finiteness of resources, that support might be removed from where excellence already exists (at the Royal Opera House, say, or the National Theatre) to where it doesn't yet, and this might be considered very risky. There are local versions of these tensions between access and excellence, too. Should a regional museum or theatre spend its money on an education and access officer, or on paying for a superb curator or director to come in and shake up what is on offer? New Labour's cultural policies repressed acknowledgement of fundamental tensions between excellence and access, partly by emphasising education's role in broadening audiences for what was already there (see Chapter 7 for comments on the ultimate inadequacy of these efforts), and partly by pressuring organisations through audit to achieve both goals, as much as possible, at the same time. The response from cultural institutions was often inspiring in terms of educational and access efforts. But enormous moral and administrative pressure was placed on those institutions and their workers (at all levels), a fact seemingly unrecognised by New Labour.

3.9   Assessing New Labour's arts policies

New Labour's boost to public expenditure on art and culture, however problematic its sources in a lottery system developed by the previous Conservative administration, helped stave off privatisation of a kind explicitly advocated by the Coalition government that followed them. Nevertheless, New Labour did very little to resist the international tendency towards top-down regeneration projects, some of which were ill-conceived, and many of which seem to have been mismanaged, at least in the early years of New Labour.

We might also ask: how much credit should we give to New Labour for their increased spending on arts and culture? After all, money was available because they were beneficiaries of an unprecedented economic bubble in the UK. Economic growth in the UK boomed from 1995 to 2006, and this enabled the second Labour administration to allow marked increases in public expenditure because of rising revenues. Yet, by 2009, it had become apparent that economic growth had been the product of an inflated property market and an outsized financial sector that was reaping the rewards of unregulated markets. When the bubble burst, funding cuts hit very quickly. Although it is a fallacy to say that Labour were unreasonably profligate in their spending (a claim regularly made by the Conservative Party and their powerful press allies – see Chapter 8), it is true that they failed to spot the property and financial services bubbles and to take ameliorative measures, as senior Labour politicians have since acknowledged.

Just as problematically, the intensified use of audit and NPM techniques were aspects of Labour cultural policy which were both ineffective and damaging to arts and cultural practice in the UK. NPM undoubtedly derives from the deep suspicion of the public domain and of public sector workers that characterised New Labour's take on 'Third Way' politics. The acceptance of such 'neo-liberalesque' views by politicians, policy makers and the media put public services on the defensive, and New Labour were far too willing to adopt dubious forms of public management, rather than to defend public services and the public domain. What's more, as we shall now consider in the next two chapters, New Labour cultural policy involved a rebalancing of relations between culture and economy, in ways that often (though not always) derived from forms of thinking that could reasonably be called 'neo-liberal'. This was at odds with remnants of the egalitarianism of social democratic cultural policy in its 'cultural democracy' forms.

4
What Was Creative Industries Policy? Film, Copyright and the Shift to Creative Economy

4.1 Creative industries: More than a policy vacuum?

No idea is more strongly associated with New Labour's cultural policies than that of the 'creative industries'. The term and some aspects of the way in which New Labour used it were picked up by national and local governments across the world (Cunningham, 2007; Flew, 2012; Ross, 2009). They were attracted not only by its seeming potential for justifying cultural expenditure of various kinds, but also by its association with the electoral success and modernising image of New Labour and its figurehead Tony Blair.

Yet identifying actual creative industries policies is not easy. Certainly, there were many documents, mapping exercises, committees and speeches that used the term, in Britain and beyond. But where were the actual policies? One possible answer to this question is simple: creative industries policies happened mainly in the *regions* of the UK, under the auspices of New Labour's regional policies, and drawing on thinking about culture-led regeneration. We consider these developments in detail in Chapter 5. But what about the *national* level? For all the international policy success of the concept, and the thousands of academic discussions of its transformative role in cultural policy, there have been suggestions that the term 'creative industries' masked a vacuum, that it served as a glossy piece of political rhetoric, rather than as a solid basis for practical policy activity (Banks and O'Connor, 2009; Oakley, 2006; Pratt, 2009). How true is this?

Here we return to issues raised in Chapter 2. As we saw there, New Labour's use of the creative industries concept indicated that they were going to differentiate themselves from the Conservative vision of cultural policy as national heritage, preservation and canon. Equally, it suggested a move beyond traditional social democratic notions of cultural policy, centred on the use of subsidy to promote artistic inno-vation and, often, grassroots and community cultural activism. A classic piece of New Labour 'Third Way' policy innovation, the concept of cre-ative industries proclaimed that New Labour understood the importance of commerce in modern culture, and that they were not particularly troubled by changing relations between culture and economy. It was shaped partly by the actions and interests of a policy group built around the interests of the copyright-holding cultural industries, specifically those with strong ties to the international and corporate level of the industry. Although these ties were forged before Chris Smith became Culture Secretary, they legitimated the efforts of Chris Smith and others within the DCMS (civil servants, special advisers and other politicians) to expand the importance and remit of the DCMS. The focus on cre-ativity also drew upon various ideas related to ideas about the 'new economy' and the information society, many of them developed and circulated by policy intellectuals and think tanks.

The term drew upon, and consolidated, an emerging, and in some respects quite proper, recognition of the increasing importance of cul-ture (as knowledge and aesthetic expression) in economic life, govern-ment, politics and society. As we saw in Chapter 3, it seems to have played a role in helping to leverage increases in spending on the arts. Yet our analysis below shows how difficult it was for the concept of creative industries policy to make any meaningful difference to the status of cul-tural policy, and of the DCMS, even in policy that was relevant to the cultural industries. We show this in relation to two areas of policy which might be considered principal cases of 'real' creative industries policy sectors at the national level: film policy (Section 4.2) and copyright (Section 4.4).[1] In the intervening section, we discuss how the creative industries concept was modified, partly in response to these difficul-ties, and partly because policy makers and policy shapers (think tanks and so on) need to differentiate what they do from earlier, supposedly 'outmoded' phases of policy. There was a shift to a notion of creative economy, involving greater attention to digitalisation and the internet, and also, crucially, to *skills*. These were all aspects that had been curi-ously marginal or absent in the early versions of the concept. Yet the

---

[1] The section on film policy draws less on our own research than other chapters, because Philip Schlesinger, Gillian Doyle and their colleagues had just conducted a research project on UK film policy, and we were able to draw upon their valuable findings. See the citations in that section.

way in which digitalisation, the internet and skills were treated, in the Creative Economy initiative of later New Labour and in copyright policy, suggests how far removed from any democratising intent creative industries policy turned out to be. The relations between culture and economy in government moved strongly in the direction of the latter.

4.2   New Labour's film policy

From the 1920s onwards, government support for film industries across much of the 'developed' world sought to address the growing international dominance of the US industry, which over many decades took advantage of its large domestic market, strong federal support, and large integrated studios, to achieve a high-percentage market share in most countries (Jarvie, 1992). Governments often sought to develop local integrated oligopolies that would serve as a domestic counterweight to Hollywood. Hollywood itself often bought stakes in these businesses, and with the decline of cinema and the rise of television and other leisure forms in the 1960s and 1970s, many national film industries hit trouble (including, for a while, Hollywood itself). But, as John Hill (2012: 337) has pointed out, 'given the precarious economic position' of industries such as the UK's, 'film policy has rarely been a matter of economics alone'. It was also based on social and cultural rationales (echoing the themes of cultural policy as a whole that we discussed in Chapter 1), for example recognition of the important role that cinema and film play in constituting and contesting cultural identity within a nation, or the promotion of diverse, innovative and enriching artistic experiences. Film policy, then, has combined cultural, social and economic rationales, and many countries operated 'parallel support mechanisms for film as industry and film as culture' (Dickinson and Harvey, 2005: 421).

British film has been considered particularly vulnerable to Hollywood domination, partly because of the USA's and the UK's shared language. UK government support for film included quotas concerning the proportion of British films shown in British cinemas (a policy introduced in 1927, and ended in 1960) and two measures introduced by the Labour government of Clement Attlee (1945–1951): the 'Eady Levy', by which a proportion of box office receipts was returned to UK producers (made compulsory by the Conservatives in 1957), and the National Film Finance Corporation (NFFC). The British film industry struggled in the era of the decline of cinema, and in the 1960s the big British film companies withdrew from the risky business of film production to focus on distribution and cinema exhibition. However, high levels of training, shared language and other factors made the UK an early favoured destination for Hollywood overseas production. Attracting 'inward investment' in the form of such 'runaway productions' became an increasingly important part of film policy from the 1970s onwards, at both national and sub-national levels, in the UK and elsewhere (see Goldsmith et al., 2010; Miller et al., 2005).

The Thatcher Conservative government of the 1980s ended the by then outdated Eady Levy, but did not replace it with other support, such as a tax on video cassettes briefly supported by the Labour Party (David Puttnam, interview). The NFFC was 'privatised' as British Screen Finance (Hill, 2012: 335). Film policy drifted, and by the end of the Thatcher era, British film production and Hollywood investment in UK-based production of their own films were at a historically low ebb. Partly 'in response to mounting criticism of the government's neglect of film' (Hill, 2012: 336), the Major Conservative government made two significant interventions: tax relief on large-budget films (over £15 million), introduced in 1992, and the allocation of revenue from the National Lottery to the film industry. This was initially administered via the national Arts Councils. In spite of the presence of figures such as Puttnam on the Arts Council's lottery board, this suggested some of the problems surrounding film as a specific cultural and economic form.[2] The films produced were 'very literary...a Thomas Hardy film, a Shakespeare film, a Jane Austen film. These were films that everyone around the table recognised as culture and then only when it cuts loose from the Arts Council do they do "movie movies"' (Christopher Frayling, interview). From 1997 to 2003, lottery money was distributed via franchises intended to develop vertically integrated companies in the UK: these three franchises operated under New Labour but were a product of Conservative policy. They were intended to be more commercially attractive than the Arts Council films – here, there was strong continuity between the last stage of Conservative film policy and New Labour. But, if anything, New Labour's policies showed stronger signs than Conservative policies of the influence of the cultural industries policy group (see Chapter 2), which had particular goals with regard to film industry and film policy.

---

[2] We were absolutely hopeless at it. I mean hopeless, just hopeless. Hopelessly inept. I remember Grey Gowrie [then Head of the Arts Council] interfering, reading a script, *reading a script of a film*, and going, 'no, I don't like the idea of this'. I'd go 'what the fuck do you know? You're Lord Gowrie!' (Ruth MacKenzie, interview).

In opposition, as we saw in Chapter 2, New Labour courted the British film industry – David Puttnam's role was key here. The film industry was absolutely central to the new focus on 'creative industries', and in many ways the concept was initially developed in order to brand New Labour's commitment to supporting the film and music industries, including via copyright. As with other aspects of its cultural policy, New Labour's inherited spending plan commitments meant that film policy had to go through an interregnum or phoney war of mapping, task forces and review groups before policies were launched (see Chapter 2). However, there was an exception: in contrast with its indifference to arts-related policy, and towards the concept of 'the creative industries', the powerful Treasury took action on tax policy. This was 'a big hobby horse of Gordon [Brown]'s – that was the biggest thing of interest for him in arts and cultural policy', Stewart Wood told us. For Chris Smith (interview),

> The one thing that Gordon really got excited about, very early on, was supporting the film industry through tax incentives and it was very much his personal endeavour that got that put in place, against the wishes of some of his officials.

In 1998, the big-budget tax breaks introduced by the Major government were extended to low-budget productions, and tax breaks became one of two key elements of film policy under New Labour.

The other was the eventual creation in 2000 of a single body to provide strategic leadership on film policy, the UK Film Council (UKFC), combining various other bodies, including the Arts Council's Lottery Film Department, British Screen Finance, and the production-funding aspect of the British Film Institute. The idea of forming a single body for film policy had been around for many years, and was taken up with enthusiasm by Chris Smith and David Puttnam. A Film Policy Review Group was established, but Philip Schlesinger (2015) argues that 'private conversations outside the formal review process' were crucial, and that 'the direction of travel' was set well before the deliberations – indicated by the fact that the announcement of a body bringing together film policy was announced in the Review Group's report, in the form of 'a page at the back which basically, literally in the small print, said, "by the way, we are going to rationalise the machinery"' (John Woodward, Chief Executive of the UKFC, 2000–2011, quoted by Doyle, 2014: 132). This direction of travel was one that involved rationalisation in the interests of putting business and economic aspects of film well above its cultural dimensions, and a logic whereby senior film insider expertise was considered 'credible and effective' and the contribution of previous organisations was disavowed. Notably this was true of the British Film Institute (the BFI), protected from abolition by its Royal Charter, but continuing only as a shadow of its former self, and dealing with now rather residual cultural aspects. All this was achieved through the power of the 'big' film industry policy actors with ties to Hollywood (as opposed to the independent production sector).

The UKFC adopted 'industry sustainability' as its key goal (Doyle, 2014: 133–4; UK Film Council, 2000). It inherited the existing lottery franchises, but launched new funds out of lottery money, a Premiere Production Fund (£10 million per year), a Film Development Fund, oriented towards script development, a New Cinema Fund intended to support 'cutting edge films' and 'film-makers who didn't really fit into the normal commercial bag' (Woodward, quoted in Doyle, 2014: 135), and a smaller Training Fund. The first two funds were designed to fund bigger productions aimed at making profit and attracting sizeable audiences, in line with the industry sustainability goal. This affirmed the move in the direction of commercial success begun with the three lottery franchises, as did an increasing orientation towards a 'distribution-led' strategy that marginalised smaller independent producers (such as those interviewed by Doyle and her colleagues – see Doyle, 2014: 136–7). Yet, as John Hill notes, the same press that had attacked earlier lottery films for their highbrow lack of commercialism attacked the funding of films on a commercial basis (Hill, 2012: 339).[3] What's more, the goal of 'sustainability' and commercialism raised expectations. When the Premiere Fund fell short of its recoupment target of 50 per cent (it had achieved 34 per cent by the end of 2008), a 'good rate return for a conventional system of cultural subsidy', it was 'less impressive for a fund designed to operate on a commercial basis' (Hill, 2012: 340), and the UKFC came in for considerable media attack. The media were much quieter about the artistic and occasional commercial success of films supported by the New Cinema Fund, such as *Man on Wire* (2007). Again, the important, though often neglected, role of the media in public policy making is apparent here. What is most indicative of New Labour in all this is the way in which film policy, like much else in its cultural policies, delivered considerable subsidy (via the lottery) but implicitly accepted and reinforced

---

[3] This was most evident in the case of the film *Sex Lives of the Potato Men* (2003). See Caterer (2011) for a comprehensive treatment of UK lottery-funded films.

the view that cultural rationales for subsidy were illegitimate, or at least hard to defend.

Tax breaks were much easier to defend in such a climate, as they were part of industrial policy, and delivered by the Treasury, rather than the DCMS. Maggie Magor and Philip Schlesinger (2009) have provided an authoritative account of their development under New Labour. There was strong consensus about the value of tax incentives, including from the famously powerful Hollywood lobbyists, the Motion Picture Association of America, headed by Jack Valenti, who met with the UKFC and then Gordon Brown in 2001. The sudden closing of a tax loophole by the Treasury in 2004 created a furore among producers, and revealed the powerlessness of the UKFC when they fruitlessly lobbied for exemption or compensation for the productions affected. All this, however, was only the prelude to the introduction in 2005 of a new fiscal measure, the Film Tax Credit (FTC) – designed by the Treasury with very little consultation with either the DCMS or the UKFC, whose roles were limited to developing a 'cultural test' that would define films as sufficiently British to merit support, and to conform with the European Commission's competition and cultural policies. The EC pushed the test further in the direction of 'cultural factors'. This incident makes clear how far New Labour had moved in the direction of economically driven understandings of the rationale behind film and cultural policy.

Film tax relief is an economically driven policy primarily intended to allow production facilities 'to compete with other potential rivals for Hollywood investment' – not with Hollywood (Dickinson and Harvey, 2005: 427). The aim is to attract 'inward investment' rather than to pursue any particular cultural goal, be it nation building or artistic enrichment. Film tax credits might be part of a desirable social democratic cultural policy, but they often serve as a subsidy to Hollywood, and they lead to massive destabilisation of cultural workers, as film capital moves around, seeking the best deal from nations hungrily competing for global Hollywood's dollars. The Treasury's complete dominance of this measure, revealed by Magor and Schlesinger (2009), shows that industrial policy still trumps cultural policy. It suggests that the creative industries rhetoric adopted by the DCMS to raise its status was very much limited in its effectiveness. As we shall now see, this was also manifest in two other important areas of policy development.

4.3   'Creative economy' and 'Creative Britain' (revisited)

We saw in Chapter 2 that, during the period (in 1997–1999) when cultural policy making was in effect put on hold as New Labour awaited the results and implementation of the Treasury-led comprehensive spending review, Chris Smith and the DCMS filled the gap by setting up a Creative Industries Task Force and undertaking a 'mapping' of the sector. Although computer software was controversially, and rather dubiously, included in the creative industries category, there seems to have been very little effort in these early years to conceptualise the impact of digital technologies on culture and economy, given that the internet and digitalisation were already major topics of futurological prediction and speculation in the mid-1990s (e.g., Negroponte, 1995). This was to change.

When Chris Smith was replaced by Tessa Jowell as Culture Secretary in 2001, the creative industries concept almost disappeared from national government discourse. Jowell and the DCMS were heavily focused on a new Communications Act, which passed before parliament in 2003, and in preparing a bid for London to host the Olympic Games in 2012. But in 2005, the junior ministerial portfolios were changed. A Minister for Creative Industries and Tourism was appointed, namely James Purnell.[4] Purnell had emerged from the world of centre-left think tanks (he was associated with the Institute for Public Policy Research and later with Demos), which had played a key role in providing an intellectual basis for New Labour's embrace of creativity within knowledge economy discourse. He sought to revivify the creative industries agenda – aimed at increasing the power of the DCMS within government – and to give it a more secure policy footing. The original DCMS programme had come under attack from even sympathetic academics for its failure to differentiate the different types of industrial activity within the 13 industries included in the original DCMS category. While the original creative industries concept had barely addressed how digitalisation and the internet were changing – or about to change – the cultural industries, this issue was unavoidable in 2005–2006. An enormous wave of media discourse, much of it emanating from the USA, revived the notion of 'the new economy', but under new names and guiding concepts influenced by enthusiasm for the dynamism of the information technology industries. The 'new economy' idea had been somewhat lost in policy discourse after the bursting of the dot.com bubble in the USA in 2000–2001, but in 2005 there was new talk of an era of Web 2.0, 'user-generated content', and 'prosumption' (consumers turning into producers – see Ritzer and Jurgenson, 2010; Toffler, 1970). Much of this

---

[4] In official language, 'Parliamentary Under-secretary of State for Creative Industries and Tourism'. Junior ministers or under-secretaries work under the Secretary of State or Minister, and do not have a seat in the Cabinet.

was drivel, but it added urgency to the genuine need for government to respond adequately to the effects of digitalisation, and to lay the basis for strategy.

The second phase of New Labour engagement with creativity had another significant dimension. Education had been one of the four main elements of New Labour cultural policy outlined in its first term (see Section 2.7). A key change since the late 1990s had been the rise up the political agenda of the concept of *skills*, signalled by the renaming of the Department of Education and Employment in 2001; employment was moved to a new Work and Pensions ministry, and its place in the name of the department was replaced by skills, to form the Department for Education and Skills (DES). In 2004, the Treasury published a report on *Skills in the Global Economy* (HM Treasury, 2004), and in the same year the Treasury and the DES, both big-hitting departments, commissioned New Labour insider Sandy Leitch to conduct a review into what skills the UK economy would need by 2020. Leitch, an insurance businessman with a strong IT background who had overseen Labour's 'New Deal' programmes (see Chapter 2), provided an interim report in 2005 and a final report at the end of 2006 (Leitch, 2006).

It was in this context that the DCMS and Purnell launched their Creative Economy Programme. As we saw in Chapter 2, the term 'creative economy' had been used alongside 'creative industries' in the early New Labour years. But its adoption here represented an effort to revive the concept on new terms. The programme consisted of seven working groups, including 'competition and intellectual property', 'technology' and 'education and skills'. In contrast to Chris Smith's Creative Industries Task Force, which had been designed to legitimate the creative industries agenda in the eyes of business and the media, the programme was technicist: the policy-making circles were groups 'overwhelmingly drawn from public sector bodies', and in industry circles 'this recruitment was seen as reducing the credibility of the exercise' (Schlesinger, 2009a: 13–14).

Purnell was moved to pensions in 2006. He was brought back to the DCMS as Culture Secretary in the reshuffle following Brown's succession as Prime Minister in 2007, but in the meantime, according to Schlesinger's primary research conducted at this time, the new Creative Industries Minister, Shaun Woodward, wanted to put his own stamp on the Creative Economy Programme. Schlesinger notes that this is a feature of ministerial change: politicians vie to associate themselves with distinctive agendas. The result was that the creative economy agenda descended into incoherence and fragmentation in the last years of New

Labour. Woodward brought in a former BBC colleague Will Hutton to inform the production of a consultative Green Paper derived from the working groups. Hutton had briefly been a New Labour policy intellectual insider in the 1990s, but had come to be seen as a maverick outsider for his attention to inequality, the downsides of globalisation, and labour conditions (e.g., Hutton, 2010). He had turned an organisation called The Industrial Society into something more like a think tank under the name The Work Foundation, and Work Foundation staff worked with DCMS staff to produce the Green Paper. But there were multiple conflicts and problems. DCMS officials apparently felt that the Work Foundation's perspective was based too much on 'blue sky thinking', of a kind that they associated with think tanks or, even worse, academics. Woodward himself was replaced by Margaret Hodge, who, according to Schlesinger (2009: 16), was seen within the DCMS as being sceptical about the actual economic role of the creative industries, a scepticism derived from her previous position at the Department of Trade and Industry. The process of producing a set of policies derived from the Creative Economy Programme also became caught up in the uncertainties surrounding the leadership transition from Tony Blair to Gordon Brown in 2007, and things got worse following Brown's succession as party leader and Prime Minister. Over the following years, under the shadow of a huge economic crisis, there were frequent changes of government departments, portfolios and ministers, as well as increasing divisions within the party. Departments with new, unwieldy names (Innovation, Universities and Skills; Business, Enterprise and Regulatory Reform) were brought into the action, further complicating the process, and making The Work Foundation's efforts even more remote from policy. The Work Foundation published its own report, *Staying Ahead*, in June 2007, but the strategy paper based on the Creative Economy Programme only appeared in February 2008 as *Creative Britain: New Talents for the New Economy*. While the title repeated that of Chris Smith's 1998 book, based on his speeches (Smith, 1998), the tone was notably less inspirational, in spite of occasional passages of rhetoric about the exciting world of creativity to be found in contemporary Britain. The detail was almost entirely about education and training. The aim was to provide a 'solid platform for creativity from the grassroots to the global stage' (DCMS, 2008: 5).[5] This was to be achieved mainly through a

---

[5] All page numbers in the next two paragraphs refer to this source. We draw here on material previously published in Banks and Hesmondhalgh (2009).

mixed programme of education and training-based initiatives designed to ensure that (mainly) young people, school leavers and students are sufficiently equipped to 'make the most effective contribution they can to the creative economy' (p. 76). The emphasis was on preparing young people for their entry into labour markets, mainly through training initiatives linked to industry-specific and wider national economic priorities. But the policies were thin. One was a 'Find your Talent programme' involving 'five hours a week provision of quality culture' for children in schools. This garnered some press and broadcasting coverage at the time of the document's release, as it promised that school students would attend top-quality theatre, dance and musical performances, learn instruments, visit exhibitions and museums, and so on. However, having made this strong link between the creative industries and the most glamorous and prestigious aspects of culture, *Creative Britain* went on to present a much more prosaic picture of the creative industries, one where 'industry demands a much greater range of skills' (such as 'backstage' business, ICT and technical skills) than the artistic careers destined for the 'gifted and talented' targeted by the 'Find your Talent' programme. Essentially, what was being offered was careers advice for those who did not understand the difficulties of gaining access to the more exciting enclaves of the creative industries.

The problematic concept of diversity (Malik, 2013) made an appearance in the document, and the DCMS declared its intention to 'work with its non-departmental public bodies to promote a more diverse workforce' (p. 23). However, this turned out to be built on 'diversity in skills' (p. 23). Underpinning this, it transpired, was an increasing emphasis in UK higher education policy on providing skills 'to meet the needs of business' (p. 24). Diversity turned out to mean a greater diversity of higher education, providing a more diverse set of services to business. Finally, there was a commitment to create 5,000 creative sector apprenticeships, in partnership with various prominent institutions such as Tate Liverpool (a leading UK gallery of modern art) and Universal Music Group (the world's biggest record company). In one respect, the continuity with the earlier phase of 'creative industries' was abundantly clear. The issue of work and employment conditions was entirely elided; the Work Foundation's mild centre-left concern with these problems had disappeared.

Creative Britain, then, shows how far the concept of the creative industries and creative economy were from the social democratic concerns that led to the creation of the Labour Party in the early twentieth century. It also shows how these animating concepts, which had for a while led to an accommodation of the interests of both arts and (mainly corporate) cultural industry policy groups, ultimately failed to raise the status of the DCMS within government. The skills agenda, associated with other departments (Business, and, of course, Education and Skills), dominated what was presented as creativity policy in this later phase of New Labour government.

4.4 Copyright policy and debates

While the Creative Economy Programme represented an attempt to rethink the creative industries concept for a digital age, it is striking that the publications that came out of it had almost nothing to say about digitalisation in terms of policy. New Labour's response to digitalisation and the rise of the internet took place elsewhere, in education and, closest to the cultural policy domain that is the focus of this book, in struggles over copyright policy.

Behind New Labour's approach to copyright lies the increased economic significance afforded to intellectual property by policymakers from the 1990s onwards, itself influenced by the information society/knowledge economy thinking that, as we discussed in Chapter 2, New Labour had taken up enthusiastically. Yet, despite the undeniable significance of copyright policy in terms of its impact on citizens and public and private sector organisations, not to mention equitable global development (May, 2000), much of the policy discussion and activity occurred below the radar of public interest, within specialised circles. Policy development was dominated by technical discussion and by thinking that put economic development ahead of cultural benefits, or equated the latter with the former.

Our position in this book is that copyright is cultural policy; that cultural policy cannot be understood without engaging with copyright policy and policy making; and that New Labour's cultural policies cannot be understood without examining the place of copyright and intellectual property within New Labour policies. Yet copyright has historically been neglected by cultural policy scholars, with academic discussion largely confined to the academic fields of law and business.

The question of copyright is central to contemporary cultural industries, because a huge amount of the revenues of cultural businesses derives not from direct sales or advertising, but from activities associated with the ownership of 'rights' of various kinds in creative works. Since the 1980s, driven by neo-liberal modes of thought, governments around the world have increasingly come to see ideas and information as 'ownable' and of strategic commercial interest (Hesmondhalgh, 2013a: 160), and this has pushed intellectual property (comprising patents, trademarks, copyright and design rights) higher up policy agendas. Copyright is the aspect of intellectual property that has by far the strongest bearing on culture and the arts, as it is explicitly designed to cover creative works, starting with printed publications and later extended to cover many other kinds. Copyright law allows rights owners to do things with creative works that non-owners aren't allowed to do, notably copying, adapting, distributing, performing and broadcasting them, or parts of them (Frith and Marshall, 2004: 7): copyright thus actually refers to a set of rights rather than a single right. The important point is that a great deal of the money and finance to be gained from cultural production and distribution depends on the ownership of such rights. Such ownership is dominated by cultural corporations, and such companies have – often through the trade associations that they control – been powerful advocates of copyright laws that enshrine longer periods of ownership (before works enter the 'public domain', after which they can be used without payment to rights holders) and stronger enforcement. Creative workers and artists also stand to make some money from their ownership of rights, or via contracts with corporate rights holders, and they and their organisations have also tended to argue for longer, stronger copyrights. Against such pro-copyright lobbyists have stood consumer electronics and, more recently, IT companies, many of whose products have been based on making it easier for consumers to copy and distribute works themselves. New Labour had to find a way to mediate between these two policy groups.

An account of copyright policy under New Labour has to consider the context of digitalisation carefully. New Labour's rise to power in 1997 was synchronous with the public emergence and uptake of digital technologies, including the internet.[6] Globally, policy makers from the late 1990s onwards were struggling with the impact of digitalisation on the cultural industries. The recording industry was the first cultural industry to be strongly affected by the internet. From the very late 1990s onwards, mass circulation of copyright-protected material via peer to peer (P2P) networks became possible (Hesmondhalgh, 2009). In the face of this threat to potential revenues, the cultural industries lobbied for stronger copyright measures. Meanwhile, the telecommunications

---

[6] Although many of the technological innovations that led to digitalisation took place before this period, they only started to become publicly available and utilised on a mass scale from the late 1990s onwards.

and IT industries fought back in order to protect their own burgeoning revenues. They were supported by activist groups concerned by stronger copyright enforcement, such as the Electronic Frontier Foundation (EFF), and, in the UK, the Open Rights Group, and, in turn, these groups were often supported by prominent academics, among them James Boyle and Lawrence Lessig.[7] As a result, New Labour's position on copyright regulation shifted, in the many policy reviews that took place between 1997 and 2010, from arguments that favoured a weaker copyright regime, to those that favoured punitive measures for infringers, and back again.

Three key copyright policy 'events' during the New Labour period help to illustrate the tensions and problems just indicated: the EU Copyright Directive in 2001, the Gowers Review in 2006 (Gowers, 2006) and the Digital Economy Act in 2010, which allow us to examine the changing dynamics of copyright policy during New Labour's governance. We shall deal with each in turn.

The EU Copyright Directive (EUCD) of 2001 came in the wake of the 1996 World Intellectual Property Organization (WIPO) conference in Geneva, where signatories agreed to update their national laws to extend copyright to cover the internet and other computer networks. As a result, the highly controversial US Digital Millennium Copyright Act (DCMA) was passed in 1998. Subsequently, the European Union agreed the EUCD in May 2001 (European Parliament, 2001). Both acts legislated for the extension of rights in the online context and were the product of intense industry lobbying by the cultural industries, in particular powerful American media corporations. The EUCD demonstrated the power of rights-owning companies to shape the policy agenda around copyright at this time. As with the development of the DCMA, the EUCD gave cultural industries the opportunity to try to push through proposals that had been rejected by the diplomatic conference that led to the WIPO treaties in 1996, in particular anti-circumvention rules that were proposed by the USA but had been initially rejected in favour of a more flexible approach, as seen in Articles 11 and 18 of the final WIPO Copyright and Performance and Phonogram treaties. Copyright user organisations were 'grossly underrepresented compared to the number of industry lobbyists in Washington DC and Brussels in the lead up to both the DCMA and the EUCD, and the stage was set for the outlawing of acts of circumvention and devices that enabled it'

---

[7] See Boyle (1996) and Lessig (2001) for examples of their perspectives.

(Brown, 2003: 9–10). For some commentators, such as Schaffner (2004), this led to a myriad of unanticipated negative effects on innovation and free speech that occurred as a result of the restrictions on the use of cultural works put in place by their owners.

Following the EUCD, signatory nations were given 18 months to implement the directive in their own countries, a process which proved to be protracted, controversial and complex. In the UK, the Patent Office's consultation over the implementation of the directive received over 300 responses, and while some responses called for less restrictive measures, the final legislation indicated that these contributions had little impact on the eventual implementation of the directive, while the industry voices of organisations such as the British Phonographic Industry (BPI) were highly influential (Brown, 2003).

The implementation of the EUCD in Britain was a key policy moment when copyright was extended and made more powerful, in favour of the major copyright-holding companies. The directive required that member states provide 'adequate legal protection' against the deliberate circumvention of technological measures – regardless of whether this act infringed copyright. As Brown pointed out, 'even fast-forwarding through a commercial at the start of a DVD could therefore be illegal if restricted by the rights holder' (2003: 16). However, this draconian approach to copyright received a great deal of negative publicity (Hesmondhalgh, 2009). At the same time, a discourse of 'innovation' and 'commercialisation' was gaining ground, in which technology companies were seen as engines of economic growth (Oakley, 2012).

It was in this context that *the Gowers Review* was commissioned by the Treasury. In effect, the committee was set the task of trying to mediate between these different sets of interests. Crucially, in spite of the association of the 'creative industries' with New Labour (a concept that in any case, as we have seen, blurred the distinction between content-producing industries and the very different IT sector), the IT industries had the ear of the Treasury, which saw economic growth as flowing from investment in these 'knowledge-intensive' sectors. The Gowers Review was praised by some commentators for taking a more balanced perspective than the EUCD and DCMA, including rejecting an increase in copyright from 50 to 95 years, stating that it would cost industry, the consumer and future innovators, while only providing a marginal benefit to performers. It suggested that education was the way to tackle piracy, and did not recommend legislation to tackle file sharing. Instead, it advocated collaboration between internet service providers and rights owners. The tone and focus of the report clearly echoed some of the concerns of the technology and software industry, shared by key decision makers within the Treasury. Dubbed the 'Google review' by its detractors (Feargal Sharkey, interview),[8] Gowers made a number of concessions to those calling for relaxations on copyright to be introduced, including a recommendation for a limited private copying exception for 'format-shifting' to be introduced by 2008 (Gowers, 2006: 6).

Jamie Cowling, a special adviser to DCMS from 2004 onwards, described the tensions around copyright policy not only across departments but also within the Treasury itself in the run up to Gowers:

[O]ne bit of the Treasury was for getting rid of copyright altogether... [a]nd then the other bit of the Treasury said, 'God, the creative industries are worth X billion to the UK economy and they're telling us this is a big problem, we're for tightening up controls... making it tougher'.

(Cowling, interview)

A key individual involved in the Gowers Review was the political adviser to the Treasury, Richard Sergeant, who ran the review, and wrote much of the final report. According to Cowling, 'the brilliant thing about Gowers and the way Richard ran it, was that it brought evidence to the debate – which I thought was really useful'. Sergeant left government soon after the review was published and went to work for Google as their UK public policy manager, where in 2009 he called for reforms to incorporate exemptions similar to the US fair use doctrine into UK and Europe copyright law – interesting in relation to Feargal Sharkey's comment about 'the Google Review', above. There were other close links between technology companies and the Treasury. A number of high-profile technology figures were key funders of New Labour at various points, including David Potter, the founder of the British technology firm Psion (Swinford, 2007). For Cowling, Chancellor Gordon Brown's influence on the final report was decisive. Reflecting on the final review, which was widely seen as advocating a more technology sector-friendly view, with arguments in favour of format shifting and shorter copyright

---

[8] Sharkey, former lead singer of the Northern Irish punk band the Undertones, was a significant lobbyist for the UK's commercial music industry during the New Labour period. In 2004 he became Chairman of the UK government task force on live music, and in 2008 became Head of UK Music, a body that represents the interests of the UK's commercial music sector.

terms, Jamie Cowling told us: 'The Chancellor's view is what Gowers said. It would not have been published if it hadn't have been the Chancellor's view. No way.'

Although it was welcomed by copyright campaigners such as Lawrence Lessig, the Gowers Review did not go down well with the rights holders of the cultural industries. For example, the BPI, the trade association of British recording companies, responded to his conclusions against extending copyright terms by saying that 'Gowers' failure to recommend term extension is a missed opportunity', and that the copyright industry would 'press on' with their calls for reform at the European Union level (BPI, cited in Hogge, 2006). For these critics, Gowers and the Treasury had failed to understand the concern of rights holders (Feargal Sharkey, interview). The following year, in 2007, Brown left the Treasury to become Prime Minister, and within three years the DCMS-led Digital Economy Act would be published, which would make very different recommendations, marking a return to the rather tougher approach to copyright that had been manifest in the early days of New Labour.

The *Digital Britain* report of 2009, and the *Digital Economy Act (DEA) of 2010* which ensued from it, were put together in the shadow of the global financial crisis of 2008. The UK experienced one of the most prolonged recessions of the OECD economies. The effects of the crisis can be seen in the tone and recommendations of the report, which stressed the need for the cultural industries to focus on growth and encouraged industrial policy measures which would allow them to be 'scaled and industrialised', as other high-tech knowledge industries had supposedly been. It also implied that the Gowers Report, released only three years before, was already out of date by this time, indicating that copyright modernisation was needed in relation to streaming subscription services such as Spotify, Netflix and Hulu, in order to allow these legal subscription providers to make commercially viable deals with copyright owners. The tone of *Digital Britain*, and consequently the DEA, was also considerably more focused on dealing with copyright infringement than Gowers had been, and copyright legislation was the most controversial aspect of the act. It included enforcement measures requiring internet service providers (ISPs) (via the media and communication regulator Ofcom, established by New Labour under its Communications Act of 2003) to intervene with measures such as handing over user information to allow infringers to be taken to court, reducing the broadband width/speed of persistent copyright infringers, and requiring ISPs to block sites hosting infringing content. Rights holders could seek a court order to obtain personal details, which would then allow them to bring legal action against infringers. The economic impact of inaction is also clearly signalled in the act: the impact assessments published alongside the DEA estimated that, without intervention, the costs to copyright owners (including television, cinema, music, entertainment software and video games) in terms of displaced sales due to illegal file sharing would be in the region of £400 million per annum. The act presented 'piracy' as a problem endemic across the UK (Edwards et al., 2013, 2015).

Again, extensive and aggressive lobbying took place in the lead up to the act's publication, most forcefully from the copyright-owning cultural industries. This lobbying was the subject of some media coverage, a mixture of fact and rumours. The heart of the coverage concerned Peter (by now Lord) Mandelson, Business Secretary in the period leading up to the DEA, and, as we saw in Chapter 1, one of the three key figures in the creation of New Labour.[9] As a result of a freedom of information request made by the BBC in 2010, there is evidence that numerous letters were sent to him lobbying for strengthening of copyright measures throughout 2009 during the drafting of the bill, including communication from major Hollywood film companies urging him to put the DEA through before the election in 2010.[10]

For example, in July 2009, a lobby group called Respect for Film, representing major Hollywood studios including NBC Universal, Twentieth Century Fox, Walt Disney, Warner Bros and Paramount, wrote to Lord Mandelson demanding that he put copyright enforcement legislation through parliament before the 2010 election, and praising him for accepting their notion that ISPs should share responsibility for copyright enforcement (Horten, 2013: 190–1). The letter reminded Mandelson of the group's view that ISPs should share responsibility for tackling digital

---

[9] 'Business Secretary' is the commonly used term for the minister in charge of the department that deals with industrial policy. Revealingly, the name of this department changed in 2007 from 'Trade and Industry' to 'Business, Enterprise and Regulatory Reform', and then in 2009 to Business, Information and Skills, when it merged with the department responsible for science and universities – a move that showed the influence of information society thinking: universities and science would be administered as part of business strategy. The replacement of 'industry' by 'business' is noteworthy.

[10] See Horten (2013: 248–65) for a full account of how the bill was rushed through before the general election of 2010.

'copyright theft', and expressed pleasure that the *Digital Britain* report accepted this principle. It continued:

> It is crucial to the success of content providers in a digital economy that this legislation gets onto the statue [*sic*] book before the General Election. To that end, we are keen to work with you to ensure that politicians on all sides understand how urgently this legislation is required and to work through any issues that might arise... We hope that both industry and political consensus can be reached in the months ahead that will facilitate that process.
>
> (quoted in Horten, 2013: 191)

Just weeks after this letter was sent, Mandelson announced that the bill would be toughened up, bringing in technical measures to ensure that repeat offenders would be disconnected temporarily from the internet for illegal file sharing.

Other letters to Mandelson from cultural industry groups during this period confirm a pattern of lobbying, and 'show a sustained campaign of lobbying in favour of the Digital Economy Bill by music-industry trade bodies' (Cellan-Jones, 2010). For example, Paul McGuinness, manager of the rock band U2, wrote to the Secretary of State for Business, Peter Mandelson, welcoming his tougher stance, and warning that it was crucial that the new measures were implemented as soon as possible, and Mandelson also met with film and music mogul David Geffen in Corfu – though Mandelson denied that internet piracy was discussed there (Cellan-Jones, 2010). Lobbying was also undertaken by opponents to the bill (predominantly the IT industries, in league with copyright liberationists such as the Open Rights Group) in an effort 'to persuade Lord Mandelson that some of its measures will be damaging to civil liberties, as well as being costly and ineffective' (Cellan-Jones, 2010). Telecommunications company Orange wrote to Mandelson stating that the measures would be 'expensive to implement and operate', and 'could exacerbate the problem of copyright infringement by encouraging users to encrypt their data'. However, their lobbying efforts seem to have failed.

Following the Gowers Review, with its arguably more measured, technology-friendly approach, the DEA represented a swing back in favour of the agenda of rights holders, and, like the EUCD discussed above, demonstrates the power of the lobbying arguments put forward by the cultural industries in defence of their revenues from IP, despite extensive campaigning from users, citizens and public interest groups opposed to the restrictions legislated for in the bill. It is also instructive to note that these letters were addressed to Mandelson, the Business Secretary at the time, rather than the two Culture Secretaries who held office during the drafting and eventual publication of the DEA, Andy Burnham (2008–2009) and Ben Bradshaw (2009–2010). This was despite the fact that the bill was emerging from both the Business and Culture Departments. This indicated where the power was perceived to lie in the formation of the DEA, and further confirms the weakness of the DCMS in relation to other departments, in spite of many years of the creative industries/creative economy agenda. It suggests that in terms of key policy and legislation affecting creative industries revenues, the DCMS had not transcended the marginal position usually afforded to culture departments of government.

A number of points emerge from the above discussion of New Labour's copyright policies. New Labour's approach to copyright policy was highly economistic, focusing on growth and commercialisation, discursively framed against the background of increasing global competitiveness as well as the perceived threat of market failure as a result of digitalisation. However, this focus oscillated over time between policies, reviews and attitudes within government which implicitly promoted the telecommunications and technology companies as the source of growth, and those which focused on the creative industries as drivers of economic growth. Ultimately, when it came to hard policy making and legislation, as opposed to reviews, New Labour's approach was to favour the arguments of the large multinational rights holders, as opposed to policies in favour of a less restrictive, weaker copyright regime. Therefore, while Gowers proposed measures which would have been more amenable to both the technology sectors and the libertarians, the EUCD and DEA, the two key pieces of copyright legislation during the New Labour period, were explicitly in favour of restrictive, punitive measures to control the consumption and use of intellectual property. What's more, New Labour policy makers were involved in international discussions and agreements, and can be seen as key players in global policy alliances which sought to increase copyright protection, as well as in the dissemination of rhetoric which sought to justify this position (Freedman, 2008).

Our analysis, drawing on interviews as well as other secondary materials, also allows us to see the relative power of the Treasury and Business Department as opposed to the DCMS. This reflects DCMS's size, of course, but more importantly its weakness as a deliverer of government policy. Larger, more powerful departments were seen as the main forces in policy making where bills leading to legislation were concerned. However, there was no single uniform view on copyright within New Labour. This was surely reflected in the hectic period of review and legislation in the final period of New Labour's period of government. Finally, we can see the crucial power of lobbying in the formation of copyright policy during the period. In the end, the interests of the cultural industries won out over views that favoured a weaker copyright regime, though the battle continues to this day (see Chapter 8).

In this chapter, we have examined three aspects of national policy that might be considered under the heading 'creative industries'. We have shown that film and copyright policy under New Labour involved greater emphasis on economic goals than in previous policy, a privileging of the interests of the cultural industries, and less concern with cultural factors, such as a film culture that represented a truly diverse array of experiences within the nation, or access of users and creators to cultural material. However, the copyright policy also showed that New Labour had to try to balance cultural industry interests with those of the newly powerful IT industries, resulting in policy incoherence. The case of the Creative Economy Programme, and the *Creative Britain* document that resulted from it, demonstrates the continuing emptiness of the creative industries concept in its rebranded form, and also its neglect of problematic working conditions in the sector. All of these developments represent a significant shift away from cultural policies in the social democratic tradition.

5
Cultural Policy and the Regions

5.1 A case of policy attachment

As we saw in the previous chapter, critics of UK creative industries policy have argued that there was very little actual policy at the national level, despite the volume of statements of intent, strategy papers, 'think-pieces' and rhetoric (Oakley, 2004, 2006). The majority of activity in this field took place at the regional level, through the activities and investments of a perplexing array of organisations. What we see in this case is perhaps the supreme case among many examples of 'policy attachment' (Gray, 2004) under New Labour, as the 'creative industries' concept was attached to regional economic development. In this way, what was largely a discourse at the national level – supported by rapidly gathered data in the form of the mapping documents (Channer, 2013) – became enacted through the creation of local support networks, small-scale development of workspace, programmes for skills development, and the provision of sector-specific business advice (O'Connor and Gu, 2010).

Early formulations of New Labour 'creative industries' thinking made little or no reference to regionalism. *Creative Britain*, Culture Secretary Chris Smith's book on New Labour's approach to cultural policy, does not mention the regions (Smith, 1998), and it was not until 2000 that the Creative Industries Taskforce, set up by Smith, published something on the role of the creative industries in regional development (DCMS, 2000b). However, once New Labour was in office, a number of factors shifted the focus towards regional development. Labour's reliance on its heartlands in the north of England meant that manifesto commitments had been made to invest in the regions and provincial cities after the worsening of regional inequalities during the 1980s and 1990s

(Labour, 1997a; Martin, 2010). The cultural industries were seen by Labour politicians and policy makers as playing a role in this attempt to boost the regions, in part because they seemed to offer a growing source of employment, but also because of their alleged role in regeneration and a variety of social benefits. The major cities were also keen. Cities such as Sheffield, Manchester and Glasgow had led the development of cultural industries thinking after the abolition of the Greater London Council (GLC) in 1986 (see chapters 2 and 4), and as the Regional Development Agencies (RDAs) were established, many embraced the potential of enhanced cultural investment. The economic imaginary of the 'creative economy' wasn't something forced on the regions by distant Whitehall policy makers, but something which seemed, at least briefly, to offer a way out of the UK's historically unequal economic geography (Channer, 2013).

In this chapter, we evaluate and explain New Labour's efforts to address regional differences in the realm of culture. We pay particular attention to how and why the creative industries concept was adopted at the regional level, and what this tells us about both sub-national policymaking and also the confused goals of New Labour's cultural policies. We also address policy attachment between cultural policy and economic development as it played out in the English regions.[1]

5.2   Two contexts: Regional arts and cultural industries regeneration

Two earlier developments in British cultural policy provide important context for understanding New Labour's regional cultural policies. The first is arts policy's attempts to deal with spatial cultural inequality. The second is the increasing emphasis on culture-led regeneration from the 1980s onwards (already introduced in Chapter 2).

Regional inequalities and arts funding

In many respects, the UK, and certainly England, has a highly centralised arts funding system, heavily based on the leading national institutions in London. A 2013 report by Stark et al. showed that central government spending per head on culture in London was still, in spite of numerous efforts by Labour to shift funding away from the

---

[1] In line with the limitations explained in Chapter 1, that we only have space to address UK policy, rather than specific policy in the devolved nations, we can pay only passing attention to Scotland, Wales and Northern Ireland here.

capital, nearly 15 times greater than in the rest of England in 2012/2013. Furthermore, London is the beneficiary of the majority of private investment in the UK's arts sector. London received 67.8 per cent of all business investment in the arts, and 90 per cent of individual giving in 2011/2012 (Arts and Business, 2013).

This was a major issue for arts policy makers. One of the key goals of the Arts Council of Great Britain when founded in 1946 was, in the words of the economist John Maynard Keynes (who helped to set it up), to 'decentralise and disperse the dramatic and musical and artistic life of this country, to build up provincial centres and to promote corporate life in these matters in every town and county'.[2] Its relationship with the regions has been complex and changing. Regional Arts Associations were introduced between 1956 and 1973, and the Labour government of the 1960s encouraged a model whereby they were essentially run by local government (see Gray, 2000: 67–71). They collaborated with the Arts Council, often co-funding arts organisations. The Arts Council abolished the Associations in 1991, replacing them with Regional Arts Boards. This was an act of centralisation intended to improve co-ordination and reduce costs. But there was decentralisation under the Major Conservative government too: the Arts Council of Great Britain was devolved into four Arts Councils, for each of the UK's four nations, in 1994. Throughout these various changes, regional arts under-development was a persistent problem. But by the 1990s, arts policy had come to seem only a small part of how spatial cultural inequalities might be addressed.

Cultural industries and regeneration

A new generation of policy makers and policy analysts began to argue in the 1980s that cultural policy ought to recognise the vital role of commercial culture in people's lives, and that such a recognition might help in developing cultural policies that could address spatial cultural inequality (Bianchini and Parkinson, 1993; Mulgan and Worpole, 1986). As we saw in Chapter 2, at the GLC, from 1981 to its abolition by the Conservative government in 1986, the concept of 'cultural industries' was imported from other international policy forums, and was then adopted by Labour-led city councils across the country, including Sheffield, Manchester and Glasgow. The GLC's cultural industries policy had two key strands. First, it was opposed to elitist, idealist notions

---

[2] Quoted in *The Glory of the Garden* (Arts Council of Great Britain, 1984).

of art, arguing that cultural policy should reorient itself around a recognition that most people's experiences of culture were through commercial forms. Second, it saw public investment as a means of achieving urban and regional regeneration, but with a focus on creating vibrant cultural sectors based on small-scale cultural production, local initiatives and sustainable forms of distribution (Garnham, 2005; Hesmondhalgh, 2008, 2013a). While these policies were never implemented in London because of the closure of the GLC, they were influential in framing investment and activity in the English regions, and played a role in the development of cultural industries 'quarters' during the 1990s, including the Cultural Industries Quarter in Sheffield, the Custard Factory in Birmingham, and Nottingham's Lace Market. Yet neo-liberal influence in this period produced an increasing tendency 'to think about all areas of public policy, including culture and media, in terms of a return on public investment' (Hesmondhalgh, 2008: 556). The connection of policies to promote independent cultural production with broader progressive social change, implicit in at least some of the GLC's work, was diminished by the time Labour developed its creative industries policies in the 1990s, but it still survived in some regions, as we shall see. At the same time, as urban policy and cultural policy came increasingly into contact with each other via the concept of 'regeneration' (see Chapter 2), European funding was pushing regional policy, and to some extent cultural policy, towards combating 'social exclusion'.[3] To gain access to such funds, 'instrumentalist' claims about regeneration via the arts (see Chapter 3 and below) were linked to similar arguments about the potential for growth in investment in cultural industries.

5.3   New Labour's Third Way regionalism: The Regional Development Agencies take up the creative industries idea

However, there is a third context that is just as important for understanding New Labour's cultural policies – the longstanding economic and social inequalities between the wealthy south-east of England and the other regions and nations, and New Labour's general response to

---

[3] Sources included the European Social Fund (ESF) and the European Regional Development Fund (ERDF). The objectives of the European Union's Structural Funds have been to address economic imbalances in disadvantaged areas of the EU and to promote development of those regions where economic and social conditions were lagging behind those of other member states. They are responsible for a large proportion of the EU's total budget.

them. These inequalities got worse with the decline, from the 1960s onwards, of extraction and manufacturing industries, based mainly in the English North and Midlands, South Wales, and the Scottish Lowlands. These problems deepened significantly under the British Conservative government of the 1980s and 1990s (Gregg et al., 1999). Tepid efforts had been made by the Conservatives to stimulate growth and regeneration in British regions and cities, most notably through the introduction of the Urban Development Corporations (UDCs) in the early 1980s (Imrie, 2004). But New Labour was determined to go much further, via national devolution, and a new regional policy.

Central to this policy were RDAs, established in 1998 in a parliamentary act, replacing UDCs. The RDAs represented a move to a model which sought to work with and expand the private sector, but which also recognised the social and political importance of public sector funding. In other words, this was a 'Third Way' approach to regional development, based on the public–private 'partnerships' at the core of New Labour politics (Falconer and McLaughlin, 2000). The RDAs were set up in eight English regions, with a ninth established in London in July 2000, when the London Development Agency (LDA) was created. Following devolution, Scotland, Wales and Northern Ireland similarly reconstructed their economic development bodies as responsibility for this policy area was devolved to the nations (Goodwin et al., 2005). The RDAs' role was 'to coordinate regional economic development and regeneration to enable regions to improve their relative competitiveness, and to reduce the imbalance that exists within and between regions' (Jayne, 2005: 543). Unprecedented resources were allocated to redressing spatial inequalities and rebalancing the UK economy.[4] The RDAs had numerous programmes running between 1999 and 2010, and their key goals were to enhance business development and competitiveness, to promote regeneration through physical infrastructure, and to support skills development (Work Foundation, 2012).

Crucially, these RDAs took up the creative industries concept with enthusiasm. As Chris Smith put it to us,

> The people who really cottoned on rapidly were the Regional Development Agencies and quite a number of big city authorities who got it straight away and recognised that here was something that was an innate strength for the economy. And it became something that was

---

[4] Between 2002–2003 and 2006–2007 they spent £2.2 billion annually (PWC, 2009).

very strongly picked up by quite a number of the Regional Development Agencies and there are clusters of creative businesses around
the country that have benefited quite a lot from that.

(Chris Smith, interview)

As Smith notes, the enthusiasm for creative industries was often
strongest at local and regional level; it was not imposed from the centre.
In 2000, DCMS's Regional Industries Working Group published *Creative Industries: The Regional Dimension* (DCMS, 2000b). It asserted the
economic importance of the creative industries to Britain's regional
economies, and following its publication, the creative industries idea
shifted decisively from the central to the regional government level –
as we saw in Chapter 4, the creative industries concept essentially disappeared from national government during the second New Labour
term of 2001–2005. Asked by government to identify priority areas for
economic development in 2000, five of the nine English RDAs proposed creative industries. By 2005, all but one of the RDAs placed a
strategic priority on the creative sector, with the most commonly prioritised sub-sectors being 'digital media' and film and television, followed
by design, fashion and visual art. According to Graham Hitchen, ex-
Head of Creative Industries at the London Development Agency, the
RDAs were the most significant investors in the cultural industries
during the New Labour years, investing over £30 million a year into capital projects, cluster development, skills training and business support
(Graham Hitchen, interview).

5.4 The regions and creative industries: Early autonomy and achievements

Once they became operational, the RDAs had a brief phase of relative
autonomy. Individual RDAs were able to take different approaches, best
suited to their understanding of the region's cultural economy, even
if, as Channer (2013) has noted, this understanding was frequently
based on unreliable statistics and inflated expectations. For Chris Garcia,
Director of Enterprise and Skills at the South West RDA, this autonomy
was important: 'we were given then the remit to develop our own economic strategies and business plans, and then it was for us to determine
what sectors or strategies were appropriate' (Chris Garcia, interview).
Similarly, Stuart McFarlane, Head of Digital and Creative Industries
at Yorkshire Forward, the RDA for the Yorkshire and Humber region
(2004–2011), summarises his attitude as follows:

I didn't feel that it was policy one-way ... [it was more] 'tell me what the policy is and then I'll decide' – not being arrogant – 'I'll decide how we do it regionally, just because I know what we've got. I know the team, I know the resources, I've got a feel for what's happening. So I know how we should position it and how we present it to people and how we implement it.'

(Stuart McFarlane, interview)

The period up to 2005 saw a much more explicit social policy being pursued by RDAs than in the later New Labour years, echoing the first Labour administration's focus on social exclusion and urban regeneration (Leys, 2003). While this early (though problematic) social aspect to creative industries development was relatively short-lived, for those involved within RDAs at this time it was an exciting moment, providing an opportunity for investment in creative sectors such as film, television and the rapidly emerging digital economy, with a commitment to addressing issues such as unemployment and poverty (Oakley, 2014). It was accompanied by a general political optimism, which in certain ways typified the first administration of New Labour (Toynbee and Walker, 2010).

As one of our interviewees, who had been involved in the Manchester cultural scene for some time, noted, the idea of the creative industries

enabled fairly progressive cities like Manchester to look at other opportunities to focus their regeneration effort, and I think, given the framework of DCMS, the introduction of the currency of culture and creative industries allowed them to say 'hang on, we do this, can we do it better?' So I think it was about permission, really, rather than encouragement. I don't think there was any direct line coming from government to cities like Manchester saying 'sort yourself out', I think there was a baton passed probably from early 80s cultural policy, GLC cultural policy, that was then taken up really by cities like Manchester, who thought 'okay, the time is right, let's have a look at this, and look at it in a different way, and look at other interventions'.

(Andy Lovatt, interview)

As this suggests, early RDA creative industries activity had vestiges of the municipal socialist cultural industries approach of the 1980s, but with a greater focus now on job creation, skills and regeneration through cultural investment (Evans, 2009a). Many of the early actors in the

RDAs had been involved in or influenced by the GLC.[5] A range of cultural industries strategies were instigated in northern England, including the Huddersfield Creative Town initiative, the Sheffield Cultural Industries Quarter and the Manchester Cultural Industries Development Service (O'Connor and Gu, 2010), by individuals who would become part of Forum on Creative Industries (FOCI) (see Prince, 2010b: 127–8). Yet, as we shall see, New Labour's regional vision for the cultural sectors soon departed from this particular political heritage.

Equally importantly, it provided economic development support that was supposedly tailored to the peculiarities of the cultural sector, accepting that 'lifestyle' businesses would not always have a formal business plan and, indeed, that business growth would not always be the aim of those who set up enterprises in industries such as music, web design or film. Examples of early RDA creative industry investments included the intellectual property advice agency OwnIt, capital investment for the creation of numerous 'creative hubs' in cities across the country, and a programme of research aimed at mapping regional cultural industries activity.

This approach was reflected even in the capital, where London's RDA supported a series of localised cultural industry 'hubs' just outside of the main concentrations of cultural sector employment in London – in areas like Lewisham, Haringey and Kings Cross – which combined high levels of creative industry activity with high levels of social deprivation. This co-location was not an accident. Initiatives were to be 'particularly targeted at disenfranchised groups', and London's 'rich but divided' legacy of social polarisation was to be 'actively challenged' (LDA, 2003: 15).

The combination of European money with generous RDA budgets allowed numerous capital projects to be developed, and enabled the development of cultural intermediary expertise in providing business and accommodation support for such businesses. Significant investment into creative industries workspace was made across the UK, often in places that had little history of cultural production or access to

---

[5] This included figures such as Paul Skelton, former Head of Sheffield City Council's Cultural Industries Team, and Keith Hackett, consultant and former Liverpool City Councillor from 1987 to 1995. Informal groupings such as the FOCI actively sought to shape regional policy in the early New Labour years. FOCI was a group of policy makers, local council officers and researchers in the north of England, many of whom had been working with the notion of the cultural industries during the 1980s and 1990s, and whose work was influenced by the GLC approach.

markets (Gilmore, 2013). Figures such as Manchester's Tom Bloxham and companies such as Igloo and Creative Space Management emerged to offer workspace, sometimes reusing derelict industrial spaces, funded by the public sector and designed to accommodate start-up businesses. Driving many of these projects was the desire to provide creative workers and businesses with modern workspaces, where the supposed benefits of clustering (Porter, 1998) could take place.

RDA creative industry officers were proud of their investments, pointing to projects which, they argued, transformed the cultural life of their regions, provided much-needed workspace and created growth. According to Stuart McFarlane, before their investments in this area, 'there was no appropriate business accommodation for creative and digital businesses' in Yorkshire. However, he claimed that creating creative workspaces acted as a catalyst for 'all this innovation, this creativity ... and so we started this policy of looking at how we could support and build just media centres, as we called them' (Stuart McFarlane, interview).

5.5 The limitations of clustering

Problems were evident even at the early stage of New Labour's regional cultural policy. For example, while the cultural industries approach pursued an agenda of democratisation and equality, favouring a dismantling of traditional cultural hierarchies, and aiming to provide those who had previously been excluded on grounds of race or class with the means of cultural production, the creative industries approach was focused on economic growth. It had a more individualistic orientation, centred on the notion of the cultural entrepreneur, rather than seeing cultural production as an essentially social process. The type of public intervention deemed necessary was consistent with the broadly deregulatory market-based approach that New Labour took in other areas of economic policy. It was certainly not *laissez faire*; but the focus was on supply-side measures, help for small business start-ups, skills training for workers and subsidized work spaces. Intervention in terms of ownership, pricing, or restricting market power was not considered.

Nor is it clear how much such developments really helped with local economic development. For example, geographer Brett Christophers (2008), writing about MediaCityUK in Salford (Greater Manchester), has argued that such projects function as a form of corporate gentrification, failing to improve social and economic conditions for local residents. Working conditions in the cultural industries, particularly the virtual requirement to work unpaid as an entry condition, means that these industries have not played a beneficial role in equitable economic development, to put it mildly. Some of our interviewees also felt that there was often hubris or vanity attached to creative industries development: each region wanted a creative industries sector, regardless of whether there was an infrastructure or market there to sustain one (Tom Campbell, interview).

One problem was the shift towards neo-liberal theories of business clusters. The enthusiasm of RDAs for this idea derived partly from the publication of the DTI's document *Business Clusters in the UK* (DTI, 2001), which drew on the economist Michael Porter's theory of business clustering (1998). Its unsuitability for cultural industry developments has been noted by many (O'Connor, 2004; Pratt, 2004), with geographer Andy Pratt describing it as unable 'to capture the broader spatial, temporal and organisational dynamics of production across creative industries' (Pratt, 2004: 20). Of course, there are numerous reasons why cultural businesses might locate in the same area: from the importance of face-to-face contact to the reputational effects of certain locations, such as advertising in Soho. But Porter's ideas were based on growth-focused businesses, and sidelined the mix of motivations and, indeed, business forms (from sole traders and non-profits to medium-sized commercial businesses) that characterise the cultural industries. In addition, the links between production and consumption in the cultural industries – the fact that musicians are likely to go to a lot of gigs, or filmmakers to go to the cinema – are irrelevant to a Porter model of clusters, which focuses entirely on production. Yet an understanding of circuits of production and consumption is vital to developing a cultural industry sector.

For Iain Bennett, who was Sector Leader for Digital and Creative Industries at the North West Development Agency from 2006 to 2011, the discursive power of cluster theory was pervasive, although he felt that the cluster concept was often misunderstood, and used more as a fashionable term than as a well-evidenced notion:

There's a lot of shit talked about clusters. Very few of the people who were promoting clusters as a means of organisation meant clusters in that sense or had done proper research. What they meant was some kind of concentration of individuals who were involved in some industries... And in fact one of the things of the Labour policies is that they didn't bother to criticise and they didn't exercise, I don't think, enough economic rigour in determining the investment priorities as to where was really a cluster and where was just a nice sitting room with some rather interesting graphic designers.

(Iain Bennett, interview)

Bennett's words draw attention to another aspect of RDA involvement in the cultural sectors that could be problematic. While some of those responsible for the cultural industries had expertise in the sectors – having worked on arts and leisure in local authorities, for example, or with small, sector-specific cultural networks – the overall machinery of the RDAs was set up to do conventional, growth-oriented economic development. The expertise required for the cultural sectors was only partially available.

5.6 Other problems in New Labour's regional creative industries policy

Other related problems surrounded New Labour's regional policy. We concentrate in this section on two inter-related sets of problems. The first concerns governance arrangements, the second a shift from a socially driven to an economically driven agenda.

During New Labour's time in office, the identity of the department of government responsible for RDAs changed frequently. Apart from the London Development Agency (LDA), which reported to the Mayor of London, the RDAs reported to the 'sponsoring' department of central government; at first the Department for the Environment, Transport and the Regions, and then from 2001 whatever the 'business department' was called (see Chapter 4). Unlike regional development in Scotland, Wales and Northern Ireland, and, indeed, to some extent in London, the RDAs in the English regions lacked a democratic underpinning almost from the start. This was not intentional, and New Labour showed commitment to regional democracy. Regionalism in England was closely linked to the Labour Party's longstanding commitment to devolution, and elected Regional Assemblies (RAs) were supposed to underpin the activities of the RDAs. However, adding another layer of government in the English regions proved a hard sell for New Labour. The idea of an elected RA was rejected in a referendum by voters in the north-east of England in 2004. If the vote had been yes, an elected assembly would have taken control of the RDA in that region and would have had powers of tax raising and compulsory purchase. However, nearly 80 per cent of the voters of the north-east turned the proposal down on a turnout of 49 per cent, and soon after, the policy of RAs was abandoned by the Labour Party. Labour's plan has been for a regional infrastructure in England that rested on three 'pillars': Government Offices in the Regions (GORs), whose job was to oversee national policy; RDAs, which were concerned with regional economic development; and elected RAs. After the north-east referendum, RAs were abandoned, and Labour was left with unelected, though arguably more malleable, institutions through which to pursue regional policies.

Overall, there was a series of shifts in focus, and also considerable 'mission creep', as RDAs became responsible for ever more activity. Moreover, while inter-agency working at the regional level was supposed to reflect collaboration across Whitehall departments, in fact the DCMS was often either at odds with, or ignored by, the larger-spending government ministries. As Channer (2013) notes, while the DCMS frequently encouraged agencies such as the Regional Cultural Consortia to work with RDAs, the Business Department rarely reciprocated, preferring instead to focus on the sectors with potential for higher growth, namely the digital sectors such as videogames, as opposed to the rather heterogeneous mix of businesses in the cultural industries (which, as we saw in Chapter 2, were originally identified by the DCMS as including visual and performing arts, crafts and even antiques, alongside the larger media industries).

While other researchers have examined RDA activities (BOP Consulting, 2005; Chapain and Comunian, 2010), there has been less analysis of the shift in focus of RDAs from a partly socially driven to a more economistic agenda.[6] Some have argued that Labour's strategy and interventions shifted towards a place-based approach focused on capital investment, rather than a 'people-led' approach oriented towards the development of skills (Work Foundation, 2012). While this shift was most evident in the decision in the last period of New Labour power (2007–2010) to charge RDAs with responsibility for regional spatial strategies, it was also evident across RDA activities, in terms of funding and resources. For example, much investment was focused on 'place-based' activity such as regeneration through physical infrastructure (32 per cent of expenditure) and business support activities (17 per cent), while only 8 per cent was spent on 'people-based' activities such as labour market and skills interventions (Work Foundation, 2012: 15).

---

[6] Though see Oakley (2012) on this phenomenon in London.

The changing departmental ownership of the RDAs and broader changes in policy emphasis are relevant here. The first major sponsor of the RDAs was the Department of Environment, Transport and the Regions, which led one of New Labour's many early 'task forces', the Urban Task Force, and this led to the Urban White Paper in 2000 (DETR, 2000). This White Paper was communitarian in emphasis, echoing a broader focus in early New Labour policy towards working in partnership with communities (Driver and Martell, 1997; Etzioni, 1995). It stated that 'we [government] intend to build the capacity of communities to help themselves and bring about social cohesion right across the country' (DETR, 2000: 6). Political scientist Mark Bevir has argued that communitarianism and institutionalism were two pivotal strands of New Labour's politics (Bevir, 2005: 4). Both are manifest in the formation of the RDAs and in the emphasis on regeneration through community engagement, partnership working and 'active citizenship' during New Labour's first term. Yet, as Janet Newman (2001: 2–3) has argued, the influence of communitarian ideas began to wane, as New Labour faced increasing political and economic difficulties in achieving its state modernisation ambitions through consensual means based on partnership. Ideas of individual autonomy and marketisation became dominant. This is most clearly apparent in the shift in RDA sponsorship to the DTI in 2002, which pushed the agencies towards 'competitiveness' and 'productivity' agendas (Pearce and Ayres, 2009: 540).

Deep-seated problems within regional governance structures and the relationship to central government also created difficulties in pursuing a coherent regional creative industries policy. There were tensions between central government and the regions. The need for quick, politically promotable outcomes came at the expense of a more considered, flexible and longer-term strategy. As Pearce and Ayres (2009: 540) point out, 'the Agencies were also under pressure from Whitehall to prepare their strategies rapidly, leading to rushed consultation and hampering efforts to develop policies tailored to the contrasting socioeconomic conditions in each region'.

A report reflecting on lessons learned by the South West Regional Development Agency (SWRDA) as it was wound up in 2012 outlined the nature of this tension between national government and regional governance:

National government sometimes expected us to simply act as their regional delivery vehicle implementing already agreed priorities and

actions but, at other times, expected us to negotiate regional consensus through formal and informal consultative processes. This dual
role was difficult to manage with partners often expressing confusion
about exactly what they were being offered and what precisely our
role was.

(SWRDA, 2011: 4)

The policy networks with which the RDAs interacted were local, sub-
regional, regional and national. They were expected by local partners to
prioritise local needs, yet, under very different pressures from national
government, they often they found themselves caught in the middle,
with results expected rapidly (SWRDA, 2011: 17). As Channer (2013:
184) argues, the DCMS was a small and relatively weak government
department, 'with no legislative or regulatory muscle', and had to try
to use persuasion, encouragement or exhortation to get other departments to collaborate with it. Although the use of European funds meant
access to what seemed like relatively large sums for the cultural sector,
compared with other areas of economic development the amount spent
was not great. Even those funds were won in the face of some scepticism
from the Treasury (O'Brien, 2013).

Those responsible for the creative industries within RDAs noted
a lack of central government strategy: 'I think probably I was frus-
trated that the central government wasn't consistent and didn't have
a regional policy' (Chris Garcia, interview). Despite Labour's rhetoric
of devolution, commentators have noted New Labour's democratic
centralism (Sandford, 2005), whereby the powers of government and
regional institutions remain asymmetric. While powers may be shifted
to regional spaces, state executives retain the pivotal power (Pearce and
Ayres, 2009: 539).

As tension in the New Labour project between social and economic
goals became settled in favour of a stronger focus on economic growth,
this was always likely to favour London and the south-east, and the
project of greater regional equality became more problematic (Jordan,
2005). In the case of creative industries development in the regions, this
tension was particularly noticeable, as earlier formulations of the role
that creative industries had to play in regenerating communities gradually became displaced by the language and values of economic clustering
and growth (Nesta, 2006), as discussed in the previous section. The New
Labour idea of a necessarily virtuous circle between economic growth
and equality was always flawed. But in creative industries policy, the
need to address both economic growth and issues of unemployment

or poverty was problematic, even when the desire to do so was there. The growth of a videogames sector in, for example, the north-west of England might create jobs; it might even help retain some of the region's graduates who would otherwise be lost to London and the south-east of England; but it was unlikely to offer much to unemployed people or those with little formal education.

RDAs mirrored broader creative industry policy shifts within New Labour as they became far more focused on innovation and business models with the potential for growth (Banks and O'Connor, 2009; and see Chapter 4). Funding for 'lifestyle' businesses was no longer on the agenda, causing tensions within the regional creative communities, though it was an approach favoured by some of those within RDAs. As Stuart McFarlane recalls,

> I came in from the private sector, and certainly what the RDAs did was look to bring in people from the private sector because they had a commercial approach to things, and when we're talking about economic development, I'm sorry, we are talking about a commercial approach. So therefore, my approach was that [...] everyone is entitled to do what they want to do. If an artist wants to just do their art for the sake of doing their art, with no commercial focus on it whatsoever, that's fine. But don't expect the public purse to pay for that.
>
> (Stuart McFarlane, interview)

Yet this approach failed to rebalance England's creative economy. The evidence base for creative industries and economic impact is patchy and has been much critiqued for lack of consistency, but the implications are fairly clear (Creight-Tyte, 2005; Pratt, 1997). The one consistent source of information about the economic impact of cultural industries is the DCMS's Creative Industries Economic Estimates, a yearly statistical bulletin which provides primary data on jobs and growth. It mainly provides information at the national level, and only sporadically for the regions. This led Chapain and Comunian to suggest that such data limitations 'might ... hide the fact that the creative economy is a successful story only for a few regions' (2010: 719). What little comparative regional evidence there is indicates that the creative industries continue to be highly focused in the south-east and in existing endogenous creative clusters, rather than in new clusters created though public funding. While the number of creative industry local businesses increased between 2006 and 2008, the north-east showed little change, while the north-west experienced a slight decline from 11,900 in 2006 to 11,700 in 2008. Of all the English regions, London had the largest numerical increase, up from 42,200 in 2006 to 49,300 in 2008 (ONS, 2010).

Presenting data on creative industries jobs over the New Labour period is fraught with methodological issues, largely because in 2007 there were important changes in the Standard Industrial Classification (SIC) codes used by the UK government to measure employment (DCMS, 2011: 9). However, using official government data, De Propris has estimated that, while creative industries job growth was consistent in London and the south-east between 1998 and 2008, some other regions fared less well, experiencing little growth, and in the case of the East Midlands even showing a slight decline over this period (De Propris, 2013: 25).

Research by Nesta (2010) explored 'creative intensity' in particular sectors and regions, and argued that creative labour and production remained highly stratified between the north and south of England (Nesta, 2010: 4). So entrenched is this division within the UK's 'creative economy' that it led the sector skills agency Skillset (see Chapter 3) to assert that 'Creative Industries is very much part of the new North-South divide of the knowledge economy whereby north of the Watford Gap there really is no private sector knowledge economy to speak of' (Skillset, 2011: 135).[7]

Given the optimal conditions for economic growth during the majority of the New Labour years, which drove financial investment in the creative sectors, coupled with generally favourable conditions for sales of content and products, the growth that was recorded was unsurprising. That is not to say that the RDAs failed outright, but it is to acknowledge the scale of the challenge they faced in redressing regional inequalities.

5.7   The arts and regeneration in the regions

Alongside New Labour's efforts to achieve regional development via the creative industries idea, arts agencies, notably the Arts Council, continued with their own regional strategies. Local authorities, required by central government to produce such strategies (to go alongside their economic strategies), ensured that action plans were focused on increasing

---

[7] The Watford Gap is a low-lying point between two hills, near a village called Watford in Northamptonshire (far from the large Hertfordshire town of the same name), which marks the symbolic divide between the south of England, and the Midlands and north.

participation, particularly via educational engagement, as was the case with museums (see Chapter 3). Arts agencies became accustomed to working within the confines of instrumentalist policy, in order to accrue resources for arts and cultural programmes, though, as in the case of creative industries, this was not simply an imposition from the centre (Belfiore, 2012; Gilmore, 2013). Since the birth of the National Lottery, Regional Arts Boards and arts organisations had pursued a range of activities, which combined arts practice with wider social policy issues (Selwood, 2001). Many Regional Arts Boards saw this as an opportunity to work on regional or local issues and to articulate a role for culture in responding both to industrial decline and to the promise of urban regeneration (Symon and Williams, 2002).

New Labour's commitment to culture-led regeneration was serious, backed by relatively large amounts of money and a fair amount of policy rhetoric (DCMS, 2004). In contrast to the production-focused development of workspaces and creative industry 'hubs' across the land, this more arts-led regeneration tended to focus on consumption – regeneration via galleries, museums, improvements in public space and the concomitant expansion of leisure and retail facilities. But although it left a legacy of undoubtedly improved city and town centres and improved cultural facilities, the familiar problems of gentrification that dog 'regeneration' initiatives across the world (Boren and Young, 2013; Elsheshtawy, 2012; Jakob, 2011) were also a major part of the legacy.

In UK policy parlance 'regeneration' is a broad term, encompassing environmental, social and economic aspects. It should be far more than a 'bricks and mortar'-type improvement in the local environment; it should also ensure improved employment opportunities, particularly for poorer communities, increased health and well-being, and enhanced quality of life. When the DCMS published its 'Culture at the Heart of Regeneration' report in 2004, it was accompanied by a review of the literature on the potential for cultural regeneration by Graham Evans and Phyllida Shaw (Evans and Shaw, 2004), in which they distinguished three types of culture-led regeneration: 'culture-led regeneration', 'cultural regeneration' and 'culture and regeneration' (Evans and Shaw, 2004: 5–6). The first type, 'culture-led regeneration' is the most familiar – the image that springs to mind is Frank Gehry's Guggenheim Museum in Bilbao, which brought together a declining industrial city, huge public investment and a globally famous architect in a formula for urban revitalisation that has been much replicated and much criticised. Evans and Shaw were equally critical of this type of approach and more supportive of what they called 'cultural regeneration', which would integrate arts activities and good urban design and architecture into an area strategy. But despite publishing and promoting the report, New Labour's regeneration strategy increasingly became concerned with buildings-led regeneration.

Some argued that outside London and the south-east, gentrification was not necessarily a problem. Cameron and Coaffee (2004: 14) in their study of Gateshead argued that there was a distinction between cities where gentrification was driven by commercial capital and those where what they call 'positive gentrification' was driven by public authorities. The latter, they argued, was more relevant in cities in the north-east of England, where 'private capital has to be dragged kicking and screaming into de-valourised urban locations through the initiative and investment of the public sector'.

Others have argued that smaller cities and towns are less likely to suffer gentrification, as larger cities are associated with greater levels of inequality, particularly given pressure on housing costs (Stolarick and Currid-Halkett, 2013). In the UK context, even a cursory examination suggests that 'small cities' are a heterogeneous mix, and thus the result of any sort of cultural investment is likely to differ depending on whether one is talking about Cambridge or Blackpool. Some small British cities have relatively affluent profiles and lack the factors that would make them a target for 'regeneration'. The major exception to this was seaside and coastal towns, where unemployment, poverty, lack of affordable housing, and often run-down public realms did make them a focus for regeneration efforts under New Labour (Rickey and Houghton, 2009). Culture featured heavily in some of these initiatives, such as Anthony Gormley's life-size figures on Crosby beach (near Liverpool), the De La Warr Pavilion in Bexhill and the Turner Contemporary in Margate. But as the financial crisis hit and the money for such capital projects ran out, they were often left as islands of public investment in what remain largely poor and marginalised communities.

5.8   New Labour's regional cultural policies assessed

Some have credited the idea of the creative industries with the increased levels of investment in infrastructure discussed in Chapter 3 (Newbigin, 2011). Many regional museums, galleries and theatres were beneficiaries of this increased investment, as, for a time, were small cultural businesses. The expansion of regional economic development activity under New Labour gave cultural policy something to 'attach' itself to, and arts and cultural organisations found themselves part of local economic policy making, sometimes for the first time.

At the regional level, however, New Labour faced difficulties in achieving regional economic growth, greater regional equality or even accountable regional institutions. Economically, the adherence to a cluster paradigm came at the expense of recognising the 'softer' human factors that influence creative industries development, as well as the complex nature of local production networks, where both consumption and production, and the relations between them, need to be taken into account (Oakley, 2004).

As RDA ownership moved through different, renamed and merged government departments, the policy focus shifted and was often accompanied by a reorganisation of top layers of management. This would further shift the dynamic of the networks within Regional Development Agencies to ensure that they fitted with central government, leading to 'identikit' strategies 'with no clear prioritisation or tailoring of the dominant prescriptions to suit local circumstances' (Bristow, 2005: 293). There was a shift to primarily economic goals.

Ultimately, the RDAs struggled with a lack of political legitimacy. The failure of the north-east referendum was indicative of a wider failure of New Labour's decentralising tendencies. As Danson et al. (2005) have argued, regional economic development is far less likely to be successful in places that lack political autonomy. The RDAs, while they had some autonomy, were always controlled by the centre. In the latter stages of their existence, the RDAs, charged with delivering both economic growth and regeneration, were described as 'increasingly keen to rid themselves of responsibility for "social" agendas' (ACE, 2006: 19). Moreover, business leaders felt that the RDAs became 'bloated' and 'tried to do too much' (Work Foundation, 2012: 1). In particular, the government's decision to give the RDAs responsibility for regional spatial strategies in their last term was seen to have 'sealed their fate' (Smith Institute, 2013: 6), not only by spreading the responsibilities of the RDAs too broadly, but also because it created conflict with local authorities and citizens who resented the housing growth plans that the RDAs were tasked with envisaging.

Unlike the devolved nations, however, the English regions at the time lacked a constituency that really supported devolution, and on the election of a Coalition led by the Conservatives, historically a more centralist party, the RDAs were vulnerable. It is no surprise that they were one of the first sets of institutions to be abolished in the Coalition's 'bonfire of the quangos' (see Chapter 8). In the dismantling of

RDAs, institutional memory and learning were also dismantled. It may be true that 'no one put up placards or banners or petitions or took to the streets to save their RDA', as one of our interviewees put it (Tom Campbell, interview), but they represented, to some extent at least, an attempt to address regional inequality through cultural policy. That this was ultimately unsuccessful is clearly the case – cultural industries remain overwhelmingly concentrated in London and the south-east of England – though this situation would probably have been worse had no regional interventions been made. Regional creative industries policy can perhaps be seen as an honourable failure. A more striking failure is New Labour's promise to redress overall regional imbalances. Although they governed during a period of economic growth, the ultimate reliance on financial services and property as the source of that growth meant that the UK ended the New Labour period as it began it, with stark spatial inequalities.

6
Policy Innovation: Nesta and Creative Partnerships

6.1 'Projects for change'

Despite New Labour's desire to be associated with innovation and with modernisation, some aspects of cultural policy remained remarkably consistent throughout their period of government. There was still an Arts Council at the end of the period and its client base remained remarkably stable, and, while a whole variety of organisations were renamed or given slightly altered missions (e.g., the formation of the Museum, Libraries and Archives Council), funding for design, for crafts and for museums and galleries continued to be administered in a way that was recognisable from previous administrations.[1] This was a far cry from what had been discussed in opposition, when some within the Labour Party had considered more radical changes to cultural funding, looking favourably on ideas such as the proposed 'Council for Creativity' (Arts Council, n.d.), which would have merged the Arts Council with the Crafts Council, Design Council and British Film Institute to form a single cultural funding agency. A version of this emerged later in the New Labour period, under the guise of Creative Scotland, but it was not implemented throughout the UK (Stevenson, 2014). The 'clear national strategy for the whole cultural sector' envisaged in the same document (Arts Council, n.d.) never quite saw the light of day; instead, change was more piecemeal.[2]

---

[1] The Museum, Libraries and Archives Council (MLA) was formed out of the Museum and Galleries Commission and the Library and Information Commission, and was initially named Re:source [sic]. Hewison (2014: 103–28) provides a cutting account of the reorganisation, and the effectiveness of the new body.
[2] In addition, though we do not discuss the BBC in this book, this vital cultural institution, constantly the target of criticism from its commercial media rivals

There were, however, some significant institutional innovations in the period, and two of them, Nesta[3] and Creative Partnerships (CP), will form the focus of this chapter (for discussion of the UK Film Council, see Chapter 4 and Schlesinger, 2015). Unlike the UK Film Council (UKFC), which could be said to have been at least implicit Labour Party policy for some time, a single unitary body for film having been under discussion in the party since the 1970s (Schlesinger, 2015), both Nesta and CP were very much 'New Labour' creations, and like the creative industries idea, both have garnered widespread admiration outside the UK (e.g., Cunningham, 2013). Both had a focus, although in rather different ways, on unearthing 'talent', and thus could be seen as part of New Labour's fondness for meritocratic language when supporting cultural production, an emphasis which sometimes sat oddly with its seemingly democratising stress on audience 'access'.

In addition, both were conceived and developed by informal policy networks rather than through the civil service, in a way that was also characteristic of policy in other fields, such as education and welfare (Ball and Exley, 2010; Peck and Theodore, 2010), and which sheds light on the fragility of these institutional innovations, as well as their success or otherwise. New Labour's use of informal policy networks – special advisers, think tanks, so-called 'sofa government' – has been widely discussed in the literature, though there is debate about whether, and to what degree, it was how the majority of policy ideas were really formed (Ball and Exley, 2010; Pautz, 2011; Peck and Theodore, 2010; Wells, 2011). Much of the rhetoric of public service modernisation and the existence of so-called 'wicked' social problems stressed the need for innovation in public service provision (IDeA, 2005; Mulgan, 2007), and there was a clear assumption that some of this would need to come from outside existing civil service structures. Tony Blair complained of the 'scars on his back' (Assinder, 1999) from trying to reform what he chose to characterise as civil service inertia, but as Pautz (2011) argues, the influence of think tanks on New Labour was much stronger when it was in opposition than when it was in government.

---

and Conservative politicians, was not only left intact; it was well-funded (Lunt and Livingstone, 2012).

[3] Nesta began life as the acronym NESTA – short for National Endowment for Science, Technology and the Arts. It became Nesta [*sic*] only in 2012. We have used the current form of the name throughout the whole book for simplicity's sake.

The rhetoric of innovation, so much a keyword for New Labour, was important for both Nesta and CP. In Nesta's case, as we shall see, it became the purpose of the organisation itself; for CP, it was a way of describing its mission. In discussing CP, John Newbigin reflected on the role of such institutions as 'exemplary projects for change', particularly in areas such as education, where pursuing more systemic change often seems to frustrate New Labour policy makers.

> I would say, in a way, what happened was that those grand, overarching ambitions, when it became clear how difficult it was to achieve them in an area like education, the temptation was, 'let's go for more modest, time limited and scope limited initiatives like Culture Online, like Creative Partnerships', things that could be exemplary projects for change... to help drive change in the system. I think for any politician, it's a really difficult choice you make between, do you try to go for systemic change and say, 'we've got to make the education system more creative', or do you go for incremental change where you launch little initiatives that are exemplars of good practice and help to change people's ways of thinking?
>
> (John Newbigin, interview)

The degree to which these initiatives were capable of changing people's thinking in the way that the government wanted is an important question to ask of both CP and Nesta, particularly given that both failed, as this chapter will demonstrate, to build large constituencies of support or to gain Whitehall backing beyond their sponsoring departments.[4]

6.2 Nesta as talent agency

While in opposition, the Labour Party had been thinking hard about what to do with lottery funding. It was particularly keen to broaden the range of activities on which lottery money could be spent, both beyond the requirement to spend it on capital projects, and beyond what it saw as a narrow definition of 'the arts'. While controversy attended the allocation of lottery funds from its earliest days (see Chapter 3) an

---

[4] Whitehall is a street in London around which are based many important government departments and buildings. As a result, the term is used as a metonym for British central government as a whole.

important debate was about the notion of 'additionality', the degree to which lottery funds could replace what was seen as core state funding in areas such as education, science or the arts. While it was limited to capital-building expenditure, the lottery could easily be seen as additional funding, thus avoiding this problem. But once it was extended beyond capital projects, following the National Lottery Act of 1998, there were some around New Labour who felt that the changes should go further. This included the group formed around David Puttnam, already discussed in chapters 2 and 5. This informal group was influential in a variety of ways, and Puttnam was also an early supporter of CP; but the origins of the Nesta idea came from a different source. Rory Coonan, at that time Director of Architecture at the Arts Council, had been involved in the lottery since the Council became a distributor of lottery funds in 1994. Coonan was not a Labour Party insider, or even a member, but he was in many ways well-placed to influence those who were working on party policy. His senior role at the Arts Council (which he left in February 1996), together with what he described as his social networks, including Puttnam's advisers, meant that, by his own account, access by Coonan to New Labour's policy thinking was easily obtained. According to Newbigin, Coonan came to him with the idea for Nesta 'perfectly formed in his head'.

Coonan had argued that the idea of the lottery was interesting, but not sufficient, that limiting the lottery to capital projects only was problematic, and that the exclusion of science and engineering from the original 'good causes' on which the lottery could be spent was a mistake. In the early 1990s, he began working on the idea of an endowment fund which would, free from Treasury control, be able to fund projects at the intersection of arts and science (for a fuller account of the original vision for Nesta, see Oakley et al., 2014). Struck by the public's willingness to gamble on the lottery, despite the long odds on winning anything, and following a visit to the National Endowment for the Arts in Washington DC, Coonan argued for a UK endowment fund to support risk-taking activities of a sort that the Arts Council and other lottery distributors often found difficult to justify.

In a document of 1995 (Coonan, 1995a), he set out what he saw as the problems with the existing lottery set up:

> The National Lottery is open to the charge that it recycles money from the poor to those who are already beneficiaries of the social order. It is also open to the accusation that the objects of its expenditure are too restricted. Science and the wider humanities (other than

the subsidised arts) are excluded altogether from the Lottery's 'good causes', which are defined by Parliament.

(Coonan, 1995a: 1)

The proposed remedy for this was ambitious. The lottery distributors were to be subsumed into what was variously imagined as a National Endowment for Science, Humanities and the Arts (Coonan, 1995a), a National Endowment for Science, Education and the Arts (Coonan, 1995b), briefly a National Endowment for Sports and the Arts (Coonan, ND), and by the third quarter of 1995, a National Endowment for Science, Technology and the Arts or NESTA (Coonan, 1995c). Such a fund would essentially support individuals, rather than buildings or organisations. Investment in new ideas was not the only goal of the proposed body, which also had a strong educational emphasis, described as 'part of a wider desire to re-assert in British cultural life the value of the disinterested pursuit of knowledge' (Coonan, 1995a: 1).

The way to do this, Coonan argued, was to set up an endowment, 'a body owned by and for the nation' (1995a: 3), which could be for the 21st century 'what the National Trust had been to the 20th'. As well as receiving an initial grant of lottery money, the proposed endowment was to solicit bequests of money, property and land, and acquire ownership of copyright and patents, particularly from those who had been supported by the endowment in their early days and had gone on to become successful. In Coonan's proposals, the endowment, rather than the state directly, would take over extinct copyright, an innovation he compared to the anomalous situation whereby Great Ormond Street children's hospital in London receives royalties from J. M. Barrie's book *Peter Pan*.[5]

These documents articulate a desire to create an institution comparable to the Arts Council or the Open University (both post-war innovations) and even the British Museum, which was also initially funded by a lottery (Coonan, 1995a, 1995b, 1996a, 1996b). But what is perhaps most striking in retrospect is the idea that the proposed endowment

---

[5] Coonan anticipated that parliament would in due time pass an amendment to the 'Great Ormond Street Hospital anomaly' legislation to bring other time-limited income-earning intellectual property into the ambit of 'extinct' copyright extension beyond 50/70 years after the 'author's' life. The plan would have required the seeking of a derogation from EU rules. In terms of active rights, the idea was that UK copyright owners might also 'gift' active rights under their control in some way proportional to the benefit they had received from Nesta. This element of the plan was never adopted.

should become a membership organisation (Coonan, 1996b), by way of a National Endowment card which, similar to an organisation such as the National Trust, 'could give discounted prices for a range of products and services, including reduced price entry to museums, galleries and events in the arts and sciences' (Coonan, 1996b: 2). This sort of public involvement could have partly offset concerns about the transfer of wealth from the poor to the rich that the lottery enacted, but more than that, it represented a notion of the civic importance of independent institutions, from trade unions to workers' educational organisations, which had deep roots in elements of the British social democratic tradition (Bevir, 2011).

The elements of the proposed endowment, or what Coonan called the 'national trust for talent', that appealed to Newbigin and to Puttnam were ones that seemed to attack longstanding 'British' problems:

> There was no national body of research or intellectual endeavour that's looking at where science, technology and the arts come together. So that was one strand. The second strand was... we have a fantastic history in the UK of coming up with brilliant ideas and an absolutely crap history of turning those brilliant ideas into viable businesses.
>
> (Rory Coonan, interview)

'Getting more serious about intellectual property' was how Newbigin characterised this strand of the endowment's potential work, and it was an idea that was to animate much of New Labour's cultural policy, particularly its simultaneous development of the creative industries. Coonan's idea was adopted by David Puttnam and others, and won support from Blair, Brown and Mandelson. There was a commitment to making it happen relatively quickly if Labour was elected. The mechanism for this was its appearance in the 1997 Labour manifesto, where it formed one of the few cultural promises of the document (see Chapter 2).

Nesta was set up with an endowment of £200 million in July 1998 and a degree of freedom in terms of spending money unknown to other public organisations. David Puttnam became its first Chair, and its first Chief Executive was Jeremy Newton, another ex-Arts Council employee. Positioning Nesta as a source of support for creative individuals reflected much of the first New Labour administration's professed enthusiasm for small entrepreneurial businesses, particularly in the cultural sectors, as well as its frustration about what was perceived as the 'missing middle'

of public policy, between arts funding that mostly went to large organisations, and small business support, which tended to stay well clear of
such high-risk fields (Banks et al., 2000). While Nesta was not freighted
with expectations about playing a role in urban or regional regeneration, as many small business support agencies were, expectations about
the economic success of the cultural industries and faith in small-scale
entrepreneurs to deliver this success were, nonetheless, central to Nesta's
definition and to its early activities.

These revolved around three funding programmes: the Fellowship
programme, the Invention and Innovation programme, and the Education programme. Fellowships, which could range in size from £25,000
to £75,000, were bestowed on individuals across Nesta's areas of interest,
but because 'invention and innovation' was always less likely to attract
applications from the arts than from science or technology, it became
seen as Nesta's arts-funding activity.

While it had no criticism of Nesta's selection process, the House of
Commons Science and Technology Committee, when it reported on
Nesta in 2002, noted that Fellowship awards seemed to be dominated
by the arts, while the opposite was true of the 'invention and innovation' stream (House of Commons, Science and Technology Committee,
2002). Funding or, indeed, finding projects at the intersection of arts,
science and technology proved harder than some might have hoped,
and Jeremy Newton later argued that while the Fellowships scheme supported some good artistic work, it failed to come up with more than one
or two projects that commercialised artistic innovation in a way that
would provide an economic return (Newton, interview).

The House of Commons Science and Technology Committee noted in
2002 that while an annual income of around £12 million from investments had been predicted in 1998, by 2002 it was only two thirds
of this figure, at around £8 million (even by 2011, investment return
on the endowment had only reached £15 million). Indeed, the return
on Nesta's endowment was never large enough to cement its status as
an entirely autonomous organization, and as time went on, and after
changes of personnel at the top, it sought to become less of a maverick
outsider and much closer to public policy. Moving from the intersection
of arts, science and technology and towards 'innovation' more generally
was seen as the way to do this.

Puttnam was replaced as Chairman by Chris Powell (brother of Tony
Blair's Chief of Staff, Jonathan) in what was widely interpreted as a
change of direction. Powell argues that the Nesta Fellowships scheme
had been too heavily influenced by the model of the US MacArthur

Foundation, essentially providing 'no strings' funding to talented individuals in a way that he felt was compatible with a charity, but not with a public body. Of greater concern was that funding for individuals was likely to be used in the early stages of project development, whereas the real need was slightly later on, when individuals had exhausted informal sources of funding – such as family, friends or credit card debt – and there was a need to scale up.

This shift, reinforced in 2005 when Jonathan Kestenbaum was recruited to replace Newton as Chief Executive, represented not just a change of investment policy, but a change to the organisation's primary remit, as well as the policy and scholarly communities with which Nesta engaged. It moved Nesta from being a funder of individuals, who were seen as neglected by the traditional funding system in both the arts and the sciences, towards an organisation focused on systems-level innovation. If improving Britain's GDP was to be Nesta's goal, Kestenbaum's interest was in ideas that could scale rapidly and had the potential for replicability; he wanted to develop an organisation that could work with large government departments, institutional investors and big corporations, to bring about the kinds of innovations that would lead to economic growth.

Given this, Nesta put much greater emphasis on its investment portfolio, scrapping the Fellowship programme and dividing its Innovation and Investment programme in two. 'Nesta investments' was set up as an early-stage venture capital fund, focused on high-technology investments 'operating on strictly commercial grounds' (Nesta, 2012). What were described as 'experimental' projects were relabelled as the Innovation Programme, and could wander further from the immediately commercialisable and into a variety of policy areas such as climate change and public services.

In its first phase, straddling arts, education and economic policy, Nesta had sought to stand somewhat aside from policy making, and while, like other arm's length non-departmental public bodies, it was not subject to direct government control, it did not see itself as an influence on government policy making. From 2005 onwards, and particularly from 2008, when its sponsoring department changed from the DCMS to the Department of Business, Innovation and Skills (BIS), it sought to engage fully with national and, indeed, international policy making, which meant a large scale reconstruction of its policy networks. Having once sought to fill the gaps left by both arts funding and higher education funding councils, Nesta now sought to position itself much more clearly as a research-led 'innovation think tank', close to higher education and to Whitehall.

Nesta's Policy and Research Unit, previously a very small part of the organisation, benefited from the bulk of recruitment in Kestenbaum's period in office, and the organisation began a series of collaborations with higher education institutions (HEIs) and the commissioning of research from HEIs in the field of innovation. In particular, it worked with Queensland University of Technology (QUT) in Australia on the idea of 'creativity' as an input into all sorts of economic activities, rather than something specifically associated with artistic creativity, as it had been under a 'cultural industries' approach. This work was, unfortunately, influential in helping to shift the focus of government policy, and of course Nesta's activities, from the cultural industries themselves to a purely economically driven notion of 'innovation' (see Chapter 4 in this book).

The closure of the Fellowship programme was widely viewed as a disengagement of Nesta from the arts, and certainly from artists. The emphasis on scale and replicability that animated Nesta's new take on innovation sat uneasily in the cultural sectors, where 'innovation' still carries echoes of originality (and not necessarily replicability) and attachment to craft forms of labour retains a strong purchase among producers (Oakley, 2009a). Even in the commercial cultural industries, scale and replication exist in a dynamic tension with the need for innovation to satisfy consumers and the desire for autonomy on the part of producers (Hesmondhalgh, 2013a).

Nesta's second-phase metamorphosis, however, had the effect of strengthening its position in the period after the New Labour government. When the Coalition government was elected in May 2010, it was clear that large-scale public spending cuts were in the offing, and for a while Nesta was thought to be a prime candidate for closure. Instead, this fate was visited on other New Labour institutions that operated in the cultural sphere, such as the UKFC and the Museums, Libraries and Archives Council (see Chapter 8). Nesta, instead, survived, changed its legal status, and was moved from the public to the voluntary sector, becoming a charity in April 2012.

6.3 Creative Partnerships

Unlike Nesta, which was an experiment in a field (cultural funding) that was not otherwise characterised by much experimentation, CP, New Labour's flagship cultural education programme, was set up in the already crowded and hugely pressurised world of education policy. Announced in 2001 and launched in 2002, CP was a joint departmental venture by the DCMS and the Department for Education and

Skills (from 2007, the Department for Children, Schools and Families), but managed by the Arts Council through regional offices. Designed to increase 'creativity' in children and to provide 'creative learning' in schools, CP also fitted with the social exclusion agenda, as it was targeted at the most deprived local authority areas.

Initially a pilot scheme in 16 regions, CP became a national scheme in 2004, and until 2009, when it was both renamed and reduced in size, local ACE offices administered CP in some 36 of the most deprived local authority areas in England. It was overseen by a central team based in London, and housed within ACE's headquarters. CP's remit was to broker partnerships between schools and creative practitioners, and to nurture the creativity of children and young people. Children worked on creative investigations in arts and culture with a range of specialists including artists, historians, scientists, architects, entrepreneurs, designers, technologists and musicians. The scale of the investment was significant. The programme is reported to have worked with over 1 million children, through more than 8,000 projects, at a cost of £275 million during its nine-year existence (Creative Partnerships, 2013), though it is worth noting that, as it was concentrated in deprived areas, this still represents only a tenth of all schools in England and Wales.

The idea of CP can be traced back to the report of the National Advisory Committee for Creative and Cultural Education (NACCCE), established in 1998 by the Secretaries of State for Education and for Culture, Media and Sport. The report, *All Our Futures* (NACCCE, 1999), was authored by noted educationalist Ken Robinson, and three years after its publication, CP was created to address and build on some of the recommendations. While the work for setting up CP was largely done within DCMS and the Arts Council, funding was also required from the much larger Department for Education, and it was vital for DCMS to connect its priorities to those of the more powerful department – another example of the 'policy attachment' we discuss throughout this book.

According to Alan Davey (2012), Director for Culture at DCMS (2003–2006), this was how Chris Smith 'sold' early arts and creative industries policy to the Treasury:

> What was interesting was that Chris Smith had a policy, it was around education and that was the way he sold it to the Treasury, so you got extra money for the arts but a lot of it was ring-fenced for Creative Partnerships and related activity, although some of it was just pure

extra money. He did that by deploying the importance of the arts in education and to children's futures.

In gaining support for CP within government, personal networks were important, notably the relationship between Chris Smith and Education Secretary David Blunkett. However, the key strategic move for DCMS was to make sure that CP connected to government policies, and what Jones and Thomson (2008: 720) described as 'the enduring pressures of the standards agenda'.

Even at this early stage, many of the misunderstandings and internal political wranglings that would eventually undo CP were taking shape, as different parts of government came to very different understandings of CP, its mission, and who it was for. Education policy academics Jones and Thomson (2008) have argued that, whereas the Robinson *All Our Futures* report had been critical of the existing curriculum and assessment regime, this critical edge was lost in the report's call for more 'creativity'. This call was justified in terms perfectly aligned to New Labour's understanding of the demands of the knowledge economy; in other words, that it would help children (and hence the nation) to participate in global markets, face national economic challenges, feed the fast-growing creative industries and adapt to technological and social change. Such a notion of creativity had widespread appeal to those in the community arts and education worlds who saw 'elitist' notions of creativity, which focus on individual talent, as setting up barriers to personal development. But, as Banaji et al. (2006) argue, there are dangers in a broader but bland definition of creativity. Such creativity no longer undermined or challenged social norms, but became, instead, the key to social cohesion. It was dynamic enough to bring us lots of new products in the marketplace, but not so dynamic that it had anything much to say about the problems of society.

By operating in the most deprived communities in the country, CP sought to offer access to the kinds of cultural practice that many middle-class children could take for granted. At the same time, and given its target demographic, CP had to appear to improve educational attainment. Culture Secretary Tessa Jowell may have claimed that 'creativity and standards go hand in hand' (quoted in Jones and Thomson, 2008: 722), but many others experienced this as an ultimately unmanageable tension.

Creative activities, rather than influencing the mainstream of education within the CP schools, remained separate from the increasingly disciplined and managerialist workings of the National Curriculum.

Indeed, subjects such as music were increasingly offered as extra curricula, rather than part of core education, and the mandated hours of literacy and numeracy left less and less time for experiment. Throughout its existence, CP was evaluated and its practices described by academics, research organisations and consultancies. Many different impacts were claimed, including improved attainment, student well-being and positive effects on the creative economy (Arts Council England, 2007a; BOP, 2006; Pringle and Harland, 2008). However, it was recognised within CP itself that a major challenge for the programme was 'to find a language and evidence base that captures its successes' (Arts Council England, 2007b).

In some ways, CP was a paradigmatic New Labour cultural policy innovation: it was delivered through an arms-length approach via ACE, worked in partnership with multiple local and national agencies, and represented a significant cultural and educational investment. In its broader policy agenda there is evidence of social and economic instrumentalism, whereby 'creative learning' was understood as a catalyst for social regeneration and economic development. At a 'meta' level, CP was developed and sustained through an extensive network of policy makers, researchers, quangos and the influential centre-left think tank Demos.[6] Furthermore, a huge amount of evidence and evaluation was created, also typical of New Labour cultural and education policy.

Just as with Nesta, based a few miles across London, the CP head office also firmly established itself as a fully-fledged research outfit, embodied in an extensive body of publications and research which reflected on its own work, and often more broadly on the nature of creative education and 'the rhetorics of creativity' (Banaji et al., 2006). While the core team was certainly not as large as Nesta's under Kestenbaum, CP benefited from links to a national and international network of academics and consultants working in this expanding area. However, despite these activities, at a 'micro' level, our research indicates a lack of communication between civil service, ministers and CP itself, leading to a fundamental and damaging policy confusion among ministers and their special advisers as to what CP was and what it would achieve. Its origins in an informal networks of organisation committed to creative learning were no match for the pressure to improve educational standards – meaning exam results – coming from the Education Department.

---

[6] See Ball and Exley (2010) for a mapping of New Labour's educational policy network.

At the same time, its perceived instrumentalism meant that while many individual cultural practitioners supported it, and not just because it represented an economic opportunity for them (BOP, 2006), other, more established cultural organisations were less supportive.

Reflecting on how CP had initially gained support within government, Paul Collard, Chief Executive of CP from 2005 to 2010, explained how the process of 'selling the idea' within government caused such significant problems further down the line:

> Why Creative Partnerships had such difficulty in its first couple of years is that the influence of the special advisers in DCMS, in their relationship with other ministries, is they told them different things about what it was. And that was hugely problematic because about a year in, the various people who'd been sold Creative Partnerships then began to go, 'but that wasn't what I thought this was about'. So, Gordon [Brown] was sold a concept of social transformation... Tony [Blair] was sold a completely different concept because his view was that staying in power was about taking swing voters with you and swing voters are actually a bit middle class and a bit affluent and they want better opportunities for their kids... And if you pick the poor schools, Tony's furious and if you pick the rich schools, Gordon's furious and it was a mess between the two trying to equalise the fact that different things had been sold to them, which then started this process of people beginning to ask fundamental questions.
>
> (Paul Collard, interview)

Whereas Nesta was created as a centralised, autonomous institution, CP was far more complex and heterogeneous in terms of structure, location and delivery. The national CP organisation was originally based inside ACE's London head office, although ACE was not directly involved in managing CP. Local CP areas were accountable to Arts Council regions, but also needed to provide data about expenditure and activity to national CP, which was, in turn, accountable to ACE. As national CP had no direct line management for the regional operations, it tended to see itself in a leadership, rather than a management, role (Jones and Thomson, 2008: 722). This created a focus on learning and reflection, which helps to explain why many of its externally facing publications were less focused on delivery, and tended to be more reflective and academic in tone (e.g., Arts Council England, 2007a; Banaji et al., 2006; Thomson, 2010). However, it also helps to explain why CP was unable to 'develop a normative, and perhaps more operationally effective, view of creativity, changing pedagogies and directions for school reform' (Jones and Thomson, 2008: 722).

This lack of a coherent mission for CP was compounded by the multiple claims for and against it. The think tank Demos argued for the importance of creativity in modern economies (see Chapter 2), and this was influential in making the political case for creative education (Seltzer and Bentley, 1999). As outlined above, the NACCCE report responded to this, and paved the way for the creation of CP (National Advisory Committee, 1999). Yet, CP also found itself the object of derision from the Conservative print media (Narain, 2009). More significantly, CP also found itself a target for rival political parties, who questioned the value of public money being used for what were seen as self-indulgent projects, and by the time of the 2005 election it had found its way into the manifesto of the Liberal Democrat Party as a project that they would abolish if they came to power.

Paul Collard told us that CP had become confused and already lacked a clear purpose by the time of his arrival in 2005. Although it had received significant funding from government, it was clear that senior politicians, both within and outside government, did not understand what CP was meant to achieve. Collard prioritised refocusing CP's mission. He commissioned research with the aim of generating positive 'headlines' on CP's achievements in terms of attainment and school engagement, which could be sold to ministers, with the aim of 'subtly undermining' an ongoing programme of evaluation of CP by the National Foundation for Educational Research, which he described as 'bonkers' (Collard, interview). Extensive lobbying of key politicians was then undertaken, which raised CP's profile considerably within government. This strategy was briefly successful and ensured CP's survival and procurement of greater funding. A key signifier of this was that in 2008 CP was given responsibility for the management and budget for *Find Your Talent*, the government's pilot cultural programme for all children and young people. In 2009, a consultation by the Cultural Learning Alliance suggested there was still a lack of empathy and shared language between the educational and cultural sectors (CLA, 2009), and in the same year CP was renamed Creativity, Culture and Education (CCE) and hived off from the Arts Council as an independent organisation.

This was initially presented as a move towards greater institutional autonomy, and CCE briefly became the Arts Council's largest single client, with £75 million for the next three years. In fact, CCE was being run down. Funding was withdrawn from *Find Your Talent* in 2010, and in the prolonged austerity following the financial crisis of 2008, CP proved to be highly vulnerable to economic and political change. In contrast to Nesta, it failed to secure public funding beyond New Labour, and was one of the first cultural projects to have its funding cut in 2010, with activities in schools ending in 2011.

Throughout Collard's tenure as Director of CP, there was growing resentment within the Arts Council, as it was increasingly cut out of the commissioning process for creative agents to work in schools. While regional Arts Council offices had previously been much more closely involved in this process, following Collard's arrival, and in particular CP's institutional shift to CCE (which was run as a charity and outside of the Arts Council control), they were increasingly marginalised. However, as the 2010 election approached, and in the wake of ferocious cultural budget cuts, the Arts Council argued that government should focus on funding 'excellence' and protecting the 'crown jewels' of the arts world (Needham, 2012). CP's large budget was highly attractive to them. Extensive lobbying of DCMS by the Arts Council made CP vulnerable in the lead up to the 2010 general election, and, crucially, the Education Department failed to give support to CP during this period.

6.4 Surviving beyond New Labour

Nesta and CP had faced some similar difficulties – in particular, identifying a clear mission and forming a clear constituency of interest that might come to their aid in any political battles. Nesta started out as a cross-departmental initiative, but always had difficulty keeping all stakeholders on board at the same time. It was an outsider organisation, and switched its constituency from inventors and artists to innovation policy wonks. But, unlike CP, Nesta was never in the great public policy battles of the New Labour administration – in this case, the battle for educational improvement in schools and, indeed, the battle for what was meant by educational improvement.

Nesta more successfully made the switch from DCMS to the Business Department and articulated its activities to the growing fashion for 'innovation', as this became a strong direction for economic policy, particularly in Labour's third term. Yet it could be argued that its voice on innovation is now something of an uncritical one. Concerns about the role of innovation in the economy, and the point at which it becomes socially harmful, have recently been the subject of debate, even as the term itself became a policy buzzword (Cowen, 2011; Dallyn, 2011; Turner, 2009). Many modern innovations bring only slight additional benefits to the majority of the population, though they can bring significant problems. The innovation of credit default swaps and other financial products was concentrated, in terms of use, in the top 1 per cent of the 1 per cent of the population, but when they blew up spectacularly in 2007/2008, the fallout from state support of the financial services sector was enough to ensure that almost every citizen would feel poorer and see their public services diminished. Innovation in consumer electronics has undoubtedly brought welfare benefits – and entertainment – to many, but the concerns in terms of growing electronic waste are severe (Maxwell and Miller, 2012). One role for a publicly funded innovation think tank might have been to provide space for a critical engagement with the problems of innovation thinking, but this sits uneasily with an investment role, and, while Nesta engages in policy debates, it has yet to take a very critical stance on innovation, an inclination which may, of course, be part of the secret of its survival, innovation having been taken up in the same rather unreflective way by the Coalition government as it was by New Labour.

Yet the major reason for Nesta's survival is surely its autonomy as an endowment-funded institution. Unlike CP, it was relatively free from needing to constantly make its case against shifting political agendas, particularly in a highly sensitive area like education. This is not to say that its purpose did not change, indeed, did not 'narrow' over time. Nesta was set up as a public institution with a broad public purpose, but the messiness and complexity of an experimental organisation, operating at the boundaries of science, art and technology, with a multiplicity of social and cultural aims and where economic returns were never likely to be great, proved unpalatable in a climate, later in the New Labour period, where the pursuit of economic growth became the only game in town.

The membership organisation that Coonan had envisaged was never part of New Labour's plan for Nesta, so it can hardly be blamed for not achieving it. But it failed to establish a wider constituency of interested parties in the way that the organisations to which it was originally compared could be said to have done. The artists, scientists and inventors who had welcomed its launch, even the Fellows who benefited directly from its funding, never formed an identifiable body of support. As Nesta moved away from funding individuals, they moved away from it.

Nesta's embrace of 'innovation', particularly large-scale innovation, as its sole purpose was a decision that the organisation itself took, though it was certainly one that fitted with the temper of the times (Oakley, 2009a) and through which it found a community of academics and policy makers enthused by the same vision of creative destruction (Cunningham, 2013).

Has Nesta been successful in its own terms? Ending the 'two cultures' split between science and the arts has inevitably proved difficult. Nesta is active in a range of technology fields: semiconductors, medical diagnostics, videogames and special effects as well as promotional and research activities in a variety of 'social' and 'public' innovations. When asked to point to significant cultural innovation, its support of the broadcasting of live theatrical events, originally under the banner of 'NT Live', is generally cited, and while this clearly represents an extension of audience for live theatre, and presents producers with new technological challenges, it is difficult to understand the degree to which it is an artistic or cultural innovation of great significance. The requirement for size and scalability of innovation may work against genuine artistic innovation, or may even work on the boundaries of art and science.

The degree of autonomy granted to NESTA meant that it was hugely influenced by changes of personnel, particularly of the Chief Executive. And the relative weakness of the policy networks that surrounded it led to the eclipse of various constituencies: artists and inventors most notably, but also the public, who had been integral to the original vision. This reflects not simply the ultimate dominance of corporate interests in New Labour's cultural policy, but also the weakness of any countervailing forces to those interests.

Nesta has, however, survived as an independent organisation, and, by becoming a charity, its independence may be more secure. For CP, while many of the evaluations of a much-studied programme reported positively (e.g., Eames et al., 2006; McLellan et al., 2012), evidence was difficult to prove and took time to assimilate, and, given the project-based nature of CP, the data was often piecemeal. According to Collard, this led to a feeling within DCMS that CP was a worthwhile experiment, but too patchy in its implementation, and was perceived to be inconsistent. It was plagued by being caught between the 'standards' agenda focused on numeracy and literacy, which dominated New Labour's education policy in their first term, and an 'arts in education' approach, with its intellectual roots in experimental teaching innovations of previous decades, often associated with being antithetical to a standardised curriculum approach.

It had difficulties in its relationship with local authorities and partners, due to what was called the 'terribly complex' arrangements between CP and its partners (Jones and Thomson, 2008). Furthermore, as Hall and Thomson argue, 'creativity' had to be positioned as outside of school structures and the core curriculum, within 'projects', and was to be found in artists, not teachers (Hall and Thomson, 2007).

Angela McRobbie has suggested that CP should be seen as a form of 'cultural neo-liberalism', to be placed alongside other cultural initiatives instigated during the New Labour period, through which young people were encouraged to become 'entrepreneurs of the self' (McRobbie, 2011). Her argument is that New Labour's cultural policies, including CP, were aligned with the broader aims and requirements of neo-liberalism, in particular at the level of the individual, by encouraging particular forms of subjectivity (such as competitive entrepreneurialism and individualism) that serve the neo-liberal project.

Our view is that CP needs to be understood in a more nuanced way. For one thing, it was reflective of fundamental tensions within New Labour. Specifically, CP exposes the contradiction between a dominant, standardised approach to education, with its emphasis on constant testing and audit (Bache, 2003), set against advocates of creative education within the New Labour government. CP's explicit rhetorical positioning of the importance of creativity within the 'knowledge economy' sought to surmount this contradiction.

However, despite gaining financial security and greater autonomy as it progressed, it proved to be politically vulnerable. The policy confusion about what it was, and what it was meant to achieve, meant it failed to gain a powerful constituency of support, both within and outside of government. While Nesta may have failed to gain a public constituency, its institutional structure as an independent endowment, and its close involvement in the economics of the creative industries (such as innovation policy), gave it a greater credibility with a new, more right-wing government. CP, on the other hand, was unable to prove the economic benefits of its activities, and the educational benefits of CP were either resisted by education policy makers (in the sense that 'we're doing this anyway') or not striking enough to merit further funding.

In terms of what they tell us about the sociology of public policy, both CP and Nesta had their intellectual origins outside the formal mechanisms of policy development. In the case of Nesta, much of the thinking was done before New Labour came into office, offering some support for Pautz's argument (2011) that such networks are more influential in opposition than in government. It's clear that in CP's case, stronger buy-in from the Education Department might have protected it when there was a change of government, though gaining that buy-in the first place would have required conforming more closely to a central government script about educational standards.

Schlesinger, in his account of the life and death of the UK Film Council (Schlesinger, 2015), comments on the lack of clear deliberation and policy analysis in either the creation or the destruction of UKFC. Instead, he argues that the policy actors involved – particularly those from outside of government (in UKFC's case its first Chair, film director Alan Parker, and its CEO John Woodward; see Chapter 4) – were generally chosen to endorse an existing policy as reliable New Labour associates who shared the same diagnosis of the problem. The expertise that they brought was essentially agreement with the particular project; they were rarely chosen as 'critical friends' (see also Schlesinger, 2009). We can see a similar approach in both Nesta and CP, though in the case of Nesta the policy network proved more flexible and able to adapt to changing times. As in the case of UKFC, the survival of Nesta and elimination of CP were decisions quickly taken by the Coalition government, featuring very little consultation or assessment of the wider consequences. As a result, there is almost no record of the official decision-making process, either at the birth of these organisations or at their demise. Policy groups may be most influential at the ideas-generating stage – often in opposition – but in the case of both New Labour and the Coalition, informal and seemingly ad hoc decision making remains a feature of the cultural policy landscape.

7
Heritage

7.1 Heritage in the UK

Heritage is, by definition, a matter of looking backwards to history. With its incessant stress on modernisation, New Labour was widely perceived as favouring the contemporary at the expense of the historical. In this context, it is no surprise that the party was frequently accused of neglecting or showing hostility towards heritage (Aslet, 2008; Christiansen, 2007; Hewison, 2014; Hunt, 2007). This chapter considers New Labour's record in this area and argues that the picture is rather more complex than such accusations and perceptions suggest.

As discussed in Chapter 2, the renaming of the culture ministry from the Department of National Heritage (DNH) to Department for Culture, Media and Sport (DCMS) was a rejection of the traditionalist connotations of heritage and a move that placed New Labour's modernising intentions centre stage. According to Chris Smith's book *Creative Britain*, New Labour did not view heritage as 'unimportant' (1998: 2), but the party wanted 'something more forward-looking' as the title for its culture department, 'a name that captured more accurately the spirit of modern Britain, that signalled the involvement of all' (1998: 2). As a result of its new 'democratic agenda' (Smith, 1998: 3), the heritage sector saw a reduction in its funding as money for other aspects of culture and the arts was increased.

In spite of the funding cuts, the heritage sector arguably did well during the New Labour years. When the party lost the general election in 2010, the heritage sector was far more self-sufficient than it had been in 1997, with cultural tourism, volunteering and membership levels at an all-time high. How can we understand the relationship between New Labour's funding cuts and this quiet rise in the heritage sector's fortunes? What part, if any, did cultural policy play? This chapter begins by sketching out the heritage sector in the UK. We then move on to discussing Labour's modernising intentions. The notion of heritage was reshaped during this period, largely due to the work being undertaken by the sector, which reflected the changes that were taking place in society more generally but chimed with New Labour's focus around cultural diversity. This discussion is contextualised by reference to the much more explicitly pro-heritage cultural policies of the previous Conservative government. We then turn to the attempt by the heritage sector to broaden audiences through outreach and education work. This is followed by an exploration of the funding cuts and the sector's lobbying in response to what it perceived as neglect. During this time, the heritage sector also rapidly expanded its income through increased commercial activity, which was essential to its survival under the Labour government. The chapter ends with some closing remarks about the relatively favourable status of the sector at the end of the period and, in turn, the relative limits of cultural policy.

How to define heritage?[1] The Heritage Lottery Fund (HLF) describes heritage simply as anything that can be inherited and passed on to future generations to enjoy. This broad definition is echoed by the key funding body, English Heritage, which sees heritage as 'all inherited resources which people value for reasons beyond mere utility' (2008: 71). From an academic perspective, museum studies and heritage studies are often seen as two separate fields, although there are considerable overlaps and shared interests. They are also seen as distinct in policy and funding terms. The heritage sector in the UK is made up of a number of heritage bodies, and while the majority of these are privately run, here we focus on the publicly funded heritage institutions such as English Heritage, the HLF and the National Heritage Memorial Fund (NHMF). Established in 1984, English Heritage is an arm's length body that advises government on heritage matters and manages historic properties. In forming the organisation, the Conservative government of Margaret Thatcher created a newly powerful, 'clear and visible' (Pendlebury, 2000: 40) conservation organisation. English Heritage receives the vast majority of (non-lottery) funding for heritage (roughly 80–85 per cent). The NHMF was established in 1980 and provides grants through an endowment to 'at-risk' heritage, to acquire, preserve and maintain land, buildings and structures of special interest.

---

[1] In many languages, the equivalent term to 'heritage' is closer to the rarely used English word 'patrimony' – such as *patrimoine* (French) and *patrimonio* (Spanish).

The NHMF distributes the heritage share of lottery money through the HLF, which has a remit to safeguard the UK's heritage. The private heritage organisations are important, but there is no space to discuss them in detail here, and so organisations such as Britain's biggest private landowner, The National Trust, are not covered in any detail within our assessment. The Trust is an independent charity but is governed by a series of Acts of Parliament. It does not receive grants directly from the government, but obtains some of its funding from public sources such as the National Lottery. However, this is marginal in relation to its overall income. There are also a number of private interest and lobby groups that make up the heritage sector, such as the Historic Houses Association and Heritage Alliance (these, too, are not addressed here for the same reason).

7.2 New Labour's modernisation of heritage?

Politically, in the UK, heritage has been strongly associated with the Conservative Party. The Conservatives have tended to embrace the nationalism, custom and tradition associated with heritage, even while favouring marketising policies that tend to undermine stability. But the relationship between conservatism and conservation is a matter of policy action as well as ideology: urban studies researcher John Pendlebury (2000) showed that the number of listed buildings tended to increase greatly during periods of Conservative government.

In the 18 years of Conservative administrations, from 1979 to New Labour's election victory of 1997, heritage was high on the political agenda. For Pendlebury (2000: 31), this period was characterized by 'a consolidation and strengthening of conservation policy to a previously unprecedented level'. The Conservatives passed National Heritage Acts in 1980 and 1983, establishing key heritage bodies such as the NHMF and the Historic Buildings and Monuments Commission for England (the official name for English Heritage), and solidified the protection of listed buildings, which involved extending the remit to include post-1945 buildings and outdoor spaces. The creation of the DNH in 1992 (see Chapter 2) has been described as a 'seismic shift' (Taylor, 1997: 443) in the status of heritage in Britain. For the first time, it had a Cabinet minister and dedicated department. Another critical development under the Conservative government was the introduction of the National Lottery in 1994 and the subsequent creation of the HLF, the latter described as 'the single most important heritage decision of the last thirty years' (Thurley, 2009).

While there was little relevant legislation between 1983 and 1997, heritage remained significant in policy terms (Pendlebury, 2002). The Conservative Party viewed conservation and regeneration as complementary aspects of economic growth, with urban dereliction seen as a deterrent to private investment. Simon Thurley (2009), Chief Executive of English Heritage from 2002 to the time of writing, has argued that the Conservatives' approach to heritage was, in fact, a means of exploiting the commercial potential of historic properties, rather than genuine preservation. Other analysts have criticised the party's increasing commodification of heritage through regeneration and tourism. Hewison (1987) lambasted the creation of a pseudo-historical 'heritage industry' that served to mask national decline. In a later account, he portrayed the party's harnessing of nostalgia and nationalism as a means of popularising and preserving the place of the British elite (Hewison, 1995). Corner and Harvey saw the growth of heritage as part of a 'resurgent nationalism' in response to the loss of empire and the 'perceived diminution of national identity' (1991: 45) in the face of forthcoming integration into the European Union. Yet there are reasons to think that the association of heritage with conservatism should not mislead social democrats and others on the left into rejecting heritage. Patrick Wright (1985) sought to account for the popular appeal of heritage by locating it within longstanding ideologies of 'deep England'; this provided a rich and complex portrayal of the politics of heritage, showing strong connections between British socialism, history and heritage (see also Samuel, 1994).

During the Conservative years, the heritage sector focused on conservation and large-scale national 'beacon' projects. The DNH's annual reports show a ministry preoccupied with economic development in a way that foreshadowed New Labour's economisation of cultural policy in the creative industries agenda. The strategic objectives for heritage centred on mobilising resources from the private sector through sponsorship and fundraising, obtaining value for money, and deriving economic benefit from buildings and monuments. English Heritage was continually praised for its work. In 1993, the DNH reported that its grant-in-aid increases confirmed 'the importance which the Government attached to the work of English Heritage' (DNH, 1993: 59). One annual report claimed that for every pound sterling of government subsidy, the organisation generated £2.50 (DNH, 1995).

New Labour's engagement with heritage took a very different trajectory. Heritage was redefined through a shift in the terminology as well as a broadening of the concept. Some have argued that, in line with its modernising orientation, New Labour tended to prefer the term 'historic environment' to 'heritage'. In fact, heritage remained a word that was used by New Labour government departments and politicians throughout the period, alongside 'historic environment', and a number of policy documents testify to this (e.g., DCMS, 2007a). The heritage sector readily adopted the new term (e.g., English Heritage, 2000, 2005), often using it interchangeably with 'heritage'.[2]

The shift in terminology points to some of the problems that New Labour, with its intense focus on newness, had with the concept of 'heritage'. Like many other analysts, Jo Littler saw the rhetorical transition as signalling a shedding of the 'archaic and Thatcherite connotations' of heritage (2005: 5). 'Heritage' was 'fusty' and 'of the last century' (Aslet, 2008: 26), with its 'prim' and 'static' undertones (Waterton, 2010: 12). For Baxter, the new term was far more 'user friendly and understandable' (2002: 4), and for Thurley (2009), it 'set heritage as part of a much wider and more complex environment in which we all live'.

New Labour did not provide any major legislation on heritage. The nearest the party got to this was a Heritage Protection Reform Bill, which was eventually dropped in 2008 due to the economic crisis unfolding at the time and an ongoing lack of political support. Instead, its heritage activity centred on the commissioning of reviews and research via the sector and making small yet significant 'tweaks' to terms and processes. For example, early in the New Labour period, the party made key changes to the remit of the HLF. Originally, the HLF had supported only capital spending on physical purchases and renovations, but this was changed in 1998 to include 'activities' such as genealogical research and educational projects. This meant that funding was available to local groups at a community level, in line with New Labour's social inclusion agenda, discussed in chapters 2 and 3. It also helped to address the persistent criticism that the proceeds of the National Lottery did not benefit those who purchased the tickets. In 2002, New Labour asked the HLF to consider intangible heritage, which it subsequently began to support through its grants, with the assistance of a dedicated policy adviser. This was a small but meaningful gesture, as it meant that broader forms of culture, notably traditional, popular and folk culture, were granted greater significance. The HLF reports that oral history projects accounted for the bulk of its investment, but many other areas were recognised

---

[2] The term 'historic environment' can also be found within Conservative documents (see Department of National Heritage, 1990 and 1995, for example) but the term has become largely associated with New Labour.

too, such as languages, dance, music, customs and rituals, oral history, food and folklore, as well as more ephemeral aspects such as mythology and memory. This move brought the UK in line with international developments.[3]

These changes helped to expand heritage beyond the traditional stately grandeur with which the term had previously been associated. The consequence was that the cultural forms and practices of specific groups were being recognised and made visible. The HLF began to fund projects on the ethnic traditions of refugee and migrant groups, the cultural practices of coal-mining villages and the rituals of Romany communities. The HLF funds projects via applications and so is 'responsive' in this sense. Opening out the boundaries of heritage meant that a broader range of interests and groups were eligible for support, and the applications reflected the growing number of European migrants entering Britain and overall increasing multiculturalism in the UK.

This was a contrast with the Conservatives, who understood heritage in strikingly 'non-inclusionary' terms (Pendlebury et al., 2004: 12), which tended to privilege the old and the grand, the British Empire and aristocratic rule. Academic treatments of heritage have drawn attention to problems of representation, and also to the related issue that the recognisable symbols of British heritage do not adequately reflect the less palatable aspects of the country's past. Neal (2002) referred to the 'invisible whiteness' embodied in heritage sites, and Littler noted the 'aggressive self-aggrandisement of white Englishness' (Littler, 2005: 1). There is also the notion that heritage is something 'fragile, finite and non-renewable' (Smith, 2009: 3), to be preserved as it is found, and which therefore remains static and unchanged. Conservative MP Patrick Cormack's 1970s television and book series presented heritage as 'in danger' (1976), and Trimm (2005) has argued that it was this type of discourse that helped to maintain the idea that private property belonging to privileged individuals needed protection, and that this

---

[3] UNESCO states that intangible cultural heritage includes traditions or living expressions that are inherited from ancestors and passed on to descendants, such as oral traditions, crafts, social practices, festive events and rituals. In 2001, UNESCO consulted nation states and non-governmental organisations to work towards a definition of intangible cultural heritage, which led to the creation of the *Convention for the Safeguarding of Intangible Cultural Heritage*, a treaty for its protection and promotion in 2003, which came into force in 2006 (UNESCO, 2003). Interestingly, the UK has not signed the UNESCO Convention and therefore has no legal obligation for the protection of intangible cultural heritage.

has served as justification for decades of public subsidy. Smith (2006, 2009) argued that politicians and heritage experts are responsible for perpetuating such views and that this, in turn, has helped to maintain the place of the British elite.

The museums sector had begun to engage with Britain's imperial legacy through the advent of 'new museology' (Ross, 2004), a type of institutional reflexivity. Heritage bodies were slower to respond, but by the time New Labour came to power they were 'beginning to learn how to question their own values' (Pendlebury et al., 2004: 27), recognising that heritage was something that needed to evolve to meet the changing needs of society. The country's cultural diversity and its complex history of migration and diaspora meant that there were many heritages, not just one. These concerns were discussed across a range of policy documents produced by government and the heritage sector during the New Labour years. These sources criticised the narrow definition of heritage and asserted the need for a more pluralistic notion. For example, a major policy review of the historic environment was commissioned in February 2000 by the DCMS and the then Department of the Environment, Transport and the Regions, which set the tone for later discussions. Led by English Heritage's then Chair Sir Neil Cossons, it involved multiple working groups and consultations, and new research into attitudes towards heritage (Ipsos Mori, 2000). The review, published as *Power of Place: The Future of the Historic Environment* (English Heritage, 2000), revealed that the majority of people associated heritage with tradition, stateliness and grandeur. Three quarters of respondents felt excluded and that the contribution of black and ethnic minority (BME) groups was not adequately represented by heritage. This fitted with Labour peer Lord Waheed Alli's view that the word 'heritage' was 'offensive to ethnic minorities' (Alibhai-Brown, 2004: 15). The report emphasised that 'in a multicultural society, everybody's heritage needs to be recognized' and these histories must involve 'multiple narratives' (English Heritage, 2000: 1). In the words of the cultural studies academic Stuart Hall, national heritage is a potent source of meaning and 'those who cannot see themselves reflected in its mirror cannot properly "belong"' (2005: 24). Hall advocated a revision of the national story, rather than an assimilation of alternative voices into the existing narrative.

New Labour's main pronouncement on heritage policy, *The Historic Environment – A Force for Our Future* (DCMS/DTLG, 2001), was a response to *Power of Place*. It stated that the historic environment should be open to everyone, and should be seen as something 'which all sections of the community can identify with and take pride in, rather than something valued only by narrow specialist interests' (2001: 30). This drew on New Labour's commitment to access to culture, and advocated local engagement and broader representation. A year later, the DCMS published a follow-up report, *People and Places: Social Inclusion Policy for the Built and Historic Environment*, in which cultural diversity was again discussed in terms of the need to reconsider what was meant by heritage and 'whose past is being represented' (2002: 15). In *Broadening the Horizons of Heritage*, the HLF recognised the 'disappointingly narrow' (2002: 2) perception of heritage and the need to use education to improve access, broaden the 'heritage constituency' (2002: 3) and spread funding more equitably.

There were also subtler developments around inclusion and representation. For example, the New Labour government made important additions to the type of buildings that were given listed status. These changes were small yet significant, and aimed to further expand the notion of heritage towards a more modest, everyday culture. A number of less obvious buildings were 'listed' (deemed worthy of preservation), and in some cases they were highly controversial. For example, Park Hill, the sprawling brutalist 1960s social housing complex in Sheffield, received Grade II status in 1998, and this was unpopular with locals, who saw it as a crime-ridden eyesore (Platt, 2012). A 1950s pigeon loft in Sunderland obtained Grade II listed status in 2007, which was controversial, as it sat on land that had previously been sold for development (Watson, 2007). Some new listings proved more popular. As part of a project to commemorate the bicentenary of the abolition of the transatlantic slave trade in 2007, English Heritage identified buildings and monuments with connections to slavery and its abolition, to aid understanding of Britain's role. This resulted in nine new listings, eight upgrades and 27 amendments to existing listings. Abbey Road Studios in London was allocated Grade II status in early 2010 for its significance to music making since the 1930s (Foster, 2010). Many prominent musicians, most famously the Beatles, had recorded there. Brixton's 1930s market buildings in South London were also awarded Grade II status in 2010 (following a campaign by local residents), due to their significance for the Afro-Caribbean immigrants who arrived in the capital after the Second World War.

Sceptics may argue that the listings of Abbey Road and Brixton's market buildings were primarily economic decisions. The former is a major tourist attraction and the latter an integral part of the gentrification of Brixton. There is some truth in this, but these buildings were also listed on the basis of their place in popular culture and social history, and were associated with the working classes, ethnic minorities and populist tastes. Previously, buildings were listed purely on the basis of their aesthetic or architectural merit, often understood in paternalist terms. These additions represented more democratic principles and a transition towards a more inclusive and collective conception of heritage.

But how much of this was New Labour's initiative, and how much was the sector already moving in this direction? There is evidence that the heritage sector was already moving in the direction indicated above, rather than being pushed by the government. In the private heritage sector, the National Trust was making acquisitions that related to the lives of the urban and poorer classes. For example, the Trust purchased a Victorian workhouse in Nottinghamshire, a place where the destitute were given accommodation in exchange for hard labour. It was opened to the public in 2001, telling the story of the Poor Law Amendment Act of 1834 and the institutionalisation of social welfare. In 2003, the childhood home of John Lennon (donated to the National Trust by the musician's widow, Yoko Ono) was opened to the public. In 2004, the Trust acquired the last surviving back-to-back houses in Birmingham. These were houses that literally backed onto each other around a communal courtyard and offered a glimpse into the cramped living conditions of ordinary people in the nineteenth century. After New Labour lost the general election in 2010, the trend of listing atypical buildings and sites continued. For example, the zebra crossing that featured on the cover of the Beatles' 1969 album *Abbey Road* was awarded Grade II listed status, and Lennon and McCartney's childhood homes were given Grade II listed status in 2012. And there were signs of a move towards this more inclusive notion of heritage before New Labour's victory in 1997. Several of the policy documents published by the sector prior to the general election made reference to the need for greater inclusion and a broader notion of heritage (see, for example, English Heritage, 1997). Indeed, the National Trust had begun to broaden its acquisition policy prior to New Labour. It purchased the childhood home of Paul McCartney in 1996 and a Chartist cottage in Worcestershire in 1997. Chartism was a national working-class movement that began in the 1830s, which asserted the rights of ordinary people in a campaign for political reform. Labour's social inclusion drive was a 'challenging agenda for heritage agencies whose fundamental concern is with the historic fabric' (Pendlebury et al., 2004: 19), but the sector was nevertheless 'anxious to demonstrate its non-elitist, progressive nature' (2004: 11), as the examples in this section demonstrate.

7.3 Social inclusion and the widening of audiences

The scale of social inclusion and access activity across the heritage sector under New Labour was vast. For example, the HLF's Social Impact Evaluation (Applejuice, 2008) reported that over a three-year period, it delivered 300 projects to engage new audiences from target groups. In 2003, English Heritage created a dedicated outreach team, running community projects in areas with high deprivation where the organisation had little or no profile, working collaboratively with charities, educational bodies and interfaith groups. The team ran over 500 projects between 2003 and 2011, working with over 1 million people (English Heritage, 2011a). Its publication *Outreach: Engaging New Audiences with the Historic Environment* (English Heritage, 2011b) documented the breadth of its activities.

Again, how much of this was a product of New Labour policy and how much a result of changing practices in the sector (possibly in anticipation of New Labour policy action) is open to debate. A factor here is that heritage organisations within the private sector also demonstrated a commitment to access. In 2001, the National Trust appointed Dame Fiona Reynolds as its new Director-General. Reynolds immediately implemented a structural review, and within a year the Trust's entire board had been replaced (except for the Chair, who retired two years later) and it was announced that its head office was relocating out of London, a controversial move that was deeply unpopular with many staff (Mitchell, 2001). Reynolds was described as having a 'white-hot zeal for social inclusion', and from the outset was quoted as aiming to 'create a wider interpretation of heritage and social history' (Mitchell, 2001). Interestingly, prior to her appointment, Reynolds had spent two years at the Cabinet Office, as Director of the new Women's Unit, under Tony Blair. Similarly, the advocacy group Heritage Link (now Heritage Alliance, a lobby group formed in 2002, representing 92 heritage organisations) set up an Inclusion Working Group that aimed to understand this aspect of government policy better. It initiated a two-year cultural diversity project, funded by English Heritage, undertaking a series of workshops to develop models for the sector.

The actual impact of this work is hard to ascertain. Evaluating outreach projects is difficult, because of problems in demonstrating that such policies have direct consequences. Collecting data on such activities is notoriously difficult.[4] English Heritage had gathered data

---

[4] See, for example, Selwood on 'measuring the unmeasurable' (2006: 48), and see also Chapter 3.

immediately following its projects, which show participant enthusiasm, small increases in repeat visits, and volunteering by target groups. However, it did not have data that connected its investment with longer-term impact. In early 2010, it commissioned London-based consultants Burns Owen Partnership (BOP) to develop a framework to measure and track the impact of this work. However, the outreach team was disbanded in 2011, so it was not implemented or tested, and more substantial data from its outreach work was never collected (English Heritage, 2011b).

There is also little independent critique of inclusion and access projects. Academic literature focuses on more generic heritage issues, such as those already discussed around representation. There are few analyses that attempt to evaluate the sector's activity, and analyses published in academic journals are authored by those within the sector. Examples include articles by Clark (2004), Clark and Maaer (2008), Cowell (2004) and Turnpenny (2004). Clark is the former Deputy Director of Policy and Research at the HLF, and prior to that worked at English Heritage; Maaer is the Head of Research, and prior to that was an economist for British Waterways; Cowell (2004) is a Regional Director at the National Trust and was previously employed at English Heritage; Turnpenny (2004) is a consultant commissioned by the HLF to investigate audience development. These articles by past and present sector insiders provided positive accounts of its community, access and outreach work.

Heritage bodies were also formally monitored and assessed through the Public Service Agreements (PSAs) discussed in Chapter 3. In December 2005, the DCMS published a performance report on English Heritage, which had been tasked with undertaking a 'modernisation' project in a bid to become more inclusive. This involved restructuring to give the regions greater power (within the broader context of devolution), making efficiency savings and attracting 100,000 new users from minority and socially deprived groups. The government declared that its targets for reform had been met earlier than planned. English Heritage's investments were up £3 million, it had made savings of £1 million year on year and it had attracted 323,487 new users between 2004 and 2006 (DCMS, 2005), over 300 per cent more than its target. In the words of journalist Yasmin Alibhai-Brown, English Heritage was 'now radical, inclusive, challenging and a sound treasurer of our collective national memories' (2004: 15).

Commentators have also praised the HLF for its transformation (Hewison, 2009, 2014; Pendlebury et al., 2004). According to Hewison, it had successfully moved away from a 'patrician, object-based and narrowly expert-driven' (Hewison, 2009: 106) style of management. It devolved to the regions, devoted half of its annual budget to smaller projects of less than £1 million, concentrated on socially and economically deprived areas and engaged in audience development. The HLF's Clark and Maaer (2008) claimed that every local authority had been awarded at least one grant, and around 40 per cent of funding went to the most deprived 25 per cent of local authorities in the UK.

Despite such positive developments, there appears to have been little change in the demographic distribution of participation. English Heritage's annual report from 2008 to 2009 noted that, while BME audiences were up 3 per cent, in line with New Labour's target, there was little change in attendance from lower socio-economic groups. In an attempt to better understand this, English Heritage organised a conference to identify key actions to engage priority groups. However, in 2010, it revealed that participation rates for BME, disabled people, lower socio-economic groups, children and young people had all remained low:

> New data for 2009/10 analyses participation rates by deprivation levels. It shows a dramatic gulf between the participation rates of adults living in the 10% least deprived areas (84.2% participating in the historic environment) compared to 39.8% of those living in the 10% most deprived places. Participation figures for children also show no significant change over the last few years.
>
> (English Heritage, 2010: 29)

One reason why the sector made limited progress in the access and inclusion agenda may be that the majority of heritage stock is privately owned. Baxter (2002) reported this figure at 90 per cent, while Culture Secretary Tessa Jowell (2005) stated that the figure is two thirds. While institutions in receipt of government subsidy were subject to PSAs and had their performance monitored, these private organisations had no such obligations. Although these properties and sites are eligible for grants from English Heritage, the HLF and the Arts Council, this funding is limited and somewhat negligible in terms of the scale of the sector's activity overall. It is beyond the scope of this book to look at this more closely, given our primary concern with public policy, but as heritage policy is inevitably affected by the high proportion of private organisations, it is important to provide some sense of this. The Historic Houses Association has 500 members, who collectively own more houses and gardens than English Heritage and the National Trust combined. The private heritage sector claims to attract 14 million visitors annually.[5] In the light of private ownership, New Labour's influence over the heritage sector as a whole could only ever extend so far.

This high proportion of private ownership also, perhaps, explains why the instrumental agenda did not take serious hold in the same way that it did across the arts. As the sector as a whole is not heavily subsidised in comparison with museums, for example, there was less at stake and less ingrained resistance to such policies. There was also not the critical mass of opposing voices that other sectors were able to galvanise in the battle against the culture of targets we discussed in Chapter 3.

7.4   Government funding and support for the heritage sector

Critics of New Labour frequently cite the sector's funding cuts as evidence of the party's neglect of, and hostility towards, heritage. It is indisputable that heritage endured an erosion of funding from 1997 to 2010. This section of the chapter looks more closely at this, comparing New Labour with the previous Conservative government, and funding for heritage with that for the arts.

Comparing 1997 with 2010 is not always meaningful, due to the economic crisis that began in 2007. However, the figures show cuts to heritage in real terms throughout the period, including prior to the economic downturn. Despite the government's positive response to English Heritage's meeting its targets for reform earlier than expected (see above), the organisation's annual grant settlements were consistently below inflation. Even in 1996, the previous Conservative government was funding English Heritage to the tune of £108 million, compared with Labour's allocation of £125 million ten years later in 2006/2007. The House of Commons Culture, Media and Sport Committee (2011) provided the following assessment:

Grant settlements since 1997 have been below inflation resulting in a real terms reduction of £130 million. In the last ten years Arts Council

[5] By opening their properties, private owners gain exemption from inheritance tax and generate income through admissions, although this covers only a small fraction of their operating costs. The Country Land and Business Association claimed that public funding only paid for 2 per cent, with 98 per cent paid for by owners, occupiers, philanthropists and users (CLBA, 2006).

England's budget has increased by 90% and Sport England's by 182%, while English Heritage has been subjected to an 11% cut.

As this suggests, the discrepancy between arts and heritage funding is striking. For example, in 2000–2001, the museums sector was awarded £309 million in grant-in-aid from the DCMS, compared with only £138 million for the entire heritage sector; in 2005–2006, museums got £330 million to heritage's £158 million.

While the National Lottery presented a welcome boost for heritage as a whole, lottery funding dropped throughout the period due to Labour's expansion of the number of 'Good Causes' to include health, education and the environment in the National Lottery Act of 1998. Further decreases came later, from 2004 onwards, when London was shortlisted for its bid to host the 2012 Olympic Games, which it subsequently won in 2005. All this led to sizeable reductions in the lottery money going to heritage, from £473 million in 1997 to £284 million in 2010.

The sector was understandably unhappy about the loss of funding. Simon Thurley (2009) wrote that

the DCMS poured money into museums (36% increase), to make them free; deluged money into the arts (53% increase)... Heritage meanwhile got 3%. The Heritage Lottery Fund too suffered... the financial picture for heritage has been bleak since 1997.

The Conservatives were not particularly vocal about Labour's cuts to heritage (or on matters of cultural policy more generally). In December 2006, David Cameron, then leader of the Conservative Party in opposition, approached John Tusa, at the time Managing Director of the Barbican Centre in London, to set up a policy task force to provide the party with 'fresh thinking on the arts' (Conservative Party, 2007: 2), with a view to feeding ideas into the next election manifesto. The report featured only one recommendation for heritage, which was to increase the annual funding of the NHMF from £6.5 million to £50 million. This was further acknowledgement of the relatively low funding of the sector.

Conservative MP and Shadow Culture Secretary Hugo Swire argued that the HLF was £800 million worse off under Labour, and that his party wanted to see the protection of heritage prioritised and more grants given to the restoration of cathedrals, churches and other places of worship (British Archaeology website). In June 2008, the new Conservative Shadow Culture Secretary Jeremy Hunt proposed the creation of a new 'National Lottery Independence Act', which would revert funding back to the lottery's original 'Good Causes' (arts, sport, heritage and charitable causes), potentially generating an additional £41 million annually for heritage (Hunt, 2008). This must have been a tantalising prospect for a sector that had withstood a sustained erosion of its funding for over a decade.

Private property owners within the heritage sector also felt badly treated by New Labour, despite their supposed contribution to the economy. Archival records show continuous correspondence between the lobby group Heritage Link (now Heritage Alliance) and a range of ministers and government departments during the New Labour years. The group consistently expressed 'disappointment' at a range of government actions. In a letter to Culture Secretary Tessa Jowell, it emphasised its dissatisfaction at heritage funding, comparing its treatment with other sectors (Heritage Link, 2004). This was raised again two years later. The group's Chair stated that the government's response to the sector's funding situation was 'disappointingly complacent and extremely disingenuous' and that it had failed to take any note of a 'weight of evidence' about resources (Heritage Link, 2006a: 4).

In 2007, in the run up to the Comprehensive Spending Review, *Valuing Our Heritage: The Case for Future Investment in the Historic Environment* (2007) was collectively produced by English Heritage, the National Trust, the HLF, the Historic Houses Association and Heritage Link. The report detailed the challenges faced by the sector in relation to what was perceived as its decline due to under-funding. It argued that the government needed to reinstate English Heritage's grant-in-aid to pre-1997 levels and increase NHMF's grant-in-aid to £10 million per year. Heritage Link reported that this document and its follow-up activity were effective in helping to obtain extra resources for the sector (Heritage Link, 2007b). Indeed, the following year saw a doubling of the NHMF's grant from £5 million to £10 million, yet a nominal increase of £9 million for English Heritage.

It was not only funding that the sector took issue with. There was a feeling that the government did not fully understand the sector or its work. Tessa Jowell was challenged on her personal essay *Better Places to Live: Government, Identity and the Public Value of Heritage* (2005).[6] Historians were enraged by her suggestion that listed buildings could be documented in virtual form before being demolished, an idea branded

---

[6] Jowell wrote this after the heritage sector complained that her earlier personal essay *Government and the Value of Culture* (2004) – see Chapter 3 – had been silent on heritage and architecture.

'barmy and dangerous' (Gates and Booth, 2005: 3). This was a misrepresentation. Jowell had noted a tension between the old and new: 'we have a duty to the past, but we also have an obligation to the present and to the future' (2005: 4). Nevertheless, the text is rather ambiguous:

> It is inevitable that some buildings from the past will be lost, and lost forever...I have already said that 'there is no substitute for the real thing' in heritage matters, and I firmly believe this. But when the choice is between obliterating a historic building so that nothing is left but the architect's drawings; and having a perfect digital record of every square inch, available for students and historians for all time, I know which I would rather have.
>
> (2005: 22–3)

Jowell also stated that more progress was required to move the heritage sector beyond its white middle-class interests and that it lagged behind other sectors in this respect. Another point of friction was the government's perception that heritage was seen as 'a brake on regeneration' (Heritage Link, 2007a). The *Sunday Times* argued that Jowell had sought to dismantle English Heritage because it had 'repeatedly stood in the way of what the government claims are necessary building schemes' (Brooks, 2005: 3), and had opposed developments such as London's new skyscraper 'The Shard' due to its central location among historic buildings. Heritage Link broached this issue directly with ministers (2006b, 2007a), and while there is little discussion of this, it may go some way to explaining New Labour's relatively punitive treatment of heritage financially, Jowell's proposal above, and why the sector's advocacy work often focused on restoration.

Heritage Link's internal and external communication throughout the period consistently emphasised the need for the sector to raise its profile across government and make clearer its contribution to national life. The group discussed the sector's lack of traction within government and its inability to influence key decisions. In the light of this and in the context of the funding cuts more generally, advocacy became increasingly important and the sector began 'lobbying furiously' (Jamie Cowling, interview), driven by the need to show its economic and social importance (Jubb, 2004). The annual *Heritage Counts* provides information and evidence for government lobbying and briefings (Laura Clayton, English Heritage, personal communication) and was a direct response to the need to raise the profile of the sector in the face of policy discussions 'dominated by the arts and the Arts Council' (Ben Cowell, interview).

Indeed, a House of Commons Culture, Media and Sport Committee (2011) stated that English Heritage considered itself disadvantaged in comparison with the DCMS's support for sports and arts. With each year, the level of reporting in *Heritage Counts* became increasingly sophisticated in terms of statistical breadth and depth, morphing from a dry, text-based document into a glossy, promotional brochure, featuring case studies and images of diversity and participation.

Awareness of the sector's profile and value was also raised through its engagement with the mainstream media. As a response to what the sector saw as New Labour sanctioning the demolition of old buildings and replacing them with new ones as a cheaper alternative (Thurley, 2009), English Heritage initiated the television series *Restoration* with Peter Bazelgette, a leading television producer (and later Chief Executive of Arts Council England). *Restoration* presented neglected buildings which were in need of restoration, and viewers voted on which one would receive £3 million funding from English Heritage and the HLF. It was very popular and ran from 2003 to 2009. The BBC claimed that the programme had a big impact on how the nation thought about its historic buildings, with the final of the first series attracting 2.7 million viewers (across all age ranges and social groupings), 2.3 million people taking part in the voting process (IPSOS-RSL, 2003) and 10,000 people visiting the winning site in Manchester. Clark (2004) reports that one in three viewers claimed that they felt inspired to visit heritage sites and one in ten were planning to learn a craft or become more actively involved in heritage following the programme. This was followed by a proliferation of popular TV programmes on heritage subjects, such as *The Museum* in 2007 (on the daily life of the British Museum); *Sissinghurst* in 2009 (on the National Trust property Sissinghurst Castle); *English Heritage* in 2009 (a documentary following the work of the organisation); and *Mastercrafts* in 2010 (celebrating a range of rare heritage crafts). The sector argued that the popularity of such shows demonstrated the interest and passion that the nation felt towards its heritage (Thurley, 2009).

Developments in tourism provide further evidence of this enthusiasm. Cultural tourism was seized upon by the Conservative government, and this informed critiques by Hewison (1987) and others, discussed earlier. By the time New Labour came to power in 1997, tourism was booming, due to a sustained increase in social mobility and disposable income. The party's sustained investment in cultural infrastructure may have encouraged further growth. One of our interviewees described heritage as the 'the bedrock of the tourist economy' (Ben Cowell, interview). Cultural heritage is repeatedly cited as a key driver for domestic and overseas travel (DCMS, 2007b; ONS, 2006), with international tourists making 10 million trips each year, 40 per cent citing heritage as their primary motivation (House of Commons, 2011). It is claimed that cultural tourism generates £12.4 billion a year, with 60 per cent coming from domestic income. The International Passenger Survey in 2006 claimed that over 50 per cent of holiday makers visited heritage properties (ONS, 2006). VisitBritain (2010) found that Britain was ranked seventh out of 50 nations in the Nation Brands Index for its cultural heritage, with castles and stately homes consistently the most popular tourist attractions, as validated by the quarterly monitoring reports by VisitEngland (2006–2011).

Despite the widespread recognition of the importance of heritage as a major tourist incentive, the DCMS's annual grant-in-aid to VisitBritain did not exceed £50 million throughout the New Labour period. In the ten years prior to 1997, the Conservative government gave tourism between £44 million and £53 million annually, although it is difficult to make direct comparisons due to a complex series of mergers.[7] In 2003, a PSA target was drawn up to 'improve the productivity' of the tourism industry over the next five years. However, a Select Committee the following year expressed concerns about the DCMS's dedication to tourism (House of Commons, 2004b). It could be argued, therefore, that heritage took a second funding hit in the light of the diminished budgets for tourism.

In response to the government's cuts, the heritage sector had little choice but to become more entrepreneurial. Great emphasis had always been placed on income generation by New Labour (see House of Commons, 2004a, for example), and the party pressured all cultural organisations to 'sweat the assets', an unfortunate business term for maximising revenue, which was adopted by the DCMS. For example, during the New Labour period, English Heritage extensively developed its commercial activities, rapidly increasing its income through all possible means: ticket sales, donations, membership, retail, corporate hospitality, public events and holiday cottage rentals. From the outset, English Heritage had had a commercial focus, and one of our interviewees explained that the sector was already starting to generate more income from non-public funds prior to New Labour (Ben Cowell, interview). However, the reduction in funding only served to

---

[7] There was a series of mergers, restructures and rebrandings between 1999 and 2003 involving the British Tourist Authority, English Tourist Board, English Tourism Council, VisitEngland and VisitBritain.

further increase the pace and scale of these efforts. An analysis of English Heritage's annual accounts reveals that earned income rose year on year, increasing from £2.3 million in 1984; to £11.9 million in 1990; to £18.1 million in 1996; to £30.6 million in 2001; to £54.4 million in 2010. By the end of the Labour period, its membership scheme was bringing in £17.3 million, while its membership grew from 374,000 in 1997; to 445,000 in 2001; to 719,000 in 2010. In 2002, membership income exceeded admission charges for the first time. Its retail and catering outlets were making £11.8 million in 2010, up from £5.6 million in 1997, and its legacy donations had increased from £435,000 in 2005 to over £1 million in 2010.[8] Alongside this, it is interesting to note that English Heritage's visitor numbers (to paid properties) remained fairly constant: 5.8 million in 1997; 5.5 million in 2002; 5.3 million in 2007; and 5.6 million in 2010. So, while the audience has barely increased in number or changed in demographic terms, spending per head has risen dramatically.

7.5   Assessing heritage under New Labour

The fortunes of heritage shifted under New Labour. The association of heritage with the previous Conservative government and New Labour's concern with 'modernisation' meant that the sector found itself lacking political relevance and lobbying traction, especially compared with the arts. This was particularly difficult for the sector, as it had formed the central core of cultural policy under the previous government. As a result of its declining influence, heritage withstood significant funding reductions in real terms, and while the lottery provided a much-needed boost compared with income in the 1980s, New Labour's changes to the funding structure meant that the sector received less money than originally envisaged.

---

[8] The National Trust presents a similar story. In 2000, it was claimed that there were more members of the National Trust than of all the political parties combined (English Heritage, 2000). In 2013–2014 alone, it attracted 745,424 new members, 4.1 million members in total, generating an annual income of over £150 million. The Trust's total annual income is over £460 million (National Trust, 2014). Heritage Alliance estimates that there are 500,000 regular volunteers across the sector as a whole, and the biggest single participation event is the Heritage Open Days weekend, which saw over 1 million people participate in 2010.

Heritage proponents have not always acknowledged the redistribution of cultural funding under New Labour. While funding for heritage was cut, other areas received substantial uplifts. This is an important point, as any assessment that attempts to evaluate New Labour's cultural policy making in all its complexity must look at the broader context and not view the sectors in isolation. New Labour adopted a more rounded approach and one that could arguably be seen as an act of 'rebalancing' cultural policy in the context of cultural spending as a whole.

The funding cuts were perhaps felt more sharply because not only was there far less money for the larger heritage bodies, but there were more mouths to feed, given the efforts of heritage to become more 'inclusive'. It could be argued that New Labour deserves credit for moving to a more pluralist notion of heritage. Mansfield noted that heritage was historically 'synonymous with fine art and architecture but its boundaries have been extended to include landscapes, industrial and engineering works, and vernacular constructions' (2013: 14). Dresser (2007: 190) argued that the 'very existence' of public consultations and outreach projects marked a 'sea change in the wider political culture'. However, as we have indicated, this may fail to recognise that this move was coming from the sector itself. New Labour rode the wave of a process of democratisation that was already in train, as discussed by analysts such as Patrick Wright and Raphael Samuel in the 1980s and 1990s. A 'proliferation of alternative histories' was already well underway (Urry, 1990 quoted in Littler, 2005: 3). By the time New Labour came to power, British heritage was being interrogated from the perspective of *whose* heritage was valid, and this move towards greater inclusion reflected an increasingly multicultural society.

Despite these changes, participation rates for target audiences were patchy throughout the period and remained relatively low (English Heritage, 2010), no doubt partly as a result of New Labour's failure to address structural inequality. This was also further complicated by the fact that the majority of heritage resides in private ownership, so, despite the party's best efforts, the scale of activity meant that the results were always going to be limited, as its ability to influence the sector as a whole was constrained.

It is also worth remembering that heritage constitutes only one part of the DCMS's remit. Of its 30 Non-Departmental Public Bodies, only a handful deal solely with heritage. The marginalisation of heritage may be less surprising in this context. Moreover, the political left has always been suspicious of heritage, and New Labour continued this tradition, even as the party moved social democracy to the centre. New Labour's agenda of modernisation was undoubtedly a factor here. The disparities in Labour's funding for heritage forced the sector to expand and speed up its commercialisation. English Heritage adopted a business model that was more akin to the National Trust. This chimed with New Labour's inclination towards a mixed economy funding model, whereby public expenditure supplements private income. While social democratic parties have generally advocated mixed economies, as discussed in Chapter 1, New Labour went further, and the party pressured cultural organisations across all sectors to increase their earned income. Yet this transformation may have led to a more independent and sustainable sector, and the credit for this should go to the dedicated core audience for heritage. The continuing, indeed thriving, popular interest in heritage ultimately ensured the survival of the sector.

This is perhaps to be expected. Britain was one of the first countries in the world to legislate protection over its buildings, with the 1882 Ancient Monuments Protection Act. Lyth argues that today's heritage institutions are the result of,

> the fears and passions of an educated middle-class ... the initiative for their formation often coming from influential private organisations and individuals rather than the government.
>
> (2006: 4)

One such example is the National Trust itself, formed in 1895 in response to the loss of open space for the public. This was land that lay in private ownership or was being bought by the wealthy for development, and in which the founders of the Trust saw a therapeutic value. This was particularly important for an urban society that was living in densely populated and squalid conditions. The founders set about acquiring and preserving land and property to alleviate this problem and improve the lives of working people. They drew inspiration from the open-space conservation movement in America (which had led to the establishment of the National Parks), but formed an independent charity, rather than a body owned by the government, with the protection of the public interest at its heart (Jenkins, 1995). A further example of the passion of the British public towards its heritage, and one that serves as a reminder that the political right do not have a monopoly over the concept, is the mass trespass of 1932. This was a wilful trespass by ramblers, which was staged in protest against denial of access to open countryside to walkers in England and Wales. It led to the right to walk in certain areas, such as moorland, heathland and coastal land.[9] Such histories provide important context for the survival of the heritage sector under New Labour's funding regime. The story of heritage under New Labour demonstrates the fundamental point that much about culture happens independently of public policy.

---

[9] In this vein, New Labour brought in the Countryside and Rights of Way Act in November 2000, which legislates the 'right to roam' on mapped land.

8
How Did New Labour Do on Arts and Culture? And What Happened Next?

8.1 The balance sheet

In this final chapter, we consider New Labour's record on arts and culture in the round. As part of that consideration, we discuss the relationships of New Labour cultural policies to their distinctive efforts to remould (some would say, abandon) social democratic politics for the twenty-first century. It is important for us to reiterate here that our purpose in assessing New Labour's record on arts and culture derives only partly from the intrinsic interest of what this remarkable, intriguing and deeply flawed political project achieved. Our more general goal is to contribute to thinking about how citizens and governments might pursue social justice in the realm of cultural policy, and thereby maximise individual and collective human flourishing (see Hesmondhalgh, 2013b).

Here, in Section 8.1, we provide a summary of our evaluation of New Labour; the evidence behind our assessments can be found in the earlier chapters of this book. As a way of contextualising our discussion of New Labour's record, and the possibilities of social democratic cultural policy, we then go on to examine, in Section 8.2, what happened to arts and cultural policies under the succeeding Coalition government led by the Conservatives from 2010 to 2015, and developments in the Labour Party during that time. In Section 8.3, we draw out the implications of our account for efforts to construct a socially just set of cultural policies in the twenty-first century. We established in Chapter 1 that social democracy in the twentieth century represented a sustained, though often failing, set of efforts to address problems of capitalist modernity, especially regarding inequality, freedom and identity. What lessons can be learned from the case of New Labour in terms of understanding political efforts to address these problems in the realm of culture?

184

Our emphasis in this final chapter, then, is on the third and fourth of the research questions specified in our opening chapter, and summarised in Box 1.2 – those concerning *evaluation*. We also take into account the *explanatory* elements of our analysis, concerning the way in which policy groups articulated beliefs and interests. To contextualise this evaluation (drawing on our explanation), we want briefly to address our first research question, regarding continuity and change: *to what extent and in what ways did New Labour's cultural policies maintain continuity with previous cultural policy regimes and to what extent and in what ways did they transform them?* This is important, not only because of New Labour's own claims to historical novelty, but also because of the way in which those claims have been accepted by many analysts. The idea of New Labour's creative industries policy as a new start for cultural policy, one that shed the elitism of arts policy in favour of a more democratic engagement with commercial culture and new media technologies, has been propagated by some researchers, notably 'the QUT School', associated with the Creative Industries Faculty of the Queensland University of Technology (e.g., Hartley and Cunningham, 2001). This is an inaccurate picture of what happened under New Labour, based on a populist version of cultural industries policy arguments developed in the 1980s (e.g., Lewis, 1990) but lacking any meaningful engagement with questions of social justice. In many respects, New Labour was, in fact, following international trends, especially a tendency to think about public policy in primarily economic terms. Like many putatively social democratic parties, New Labour sought to fuse such thinking with a residual progressivism. In cultural policy, economic rationales had been gaining ground rapidly since the 1980s, and this was a more significant development than anything New Labour did.[1] Politicians usually don't have the time or resources to be original or ground-breaking or distinctive, and nor do civil servants. Even policy experts and entrepreneurs (think tanks, consultants and so on) form their views from ideas circulating in academia and elsewhere, and they often revive older concepts.

That a policy direction can be understood as part of a more general international phenomenon, shared across different parties in different countries, does not absolve a government of blame if that policy can be deemed to be misguided or wrong, and it does not mean that a

---

[1] See Duelund (2008) for a surprisingly similar set of developments in the Nordic countries, where 'economic instrumentalism' gave way from the mid-1990s to a 'political colonisation' involving tightening links between arts and businesses, media deregulation, and increasing use of performance contracts.

government should go without credit for applying a good policy. But such an understanding helps to contextualise praise or blame, and to counter understandings of politics that see policies as creations of national political parties, rather than what they often are – hybrids constructed from internationally circulating ideas. It can also help us to see how deeply rooted policy tendencies can be.

This takes us to our evaluation. At the beginning of this book, we set out to consider the extent to which New Labour's cultural policies balanced the sort of goals that a democratic cultural policy might pursue: did it, for example, lead to greater equality of access to consumption and production, a higher quality of cultural goods, or the flourishing of individuals, communities and groups? In drawing up the New Labour 'balance sheet' – a phrase they would no doubt approve of! – we need to consider both the specific areas with which cultural policy is concerned and these wider questions of the contribution of cultural policy to society as a whole. We will begin with the more positive aspects of New Labour's record, and then move on to the downsides.

For the arts, as we saw in Chapter 3, the positive side of New Labour's achievements centres on the considerable increase in spending they achieved, in spite of occasional cuts (as in 2005). Arts Council allocations increased by around 150 per cent, and around 90 per cent in real terms. In addition, lottery revenue grew in size, even if the proportion of lottery funding for the arts fluctuated. New Labour also pushed hard for greater access to the arts and culture by more people, from a wider range of groups, including young people, people from ethnic minorities, and 'C2DEs', which is marketing jargon for working-class people. Although, as we shall see, the Conservative-led Coalition unleashed savage spending cuts from 2010 onwards, the principle of arts subsidy was not seriously challenged even by the Conservative right, and New Labour's pet policy of free admissions was considered untouchable – even the Rupert Murdoch-owned, conservative-populist *Sun* newspaper supported it by 2012.

The creative industries concept (chapters 2, 4 and 5) was central to New Labour's cultural policies and has been adopted internationally, albeit with local variations. The introduction of the concept enabled a greater recognition of the role of commercially produced culture in everyday life. As a tool for economic development, it helped to legitimate attention to cultural life in the regions of England and in the devolved nations – where it was never entirely separated from the arts (creative industries and arts groups were brought together, for example, in Regional Cultural Consortia). There are undoubtedly cultural institutions and businesses that benefited from New Labour's regional creative industries policy, and it is not unreasonable to assume that regional disparities might have been worse without such interventions. While, as Chapter 5 argued, and as we shall discuss further below, these investments clearly failed to redress the balance between London and the south-east, on the one hand, and the rest of the UK, on the other, the forces of concentration in these industries are strong, and it is unlikely that any amount of public support could counter them entirely.

Investment in city transport and buildings has meant that the centres of some British cities are now much more attractive than they were in the period between the Second World War devastation and the 1980s, when (even under Thatcherism) efforts began to be made in earnest to 'regenerate' cities in order to attract investment, professionals and tourism. Much of this space is given over to consumption of one sort or another, often in the semi-privatised spaces of the shopping mall. The architecture that New Labour's building boom unleashed is not without its problems. Owen Hatherley (2014) has written that some (not all) of the big lottery-funded building projects associated with New Labour regeneration are 'one-line architectural blipverts', vacuously and showily forefronting a single, catchy idea rather than being truly imaginative in their use of public space. But the general air of neglect and abandonment that many city centres wore by the mid-1990s was at least lifted; and, as Hatherley points out, excessive critique of such projects can too easily merge with conservative metropolitan sentiments that, outside capital cities, fine new buildings should not be publicly funded.

New Labour also deserves some credit for its intermittent efforts to connect cultural policy with its vital sibling, education policy. The Creative Partnerships initiative seems to have produced some positive and enriching cultural experiences for young people, many of them in deprived areas of the country. The establishment of the UK Film Council rationalised the plethora of agencies involved in film, and, by the time of its abolition by the Coalition government in 2010, had developed considerable expertise (Doyle, 2014). The New Cinema fund supported some superb films, some of which provided extraordinary depictions of ordinary life (such as Andrea Arnold's *Red Road* and *Fish Tank*), and which might not otherwise have been made without some public money. And Nesta, though ultimately it moved towards a more economically driven agenda (see Chapter 6), did open up new avenues for funding cultural production outside the false separation of 'art', 'design', 'film' and so on that New Labour inherited.

There are some reasons, then, to think that what happened to the arts and culture under New Labour justifies the boasts of government ministers and the positive assessments made by a number of commentators (see Chapter 1). We have discussed these achievements in some detail in this book. However, in many respects, as we have also shown, New Labour's record falls far short of the democratising and egalitarian aspirations of the social democratic tradition to which the British Labour Party nominally belongs. The creative industries policy concept represents a deeply problematic conception of the relations between culture and economy, and what governments should do with regard to these relations. This was apparent in the way that New Labour often understood cultural industries as essentially corporate entities, or as entrepreneurial start-ups with the potential to achieve international stature. That understanding was not unrelated to New Labour's links with senior figures in the cultural industries, and with the formidable copyright lobby. Even in the regions, where New Labour's early commitment to regional economic development brought benefits, there was a shift away from the 'regionalism' of early creative industries policy towards a more problematic focus on 'innovation'. Throughout, this classic piece of policy attachment failed to understand the particular ways in which the cultural industries operate (see Chapter 5). A similar move towards a more economistic notion of the value of creativity and innovation can also be seen in the development of Nesta (Chapter 6). And as New Labour faded amidst recession, political exhaustion and mutual recrimination, it could only recycle old ideas (as in the 2008 *Creative Britain* mess) and produce a Digital Economy Act that seemed designed primarily to respond to the lobbying interests of corporate copyright holders.

In the realm of the arts, the increases in funding, attached to all sorts of targets about access and education, failed to achieve any significant change in the distribution of funding between the major organisations and institutions in the capital and the rest of the country (GPS Culture, 2014). New Labour was successful, in political terms, in retaining close links with both the cultural industries and the arts (very different policy groups with very different policy agendas). It was the grandees of the arts that New Labour most assiduously courted, however, and the free admissions policy served as a mask for limitations in an access agenda that could really only achieve a limited democratisation of culture, rather than any meaningful effect on inequality. It has proved extremely difficult to shift the composition of audiences for subsidised art forms in the UK. Access to production, at least if we look at the composition of cultural labour markets, has become more unequal. New Labour's enthusiasm for measurement produced, for the first time, reasonably good statistics on cultural labour markets – and much of this data gathering has subsequently been undone by funding cuts and a political unwillingness to talk about questions of inequality. But the picture revealed by the statistics is bleak, and was getting bleak even in the days of New Labour – a government supposedly committed to improving access. Black and ethnic minority representation in the media sectors, for example, declined from 7.4 per cent in 2006 (a figure that already indicated serious under-representation) to 5.4 per cent in 2012. Only around 1 per cent of the cultural workforce is recorded as having a disability, way below the average for other sectors. Just under 36 per cent of jobs in the creative economy are filled by women, compared with nearly 47 per cent in the economy as a whole. The fact that New Labour ducked the issue of class when drawing up its 2010 Equality Act[2] means that social inequality does not register as one of the 'protected characteristics' and also means that we have little data on class-based exclusion in cultural work, though few commentators doubt that it is the central problem of cultural inequality in both production and consumption (Oakley and O'Brien, 2014).

So, judged in terms of the longstanding aspirations of the social democratic left to address the inequalities produced by capitalism, New Labour's record was a failure. New Labour's own response might be that, across their various policies, they had to pursue pragmatic centrist policies that would allow them to be elected, given the problems facing traditional social democratic politics (Chapter 1). But in the British context, there are reasons to think that New Labour's cultural policies represented a lost opportunity to pursue a more radical social democratic agenda, given the deep unpopularity of the Conservatives in the 1990s and the favourable economic conditions of the early 2000s. New Labour had correctly identified a new importance for culture in society and the economy. But with their eyes on electoral success, New Labour courted the arts and the cultural industries policy groups, and steadfastly avoided anything that hinted at the kinds of democratising cultural policies associated with the municipal socialism of the Greater London Council and other Labour-led local government initiatives. Questions concerning working conditions in the cultural sector were completely ignored. The irony of a party called *Labour* neglecting issues of social

---

[2] The 2010 Equality Act, which brought together a lot of previous anti-discrimination legislation, defines nine 'protected' characteristics (age, race, gender reassignment, disability, marital status, pregnancy and maternity, religious belief, gender and sexual orientation). At the time of its drafting, there were suggestions that it might include social class. In the end, it didn't.

justice in the domain of work has been pointed out so many times now that it verges on cliché. But it is hard not to be struck by it when considering New Labour's cultural policies (see also Banks and Hesmondhalgh, 2009).

Cultural policy would need a much more root and branch rethinking in order to democratise the arts, and a labour policy for the cultural industries would need to consider access to higher education, unpaid work, regional disparities and the continuing issues of sexism, racism and class discrimination. This would necessarily be linked to a much more profound engagement with the arts and culture in education, and at the local level, as well as a more general commitment to egalitarianism across other areas of policy. As policy analyst Abigail Gilmore has suggested, the issue of quality of life, a feature of 1960s Labour policy, though underdeveloped there, might be a better basis for a social democratic cultural policy in the twenty-first century than dubious claims to be able to marry excellence and access (as in the Arts Council's recent *Great Art for Everyone* programme).

The concept of instrumentalism has been a feature of many critical assessments of many critical assessments and explanations of contemporary cultural policy, including New Labour's. The problems surrounding New Labour's cultural policies do not derive from instrumentalism per se (see Chapter 3), because all policies have strong instrumental components, in any meaningful sense of that term. The real issue is New Labour's embrace of a particular kind of instrumentalism, characterised by Eleonora Belfiore as a *defensive* instrumentalism, 'deprived of the attendant effort to elaborate a positive, confident and coherent notion of cultural value' (Belfiore, 2012: 106), and which served to mask the real values that they were pursuing. The embrace of such a defensive instrumentalism, in the name of political pragmatism, is likely to make it much more difficult to construct and defend a truly democratic set of cultural policies in the next two decades. The apparatus of targets built by New Labour was supposed to achieve transparency and accountability, but in fact obfuscated crucial underlying issues. Political and ideological questions were reconfigured as technical ones. Languages of value, always prone to contestation, are marginalised in favour of supposedly objective means of judging 'what works'. Of course, discussion of value can get caught in confusion and problems of incommensurability. But New Labour marginalised political and ethical questions concerning culture to an unprecedented degree, seemingly out of an excessive reaction against what their leaders saw as the hegemony of conservatism among the British population. In this, as in other ways, they underestimated the British public.

The culture of targets adopted by New Labour, to control and monitor subsidised organisations in the name of accountability and access, also represented an excessive burden on arts and heritage organisations. Yet when New Labour finally reacted against such targets, under pressure from the powerful arts lobby, they could only turn to a deeply problematic notion of excellence as a substitute, rather than policies and values associated with the labour movement and social democratic traditions.

So the balance sheet does not look good when viewed from a social democratic position that focuses on questions of social justice in modern capitalist societies. This is not simply a matter of partisan politics. Anyone, regardless of political position, ought to be concerned by the ways in which deprivation and marginalisation deny millions of people the ability to participate meaningfully in the realm of culture. This is not a matter of 'choice': what people think they want, and what they are capable of, are profoundly shaped by their life chances, which in turn are profoundly shaped by the political, economic and cultural systems we have under modern capitalism.

In modern democracies, a common response to criticisms of a particular party's record is to ask: 'How different would things have been under a different government?' This question is important, though always difficult to answer. Some of what New Labour did would probably have been done by the Conservatives. There were indications of a softer, less Thatcherite approach to arts funding in Conservative cultural policy of the 1990s, and an increasing attention to the lobbying interests of the cultural industries would probably have been manifested in some version of 'creative industries' policies, even if the Conservatives would not have chosen to brand such policies using that term. However, the cultural policies of the Conservative-led Coalition that ascended to power in 2010 help put New Labour's record into rather more favourable perspective. Even taking into account an economic crisis, and a new vulnerability of governments to international financial speculation, the savagery of the Conservative attack on the public realm across the government's policies as a whole was shocking, and this certainly applied to the cultural domain.

8.2 The Coalition, cuts and creative economy

In 2008, a major economic crisis hit much of the world. This was the result of a massive loss of confidence in the wake of the failure of major financial institutions, a result of their greed and a lack of adequate oversight and regulation (Lanchester, 2010). Governments of major economies poured out money to rescue the international economy, and to bail out banks and other corporations. This use of Keynesian government deficit seemed to augur the end of the kind of thinking that had dominated government finance departments since the 1980s, based on the desirability of 'balanced budgets' and the benefits of markets. But in 2010, the imposition by the 'Eurozone' countries of massive austerity measures on their most struggling economies signalled a shift to a new phase of neo-liberalism. The Conservative-led Coalition elected in the UK in the same year took up the new austerity agenda with particular fervour.

The Coalition government was led by a Conservative Party that had seemed to shift towards the political centre following the election of David Cameron as its leader in 2005. Once elected, they implemented a return to Thatcherite rhetoric and spending cuts, and, together with their allies in the conservative media, blamed New Labour's public spending for the economic crisis, a demonstrably false view (see Chang, 2014) but one that seems to have been accepted by a large proportion of the British public. In the results of the Spending Review announced in October 2010, the DCMS's projected budget over the three-year period was cut by 25 per cent, with a 29.6 per cent cut to the Arts Council's budget. Just as damagingly for culture, the money provided to local government by central government was cut by 28 per cent, and was combined with measures to curb the money that local government could raise through local taxes. Because of the lack of any requirement for local government to support culture, other than libraries, this led many councils to make very substantial reductions in their culture and leisure budgets. Although an adjustment was made to lottery funding to increase the proportion of money going to the arts and heritage (each of them went up from 16.6 per cent to 20 per cent of total allocation), the cuts would have a huge impact on the arts and culture. Some local government leaderships, such as Somerset County Council and London's Westminster City Council, completely cut their arts and culture budgets (Pickford, 2014). Newcastle City Council threatened a 100 per cent cut, but reduced it to 50 per cent. These measures disproportionately affected small and grassroots cultural efforts, exacerbating the concentration of arts funding in large London-based organisations.

Libraries were particularly affected. Under the 1964 Public Libraries and Museums Act, local authorities in England and Wales have a statutory duty to provide a 'comprehensive and efficient library service'. The DCMS under New Labour had intervened in 2008–2009 to launch an enquiry into Wirral Council's plan to close 11 of its 20 libraries. The report judged that Wirral was in breach of its statutory duties, and the decision was reversed. The DCMS under the Coalition showed no such willingness to intervene in local council decisions. At least 347 libraries closed during the first two years of the Coalition government (Siddique, 2013). A House of Commons DCMS report noted a long-term decrease in library staffing, and this trend continued (House of Commons CMS Committee, 2012).

The arts lobby deployed key individuals to condemn the arts cuts. In late 2010, a consortium of over 2,000 organisations and individuals launched the *Save the Arts* campaign, spearheaded by high-profile artists and publicised through the production of new artworks. Nicholas Serota, Director of the Tate, argued that the cuts were the biggest threat to the British cultural landscape for 70 years, warning that they were likely to cause a 'slow, painful death' to the 'most innovative' organisations (Serota, 2010: 27). National Theatre Director Nicholas Hytner claimed that the arts in England were sitting 'on a knife's edge' and that the country was 'facing the same situation as we endured between 1979 and 1992 when 25 per cent of regional theatres closed down. That is what will happen. We are right at the edge' (Higgins, 2012).

Unable to galvanise lobbying support to anything like the same degree as the arts sector, public sector heritage suffered. The historical association of the sector with conservatism, discussed in Chapter 7, did not help it one bit. English Heritage's budget was cut by 32 per cent in the 2010 settlement. The HLF told the House of Commons Committee on Communities and Local Government that the loss of central and local authority funding for heritage in England would be over £500 million a year – far more than the extra income generated by the lottery changes. Local government efforts in terms of conservation and archaeology – far more important than showpiece stately homes in preserving and understanding history – were slashed. English Heritage was told by the Coalition's Public Bodies Review to lose its outreach department – a blow for any meaningful notion of widening access (to which the Conservatives had always paid lip service, even in the Thatcherite days of the 1980s). The same body demanded an overhaul of English Heritage over the next ten years, in the direction of privatisation, and a membership scheme based on the principle of the already existing National Trust (which increasingly acted as a business, and it seemed to be increasingly forgotten that its success was based on a long history of public investment and acquisition).

After such savage cuts in the Spending Review of 2010, there was some relief in the 2013 spending round that the next round of cuts were not equally severe. DCMS funding was cut by 'only' 7 per cent, whereas projected Arts Council funding was cut by 'only' 5 per cent in real terms over the 2014–2017 period. But the relief was a measure of how much lower expectations had become since 2010.

While any incoming UK government would have made reductions in public expenditure in order to try to address the UK's structural deficit,[3] those imposed by the Coalition reflected longstanding Conservative antipathy towards the public sector. Other areas of public spending were also subjected to very substantial cuts, but arts and culture cuts need to be understood in the context of the actual money being saved – a tiny sliver of total public expenditure. For example, in 2011–2012, the DCMS's budget was £1.1 billion, compared with £167 billion for pensions, £106.7 billion for health, £48.2 billion for debt interest and £37.3 billion for defence.

The Coalition placed great emphasis on replacing gaps in funding via more philanthropic giving. The first Coalition Culture Secretary Jeremy Hunt spoke of the need for cultural institutions to build endowments in the style of the big US arts organisations, and in 2011 launched an Endowment Fund, drawing on Arts Council and Heritage funds (Brown, 2011). His successor Maria Miller claimed that philanthropy had been 'shamefully neglected during Labour's 13 years in office, despite this being a time at which building sustainability should have been encouraged' (Brown, 2013).[4] The (junior) Minister for Culture, Communications and Creative Industries, Ed Vaizey, introduced a Cultural Gifts scheme in 2013, based on tax relief to corporations and individuals donating cultural treasures. It remains to be seen whether such initiatives will produce greater levels of philanthropy. As we pointed out in Box 3.2, there are many problems associated with sponsorship and philanthropy, among them the tendency for donations to favour larger institutions with already developed fund-raising capacities.[5]

What happened to creative industries and the creative economy? Here there was considerable continuity with New Labour. New Labour's embrace of the copyright-owning industries was taken up with relish by

---

[3] If only to defend the country against predatory investors moving their money into other government's bonds, and to reduce interest payments – there is nothing wrong in itself with a government being in debt.

[4] Munira Mirza, Deputy Mayor of London for Education and Culture, told us that the focus on philanthropy had become 'much more explicit' under the Coalition (Munira Mirza, interview).

[5] For further information and discussion of the Coalition's cultural policies (though not creative industries/creative economy), see *Cultural Trends* (2015), a special issue that appeared just as we were completing the book.

the Coalition, lauded in speeches by Prime Minister David Cameron and his Chancellor/Finance Minister, George Osborne. The tendency of the later New Labour years to focus primarily on the higher-growth technology end of the creative industries was intensified, and any lingering social or cultural policy objectives were quashed. Moreover, the abolition of the RDAs (see Chapter 5) meant that creative industries policy ceased to have meaningful spatial characteristics. Although the (ever-present) need to 'rebalance' Britain's economy was acknowledged by the Coalition government, the regional infrastructure that had been set up to achieve this was largely dismantled.

Perhaps the most substantial creative industry-related moves made by the Coalition involved the extension in 2014 of the film tax relief discussed in Chapter 4 to four other forms of cultural production: videogames, animation, 'high-end' television and theatre, subject to a nationality test administered by the British Film Institute. This followed years of intensive lobbying by organisations such as the UK games industry's association, Tiga (Arthur, 2014). This was part of a major international trend whereby national and regional governments increasingly compete with each other to attract inward investment by offering tax relief. Such battles have their origin in film tax relief, but are now being extended to many other cultural industries (McDonald, 2011). There needs to be a serious debate among critical researchers of cultural policy about the degree to which the enormous tax revenues given up by states in order to beat the competition result in real, sustainable cultural and economic goals. The incentive to move production around different sites destabilises cultural labour forces, and potentially provides a tax 'race to the bottom' that benefits the larger cultural corporations at the expense of public revenue.

The Coalition formed its own version of New Labour's Creative Industries Task Force, named the Creative Industries Council (CIC), stacked with figures from the corporate industries, and a few associated with the IT sector. The Council's remit was confined to England, on the slightly surprising grounds that many of the policy issues were now dealt with by the devolved nations, although this is clearly not the case with copyright. To a greater extent even than the Task Force, the CIC has been viewed largely as a talking shop, meeting relatively infrequently and failing to attract serious political support. The House of Commons CMS Committee commented on non-attendance by relevant ministers and lack of representation from the Treasury (House of Commons CMS Committee, 2013). The remit of the Council is confined to economic issues, namely finance, copyright, exports and skills (CIC Skillset, 2012).

The concern with exports, unsurprising perhaps in the face of severe economic recession, means that creative industry policy is often made manifest either in overseas markets, such as Prime Minister David Cameron's trade mission to India in 2013, or via promotional campaigns, such as the 'Britain is GREAT' campaign with which those arriving at British airports are routinely assaulted. The campaign, run by UK Trade and Investment, the government department now responsible for international trade, interestingly splits 'culture', depicted in its campaign by institutions such as the British Museum, from 'creativity', which is associated with the successful export of UK animation, film or design services. The attempt to fuse culture with creativity that characterised the early years of New Labour's creative industries policies is totally absent.

The weighting of the CIC towards representatives of media corporations (ITV, BSkyB, Warner Brothers), along with a smattering of IT corporations (Creative Industries Council, 2014), left the arts somewhat excluded, a fact not lost on the House of Commons Culture, Media and Sport Committee (House of Commons CMS Committee, 2013). Yet the relationships between arts organisations and the commercial cultural industries that had been forged in the New Labour years have not entirely atrophied. Late 2014 saw the launch of the Creative Industries Federation, an industry lobbying body, which, despite the name, continues a rather New Labour approach in seeking to bring together arts organisations, commercial cultural industries and creative education, particularly in higher education.[6] Launched and housed at Central St Martins art school in the heavily redeveloped King's Cross area of London, the organisation was the idea of designer John Sorrell, who had also been an active figure under New Labour, notably via the London Design Festival. Although the membership features many of the same corporate businesses as the CIC, there is also strong representation from theatres, galleries and educational institutions.

The abolition of the RDAs, carried out by the Coalition government more or less immediately on taking over in May 2010, was a major development for cultural policy. However problematic their role, and however much they became influenced by neo-liberal rather than social democratic notions of redevelopment, these bodies, as we saw in Chapter 5, were the basis of more integrated strategies to develop the arts and cultural businesses (smaller as well as large, corporate interests)

---

[6] See http://www.creativeindustriesfederation.com/ (accessed 4 March 2015).

in the regions. Their disbanding has left regional planning in a much more ad hoc state. It meant the dismantling of the many creative industries teams around the country, which had developed considerable local expertise and knowledge about their sectors. The Local Enterprise Partnerships, which have replaced the RDAs as the main institutional basis for regional policy in England, have very little money and no ability to fund capital projects, such as new workspaces and new infrastructure for the creative industries.[7] They are very small and under-funded, they have very little contact with businesses, and their role is largely 'strategic'. Many creative businesses now no longer know where to go for business support. It is difficult to imagine many of the big projects that took place during the New Labour years – such as Salford's Mediacity – occurring now.

The combined effects of the abolition of RDAs and cuts to arts and cultural budgets mean that the capacity of the UK to develop and deliver policies that cut across the arts, cultural industries and education has been significantly weakened under the Coalition. As RDAs disappeared, other national organisations, notably the Technology Strategy Board (later named Innovate UK), which provides some public funding for 'high growth' small firms, picked up some cultural industry clients, providing some £30 million between 2007 and 2012 (House of Commons, 2013). Unlike RDAs, however, the new agency is not responsible for stimulating economic activity. Instead, it seeks to respond to existing demand, while at the sub-national level the small and rather under-funded Local Enterprise Partnerships are now the principal agencies undertaking regional development.

The UK Film Council was also abolished in the Coalition's 'bonfire of the quangos', along with the Regional Screen Agencies (which had suffered from complex governance arrangements, being answerable both to the UKFC and to the RDAs). Many of the UKFC's functions passed to the British Film Institute (BFI), which had been marginalised under New Labour. As Philip Schlesinger (2015) has commented, New Labour's creation of the Film Council was hardly transparent, and involved very little public deliberation, based on the behind-the-scenes clubbiness that characterised so much of what New Labour did. But 'by comparison, complete opacity prevailed when the Film Council was axed' (Schlesinger, 2015: 474). The House of Commons CMS Committee and

---

[7] Funded by the Business Department, these are voluntary partnerships between local government and local businesses.

the National Audit Office pointed out a number of failings. There was no assessment of costs, and no planning of the transfer of Film Council functions to the BFI. Staggering incompetence was shown in enacting a decision motivated principally by party political point scoring.

The Labour Party, of course, opposed many of these developments, and claimed that they would have made far less serious cuts to public spending as a whole, including to the arts and culture. This was a period in which the Labour Party sought to reposition itself in the light of the financial crisis, the electoral defeat of 2010, and the increasing disillusion of party activists since the early 2000s. The new party leader, Ed Miliband, distanced himself and the party from the New Labour project, showing an interest in efforts to renew social democratic thought on different terms than New Labour.[8]

Yet Labour paid very little attention to cultural policy during the 2010–2015 period. The role of Shadow Culture Secretary was given from 2011 onwards to a senior figure, Harriet Harman, but this had to be combined with her role as Shadow Deputy Prime Minister, and pronouncements and consultations on cultural policy were markedly few. It was, therefore, something of a surprise that when Labour finally gave some indication of its cultural policies, this was in a speech by Ed Miliband himself, at London's Battersea Arts Centre, in February 2015 (Miliband, 2015). The themes were not markedly different from those of New Labour policy. There was the usual praise for the success of Britain's creative practitioners, including film, and mention of the economic and non-economic contribution of the arts. The main emphasis, however, was on education. Miliband accused the Conservatives of neglecting cultural aspects of education, and pledged measures to reinvigorate them – though he might reasonably have accused New Labour of the same neglect.[9] There was also a commitment that under a future Labour

---

[8] An example was the Blue Labour tendency associated with Maurice Glasman and Miliband speechwriter Marc Stears (see Davis, 2011), though Miliband later seemed to distance himself from it. Another was the Party's attempt to rebrand itself as 'One Nation Labour' in 2012 (see Cruddas and Rutherford, 2014). But such experiments in political thought paid very little attention to questions of culture in the sense in which the term is generally used in cultural policy, and that we use in this book.

[9] The Coalition deserves some credit for its attention to music education, in the form of its Department for Education's *Music Education Plan* (2011), which followed the *Review of Music Education* (Henley, 2011). But cultural education more generally was very much marginalised in Conservative education policy, which managed to combine New Labour's obsession with results in core literacy and

government, the arts would be made more central by forming a 'Committee on Arts, Culture and Creative Industries' chaired by the Prime Minister. There was relatively little emphasis on creative industries and economic impact, compared with New Labour pronouncements. But then, Miliband was addressing arts practitioners and advocates. He had already commissioned a report on creative industries policy by former UK Film Council Head John Woodward in January 2014. The speech reflected Miliband's careful and limited move of the Labour Party back towards the centre-left and away from the political centre where Blair and Brown's New Labour had located it. It would have reinforced what the audience already knew: that the arts and culture would gain considerably more support from Labour than from a government led by the Conservatives, who had promised further cuts if elected. But ultimately there seemed to be little fundamental difference between Miliband's Labour and New Labour on culture and the arts. There was no sense whatsoever of the cultural democracy initiatives that Labour had always neglected at the national level, but which had occasionally flourished at the more local level.

The Labour Party was defeated in the 2015 general election. The Conservative Party formed a government with a small parliamentary majority, meaning that they could govern on their own for the first time since the 1990s. The by now thoroughly marginalised Department for Culture, Media and Sport was retained. The newly appointed Culture Secretary was John Whittingdale, a respected Chair of the House of Commons CMS Committee from 2005 to 2015, and therefore considered to be unusually expert in his area for a Culture Secretary – a post often given to up-and-coming political figures who quickly move on to other departments. However, Whittingdale was known for his opposition to the BBC licence fee, signalling tough times ahead for the corporation during a period of 'Charter Review'. The arts and heritage lobbies were expecting no favours from an incoming government committed to a strongly Thatcherite, neo-liberal agenda.

8.3 Final words: Cultural policy and social justice

We have framed this study of New Labour in terms of the cultural policies of social democratic parties and movements. We did so because

---

numeracy subjects with an authoritarian–nationalist agenda redolent of the early twentieth century. See Warwick Commission (2015), which Miliband drew upon in his speech, and Bull (2015).

social democrats have most actively sought to address the problems of capitalist modernity in the realm of culture, whereas conservatives and centrist liberals have tended largely to accept the inequalities, injustices and social fragmentation of capitalist modernity as they inhere in the arts and culture. The framing we have used does not derive merely from our own political preferences. The efforts of social democrats, in cultural policy and beyond, have often been limited and problematic, as we discussed in Chapter 1. But social democracy at least has offered the hope of political measures, based on principles of equality, social justice and the benefits of shared community, which might unlock the potential of the arts and culture for enriching the lives of everyone who might choose to engage with them. New Labour's mantra of 'For the many, not the few' is a common piece of progressive rhetoric. The challenge is to construct, in cultural policy itself and in other related policy domains, policies that are meaningfully egalitarian.

In Chapter 1 we pointed out that one term for such egalitarian cultural policies is 'cultural democracy', distinguished from a narrower, rather unambitious 'democratization of culture' orientation (Simpson, 1976). We discussed in that chapter that this distinction can be made simplistically and problematically, but that, employed cautiously, it has its uses. New Labour was resolutely uninterested in cultural democracy. Its focus on a particular conception of the economic contribution of 'creativity' and the arts legitimated greater funding, but took cultural policy further away than ever from meaningful democratisation.

Perhaps the blame should not reside entirely with New Labour politicians and policy makers, or even with the conservative print media that shape so much of what politicians do and say in the UK. It may be that academics and other intellectuals committed to democratic notions of cultural policy didn't do enough to forge new ways of thinking that might have pulled policy makers away from their centrist visions and towards the 'cultural democracy' goals that had been intermittently present in the history of social democratic cultural thought.

In making our rather negative evaluation of New Labour, we are echoing the disappointment that many commentators with a commitment to social justice have expressed in relation to New Labour's policies (see, for example, the thoughtful but critical appraisal by Shaw, 2007). To what extent should we understand New Labour's failures as evidence of a terminal decline in social democratic politics? Philippe Marlière (2010) has written of the steady electoral decline of social democratic parties since the 1990s, and of the 'ideological and cultural meltdown' signalled by the uncritical support for neo-liberal globalisation and finance capitalism on the part of Third Way centrist parties such as New Labour and Gerhard Schröder's SPD in Germany. Since 2010, the Occupy movements, the rise of the leftist Syriza Party in Greece, and the development of the complex Podemos movement in Spain have given some leftists new hope of a revival in social democracy. In the months leading up to the UK general election of 2015, Britain saw a major surge in support for its Green Party, and Green parties in some countries have offered a space to the left of traditional social democratic parties that have moved to the centre in an era of neo-liberal consensus. Many Green parties have had rather little to say on the arts and culture, and have formed only nascent policies. This is unfortunate. For societies need government cultural policies that can more adequately deal with inequality and other social injustices than the instruments that were characteristic of New Labour's very British (or Anglo-American) version of centrist cultural policy: statistical access targets set from on high for well-meaning outreach departments in arts organisations, and 'creative industries' policies that answer to the needs of corporations rather than publics and citizens. The need for such policies is not just a matter for the left. Culture and the arts are important ways in which people in modern societies express themselves and find meaning, along with the media and social media that we have not had the space to address in this book (see Hesmondhalgh, 2013a for fuller consideration). Many people – perhaps *most* people – now feel powerless in the face of the massive power, wealth and privilege accumulated by others, in a way that was simply not the case before the New Right established their hegemony from the 1980s onwards. That cannot be a good thing for our ability to share life in the same societies, on the same planet. Cultural policies cannot fix such problems. But they can play a part in making culture more democratic. New Labour's failures should not make us think that a real democratisation of culture is an impossible goal.

Appendix: People Interviewed for the Project

Here we provide information about those who participated in the research, including where and when they were interviewed. We usually state their position at the time of writing (January 2015) or when interviewed, followed by the main roles that they undertook during the New Labour period as well as other positions they have held. Some further details can be found in the text. The aim is to explain why we approached them for an interview. We aimed to achieve a reasonable balance of interviewees across the various sectors discussed in this book. Our thanks again to all those who agreed to be interviewed. Principles of informed consent were followed, in accordance with the University of Leeds' research ethics policies at the time of the research.

Bakhshi, Hasan
London, 10 December 2012
Director of Creative Industries at Nesta. Prior to this, economist at the Bank of England and the Foreign and Commonwealth Office. He has also consulted for Film London and the British Film Institute.

Bennett, Iain
Leeds, 16 January 2013
Creative industries consultant, working for BOP Consulting and The Fifth Sector. Prior to this, Sector Leader for the Digital and Creative Industries at the North West Regional Development Agency.

Bianchini, Franco
Leeds, 15 November 2012
Professor of Cultural Policy and Planning at Leeds Beckett University. He previously worked as a consultant, adviser and researcher on cultural planning projects across Europe, for clients such as Arts Council England and the European Commission.

Campbell, Tom
London, 21 June 2012
Associate at BOP Consulting. Previously held a number of posts in creative industries policy, including Head of Creative Industries at the London Development Agency. Formerly Cultural Strategy Manager to the Mayor of London.

Carty, Hilary
London, 14 February 2013
Independent consultant, working for a range of cultural clients. Prior to this, she was Director of the Cultural Leadership Programme, Director of Arts at Arts Council England, and Director of Dance at Arts Council England.

Childs, Katie
London, 19 July 2012
Policy and Projects Officer for the National Museum Directors' Council. Prior to this, International Programmes Manager at the British Museum and International Cultural Policy Manager at the DCMS.

Collard, Paul
Newcastle, 18 August 2013
Chief Executive of Creativity, Culture and Education. Prior to this, led Creative Partnerships, and involved in various cultural regeneration schemes. Was General Manager at the Institute of Contemporary Arts and Deputy Controller of the British Film Institute.

Coonan, Rory
London, 19 October 2012
Previously Director of Architecture at Arts Council England, where he devised policies for the National Lottery's capital projects and worked on the formation of Nesta.

Cowell, Ben
Bury St Edmunds, Suffolk, 1 March 2013
Regional Director at the National Trust and prior to this Head of Social and Economic Research, English Heritage. Before that, Head of Museums at DCMS.

Cowling, Jamie
London, 30 July 2012
Currently works in the Department for Communities and Local Government. Prior to this, he was a Senior Strategy Advisor at the DCMS and a Research Fellow at the Institute for Public Policy Research, working on media and communications policy.

Davey, Alan
London, 20 June 2012
Currently Controller of BBC Radio 3. At the time of interview, he was Chief Executive at Arts Council England. Prior to this he was a civil servant in the Department of Health and the Department of National Heritage, and Director of Arts and Culture at the DCMS.

Frayling, Christopher
London, 17 July 2012
Writer and cultural commentator. Previously, he has been Chair of Arts Council England, Rector of the Royal College of Art, Chair of the Design Council and a Governor at the British Film Institute.

Garcia, Chris
via Skype, 8 March 2013
Creative Industries specialist. Previously held a number of posts within the South West Regional Development Agency, including Director of Enterprise and Skills, Head of Creative Industries and Head of Cluster Development.

Gowers, Andrew
London, 5 October 2012
Public relations executive at time of interview. Former Editor of the *Financial Times*. In 2005, he was commissioned by Gordon Brown to lead an independent review of intellectual property, which was published in 2006 as the Gowers Review.

Gowrie, Grey
London, 26 November 2012
Grey Gowrie was a Conservative Party politician and was Minister for the Arts in the 1980s. Following this, he was Chair of Sotheby's and Chair of Arts Council England in the 1990s.

Griffin, Theresa
Manchester, 15 October 2012
Formerly involved in regional development in the North West, worked for a time at Arts Council England and commissioned the first studies into the economic impact of the arts in the 1980s.

Hackett, Keith
Liverpool, 23 August 2012
Creative industries consultant, involved in regional development projects around Liverpool and Manchester since the 1980s, particularly around obtaining European funding for cultural regeneration initiatives.

Hewison, Robert
London, 13 May 2013
Cultural historian, journalist, critic. Most recently, consultant on a range of projects in the cultural and creative industries for clients such as Demos, the Heritage Lottery Fund and the Royal Shakespeare Company.

Hewitt, Peter
London, 5 and 18 July 2012
Currently Chief Executive at Guy's and St Thomas' Charity. Chief Executive of Arts Council England for ten years under New Labour. His early career was in local government.

Hitchen, Graham
London, 21 June 2012
Creative industries expert. Has held a number of roles in both policy-making and regional development, including as a project director at the London Development Agency and Director of Corporate Policy at Arts Council England.

Holden, John
London, 19 July 2012
Independent consultant, formerly Head of Culture at Demos. Has been involved in policy projects across the cultural sector, working with governments and arts organisations such as Tate, the British Museum and the Royal Shakespeare Company.

Holt, Thelma
London, 11 September 2012
Theatre producer who has held a number of senior positions within the performing arts, including periods at the Roundhouse and National Theatre. She was also Chair of the Drama Advisory Panel at Arts Council England.

Jones, Mark
Oxford, 12 October 2012
Master of St Cross College, Oxford. Formerly Director of the V&A, and before that held positions at the British Museum, the National Museums of Scotland and the National War Museum of Scotland.

Kelly, Jude
London, 6 September 2012
Currently Artistic Director at the South Bank Centre, including the Royal Festival Hall and the Hayward Gallery. Prior to this, she worked at Battersea Arts Centre, the Royal Shakespeare Company and West Yorkshire Playhouse.

Kestenbaum, Jonathan
London, 26 February 2013
Member of the House of Lords and currently Chief Operating Officer of an investment trust. He has had a wide-ranging career and we interviewed him in his capacity as the former Chief Executive of Nesta.

Kingsbury, Jon
London, 14 September 2012.
Head of Digital Economy at the Knowledge Transfer Network. At the time of interview, he was Director of the Creative Economy Programme at Nesta. Prior to this, he worked within content and technology roles at the BBC and Channel 4.

Leonard, Brian
London, 20 July 2012.
Chief Executive of Sporta. Prior to that, senior civil servant and Lead Policy Director at the DCMS for ten years, where he was involved in co-ordinating the local, regional and European aspects of culture, media and sport policies.

Lovatt, Andy
Manchester, 29 May 2012
Creative Economy consultant and previously Head of Creative and Digital Industries at the North West Development Agency.

MacFarlane, Stuart
London, 26 October 2012
Management consultant, interviewed because of experience within the creative industries, as Sector Manager of Digital and New Media for Yorkshire Forward.

MacKenzie, Ruth
London, 17 December 2012
Artistic Director, most recently the Director of the Cultural Olympiad, part of the London 2012 Olympic and Paralympic Games. Prior to that, she was Expert Adviser and Special Adviser to five Secretaries of State for Culture throughout the New Labour years.

McMaster, Brian
London, 21 November 2012
Senior arts administrator, previously managed the Welsh National Opera and the Edinburgh International Festival. In 2007, he was commissioned by James Purnell to undertake a review of excellence in the arts, which was published as the McMaster Review in 2008.

Mirza, Munira
London, 12 March 2013
Deputy Mayor of London for Education and Culture. Prior to that, she worked for the Royal Society of Arts, Tate and the Policy Exchange. She has written extensively about cultural and social policy in the UK.

Morris, Estelle
London, 15 November 2012
Labour Party politician and member of the House of Lords. Secretary of State for Education and Skills and Minister for the Arts under New Labour.

Mulgan, Geoff
London, 30th July 2012
Currently Chief Executive of Nesta. Previously Director of Policy at 10 Downing Street under Tony Blair, Director of the Prime Minister's Strategy Unit and Director (and co-founder) of Demos.

Nairne, Sandy
London, 21 November 2012
Director of the National Portrait Gallery. He has also held positions at the Tate, the Institute for Contemporary Arts and Modern Art Oxford.

Newbigin, John
London, 8 June 2012
Cultural entrepreneur and writer. During the New Labour period, he was Special Adviser to Chris Smith and prior to that, Policy Adviser to Neil Kinnock. He was also Executive Assistant to David Puttnam at Enigma Productions.

Newton, Jeremy
London, 22 October 2012
Chief Executive of the Prince's Foundation for Children and the Arts. He has held a range of posts within the cultural and creative industries, including Chief Executive of Nesta and National Lottery Director for Arts Council England.

Powell, Chris
London, 17 July 2012
Previously Chair of Nesta and former Chief Executive of the advertising agency DDB London. DDB was the Labour Party's advertising agency for some time, covering five general elections and responsible for the New Labour rebranding.

Purnell, James
London, 20 June 2012
Currently the Director of Strategy and Digital at the BBC. He was a Labour Party politician and was Secretary of State for Work and Pensions, and Secretary of State for Culture, Media and Sport. Also worked with Demos and the Institute for Public Policy Research.

Puttnam, David
London, 15 January 2013
Former film producer and was the first Chair of Nesta. Although he did not hold an official position within New Labour, he was fundamental to a number of policies and was seen as a trusted adviser.

Robinson, Gerry
London, 22 November 2012
Television presenter and businessman. During the New Labour period, he was Chair of Arts Council England.

Sharkey, Feargal
London, 28 November 2012
Former Chair of the Task Force on live music and Head of UK Music, a body that represents the interests of commercial music. A prominent musician in the late 1970s and 1980s, he was lead singer with the Northern Irish band, The Undertones.

Smith, Chris
London, 8 June 2012
Now a member of the House of Lords, the first Secretary of State for Culture, Media and Sport under New Labour. Prior to that he was a shadow minister in various departments: Social Security, National Heritage and State for the Environment.

Stevenson, Wilf
London, 22 October 2012
Member of the House of Lords. Under New Labour, he was Senior Policy Adviser in the Prime Minister's Office under Gordon Brown and is the former Director of the British Film Institute.

Wood, Stewart
London, 30 April 2013
Policy Adviser to Ed Miliband, Labour Party leader from 2010 to 2015, and member of the House of Lords. Under New Labour, he was Senior Policy Adviser in the Prime Minister's Office under Gordon Brown. Prior to this he worked with the think tank Policy Network.

References

Ahearne, J. (2009) 'Cultural Policy Explicit and Implicit: A Distinction and Some Uses', *International Journal of Cultural Policy*, 15(2), 141–153.

Alexander, V. (2008) 'Cultural Organizations and the State: Art and State Support in Contemporary Britain', *Sociology Compass*, 2(5), 1416–1430.

Alibhai-Brown, Y. (2004) 'British Heritage Is Our Heritage Too, Lord Alli', *The Evening Standard*, 26 October.

Applejuice Consultants (2008) *Social Impact of Heritage Lottery Funded Projects: Evaluation Report on Research Conducted for Heritage Lottery Fund during 2006–2007*, Norwich: Applejuice. British Archaeology website. http://www .archaeologyuk.org/ba/ba82/letters.shtml, accessed 14 May 2015.

Arthur, C. (2014) 'UK Video Games Tax Breaks Expected to Protect More Than 10,000 Jobs', *The Guardian*, 16 June.

Arts and Business (2013) *Where Is Private Investment to the Arts Going?* http:// artsandbusiness.bitc.org.uk/sites/default/files/kcfinder/files/artsandbusiness/ artsandbusiness-pics-2011-12.pdf, accessed 3 February 2014.

Arts and Business (2015) 'About Us', http://artsandbusiness.bitc.org.uk/about-ab, accessed 7 January 2015.

Arts Council England (2006) *Looking Back, Looking Forward: 10 Years of Arts Council Work in the Creative Industries* (London: ACE).

Arts Council England (2007a) *This Much We Know... Creative Partnerships: Approach and Impact* (London: Arts Council England).

Arts Council England (2007b) *This Much We Know... Thinkpiece: The Challenge of Defining Impact* (London: Arts Council England).

Arts Council England (not dated) *Creative Futures: Supporting Creativity in the Next Century. A Proposal from the Arts Council of England* (London: ACE).

Arts Council of Great Britain (1985) *A Great British Success Story* (London: ACGB).

Aslet, C. (2008) 'Britain's Second Stone Age', *The Daily Telegraph*, 19 July, p. 26.

Assinder, N. (1999) 'Blair Risks Row over Public Sector', BBC, 7 July, http://news .bbc.co.uk/1/hi/uk_politics/388528.stm, accessed 10 December 2013.

Babbidge, A. (2000) 'UK Museums: Safe and Sound?' *Cultural Trends*, 10(3), 1–35.

Bache, I. (2003) 'Governing through Governance: Education Policy Control under New Labour', *Political Studies*, 51(2), 300–314.

Bakhshi, H., Freeman, A. and Higgs, P. (2013) *A Dynamic Mapping of the UK's Creative Industries* (London: Nesta).

Ball, S. J. and Exley, S. (2010) 'Making Policy with "Good Ideas": Policy Networks and the "Intellectuals" of New Labour', *Journal of Education Policy*, 25(2), 151–169.

Banaji, S., Burn, A. and Buckingham, D. (2006) *The Rhetorics of Creativity: A Review of the Literature* (London: Arts Council England).

Bangemann, M. (1994) *Recommendations to the European Council: Europe and the Global Information Society* (Brussels: European Commission).

Banks, M. and Hesmondhalgh, D. (2009) 'Looking for Work in Creative Industries Policy', *International Journal of Cultural Policy*, 15(4), 1–16.

Banks, M. and O'Connor, J. (2009) 'After the Creative Industries', *International Journal of Cultural Policy*, 15(4), 365–373.

Banks, M., Lovatt, A., O'Connor, J. and Raffo, C. (2000) 'Risk and Trust in the Cultural Industries', *Geoforum*, 31, 453–464.

Barker, A., Byrne, I. and Veall, A. (1999) *Ruling by Task Force: The Politico's Guide to Labour's New Elite* (London: Politicos).

Bartlett, K. (2008) 'A Rich Mix of Politics in East London', *The Times*, 15 July.

Baxter, I. (2002) 'Auditing the Historic Environment: Measurements, Datasets and English Heritage's State of the Historic Environment Report 2002', *Cultural Trends*, 12(46), 1–31.

Beckert, J. and Lutter, M. (2009) 'The Inequality of Fair Play: Lottery Gambling and Social Stratification in Germany', *European Sociological Review*, 25(4), 475–488.

Belfiore, E. (2002) 'Art as a Means of Alleviating Social Exclusion: Does It Really Work? A Critique of Instrumental Cultural Policies and Social Impact Studies in the UK', *International Journal of Cultural Policy*, 8(1), 91–106.

Belfiore, E. (2004) 'Auditing Culture: The Subsidised Cultural Sector in the New Public Management', *International Journal of Cultural Policy*, 10(2), 183–202.

Belfiore, E. (2009) 'On Bullshit in Cultural Policy Practice and Research: Notes from the British Case', *International Journal of Cultural Policy*, 15(3), 343–359.

Belfiore, E. (2012) ' "Defensive Instrumentalism" and the Legacy of New Labour's Cultural Policies', *Cultural Trends*, 21(2), 103–111.

Belfiore, E. and Bennett, O. (2008) *The Social Impact of the Arts: An Intellectual History* (Basingstoke: Palgrave Macmillan).

Bell, D. and Oakley, K. (2014) *Cultural Policy* (London & New York: Routledge).

Bennett, T. (1998) *Culture: A Reformer's Science* (London: Sage).

Bennett, T., Savage, M., Silva, E. B., Warde, A., Gayo-Cal, M. and Wright, D. (2009) *Culture, Class, Distinction* (Abingdon: Routledge).

Bevins, A. (1996) 'Cool Britannia: Major Claims the Credit', *The Independent*, 12 November, http://www.independent.co.uk/news/cool-britannia-major-claims-the-credit-1351900.html, accessed 11 January 2015.

Bevir, M. (2005) *New Labour: A Critique* (London: Routledge).

Bevir, M. (2011) *The Making of British Socialism* (Princeton: Princeton University Press).

Bevir, M. and Rhodes, R. A. W. (eds) (2006) *Governance Stories* (London & New York: Routledge).

Bianchini, F. (forthcoming, 2016) *The Labour Party and the Arts: A History* (London: Lawrence and Wishart).

Bianchini, F. and Parkinson, M. (eds) (1993) *Cultural Policy and Urban Regeneration: The West European Experience* (Manchester: Manchester University Press).

Bird, L. (2000) 'Art and Design Education: Historical Overview', Working Papers in Art and Design, University of Hertfordshire.

Blackstock, A. (2011) *The Public: Lessons Learned by Arts Council England* (London: Arts Council England).

Blair, T. (1997) 'Speech to the CBI', http://www.ukpolitics.org.uk/category/uncategorized/, accessed 2 January 2015.

Blair, T. (2007) 'Blair's Speech on the Arts in Full', *The Guardian*, 6 May, http://www.theguardian.com/politics/2007/mar/06/politicsandthearts.uk1, accessed 13 January 2015.

Bogdanov, M. (1998) 'Love for Labour Lost', *New Statesman*, 27 February.

BOP (2006) *Study of the Impact of Creative Partnerships on the Cultural and Creative Economy* (London: Burns Owens Partnerships).

BOP Consulting (2005) *Creative Industries Development Framework in the English Regions* (London: DCMS).

Boren, T. and C. Young (2013) 'Getting Creative with the "Creative City"? Towards New Perspectives on Creativity in Urban Policy', *International Journal of Urban and Regional Research*, 37(5), 1799–1815.

Bowerman, M., Raby, H. and Humphrey, C. (2000) 'In Search of the Audit Society: Some Evidence from Health Care, Police and Schools', *International Journal of Auditing*, 4(1), 71–100.

Boyle, J. (1996) *Shamans, Software and Spleens* (Cambridge: Harvard University Press).

Bragg, M. (1999) 'Sorry, Sir Peter, But Things Are Getting Better for Theatre', *The Independent*, 26 February, http://www.independent.co.uk/arts-entertainment/sorry-sir-peter-but-things-are-getting-better-for-theatre-107 3190.html, accessed 2 January 2015.

Bristow, G. (2005) 'Everyone's a "Winner": Problematizing the Discourse of Regional Competitiveness', *Journal of Economic Geography*, 5(3), 285–304.

Brooks, R. (2005) 'You're History: Jowell in Threat to English Heritage', *The Sunday Times*, 13 March, p. 3.

Brown, I. (2003) *Implementing the European Union Copyright Directive* (London: Foundation for Information Policy Research), http://discovery.ucl.ac.uk/40795/.

Brown, M. (2011) 'Hunt Outlines £55m Fund to Help Build Endowments', *The Guardian*, 4 July.

Brown, M. (2013) 'Tories Hit Back at Labour over Arts Funding', *The Guardian*, 3 July.

Bull, D. (2015) 'Culture in a Cold Climate', *Cultural Trends*, 24(1), 46–50.

Bunting, C., Chan, T. W., Goldthorpe, J., Keaney, E. and Oskala, A. (2008) *From Indifference to Enthusiasm: Patterns of Arts Attendance in England* (London: ACE).

Bunting, M. (2005) *Willing Slaves: How the Overwork Culture Is Ruling Our Lives* (London: Harper and Collins).

Cabinet Office (1999) *Giving Time, Getting Involved: A Strategy Report by the Working Group on the Active Community* (London: HMSO).

Cairney, P. (2012) *Understanding Public Policy: Theories and Issues* (Basingstoke: Palgrave Macmillan).

Cameron, S. and Coaffee, J. (2004) 'Art, Gentrification and Regeneration: From Artist to Pioneer to Public Arts', *European Journal of Housing Policy*, 5(1), 39–58.

Caterer, J. (2011) *The People's Pictures: National Lottery Funding and British Cinema* (Newcastle upon Tyne: Cambridge Scholars Publishing).

Cellan-Jones, R. (2010) 'Digital Economy: The Mandelson Letters', http://www.bbc.co.uk/blogs/legacy/thereporters/rorycellanjones/2010/03/digital_economy_the_mandelson.html, accessed 30 August 2014.

Chang, H.J. (2014) 'Why Did Britain's Political Class Buy into the Tories' Economic Fairytale?' *The Guardian*, 19 October.

Channer, J. (2013) *Forms, Fields and Forces: An Exploration of State Governance Relating to the Creative Industries in South West England* (PhD thesis, University of Exeter).

Chapain, C. and Comunian, R. (2010) 'Enabling and Inhibiting the Creative Economy: The Role of the Local and Regional Dimensions in England', *Regional Studies*, 44(6), 717–734.

Chartrand, H. and McCaughey, C. (1989) 'The Arm's Length Principle and the Arts: An International Perspective – Past, Present and Future', in M. Cumming and M. Schuster (eds) *Who's to Pay for the Arts? The International Search for Models of Support* (New York: American Council for the Arts Books), pp. 43–80.

Christiansen, R. (2007) 'Why the Outlook for 'Heritage' Is Bleak', *The Daily Telegraph*, 4 July.

Christophers, B. (2008) 'The BBC, the Creative Class, and Neoliberal Urbanism in the North of England', *Environment and Planning*, 40(10), 2313–2329.

Clark, K. (2004) 'Why Fund Heritage? The Role of Research in the Heritage Lottery Fund', *Cultural Trends*, 13(4), 65–85.

Clark, K. and Maaer, G. (2008) 'The Cultural Value of Heritage: Evidence from the Heritage Lottery Fund', *Cultural Trends*, 17(1), 23–56.

Cloonan, M. (2002) 'Hitting the Right Note? The New Deal for Musicians', *Journal of Vocational Education & Training*, 54(1), 51–66.

Cloonan, M. (2007) *Popular Music and the State in the UK: Culture, Trade or Industry?* (Farnham: Ashgate).

Clotfelter, C. T. (2000) *Do Lotteries Hurt the Poor? Well, Yes and No*, http://sanford .duke.edu/news/newsletters/dpn/summer00/lottery.html, accessed July 2013.

Clotfelter, C. T. and Cook, P. (1989) *Selling Hope: State Lotteries in America* (Cambridge: Harvard University Press).

Clotfelter, C. T., Cook, P. J., Edell, J. A. and Moore, M. (1999) *State Lotteries at the Turn of the Century: Report to the National Gambling Impact Study Commission* (Durham: Duke University Press).

Conservative Party (2007) *A New Landscape for the Arts. The Arts Task Force: Submission to The Shadow Secretary of State for Culture, Media and Sport* (London: Conservative Party).

Coonan, R. (1995a) The National Endowment for Science, Humanities and the Arts (unpublished).

Coonan, R. (1995b) The National Endowment for Science, Education and the Arts (unpublished).

Coonan, R. (1995c) A National Endowment for Science and the Arts (unpublished).

Coonan, R. (1996a) The National Endowment for Science, Humanities and the Arts (unpublished).

Coonan, R. (1996b) Letter to Lord Chadlington, 29 November 1996 (unpublished).

Cormack, P. (1976) *Heritage in Danger* (London: New English Library).

Corner, J. and Harvey, S. (eds) (1991) *Enterprise and Heritage: Crosscurrents of National Culture* (London: Routledge).

Country Land and Business Association (2006) 'Who Pays for Heritage?' http:// www.cla.org.uk/sites/default/files/2005-06%20CLA%20Heritage%20Survey% 20report%2020060620.pdf, accessed 22 December 2014.

Cowell, B. (2004) 'Why Heritage Counts: Researching the Historic Environment', *Cultural Trends*, 13(4), 23–39.

Cowell, B. (2007) 'Measuring the Impact of Free Admission', *Cultural Trends*, 16(3), 203–224.

Cowen, T. (2011) *The Great Stagnation: How America Ate All the Low-Hanging Fruit of Modern History, Got Sick, and Will (Eventually) Feel Better* (New York: Dutton).

Cowling, J. and Keaney, E. (2003) *Arts for Wellbeing?* (London: IPPR).

Creative Industries Council (2014) *Create UK: Creative Industries Strategy* (London: Creative Industries Council).

Creative Industries Council Skillset (2012) *Creative Industries Council Skillset Skills Group Report to Creative Industries Council*, http://cicskills.skillset.org/data/ the_creative_industries_council_skillset_skills_group_report, accessed 12 January 2015.

Creative Partnerships (2013) *About Creative Partnerships*, http://www.creative -partnerships.com/about-creative-partnerships/, accessed 12 November 2014.

Creight-Tyte, A. (2005) 'Measuring Creativity: A Case Study in the UK's Designer Fashion Sector', *Cultural Trends*, 14(2), 157–183.

Crouch, C. (2013) *Making Capitalism Fit for Society* (Chichester: John Wiley & Sons).

Cruddas, J. and Rutherford, J. (2014) *One Nation: Labour's Political Renewal*. E-book available at http://b.3cdn.net/labouruk/7d780d9fb7f25e85bd_1rm6iywub.pdf, accessed 27 March 2015.

Cultural Trends (2011) *'Golden Age'? Reflections on New Labour's Cultural Policy and Its Post-Recession Legacy* (journal, special edition), 20(3–4).

Cultural Trends (2015) *Cultural Trends*, election special, 24(1).

Cunningham, S. (2007) 'Creative Industries as Policy and Discourse outside the United Kingdom', *Global Media and Communication*, 3(3), 347–352.

Cunningham, S. (2013) *Hidden Innovation: Policy, Industry and the Creative Sector* (Brisbane: University of Queensland Press).

Dallyn, S. (2011) 'Innovation and Financialisation: Unpicking a Close Association', *Ephemera*, 11(3), 289–307.

Danson, M., E. Helinska-Hughes and M. Hughes (2005) 'RDAs and Benchmarking: Learning from Good Practice When the Model Has Broken', *Public Policy and Administration*, 20(3), 4–22.

Davies, W. (2014) *The Limits of Neoliberalism: Authority, Sovereignty and the Logic of Competition* (London: Sage).

Davis, R. (2011) *Tangled Up in Blue: Blue Labour and the Struggle for Labour's Soul* (London: Ruskin).

Department for Culture, Media and Sport (1998) *Creative Industries Mapping Document* (London: DCMS).

Department for Culture, Media and Sport (1999) *Policy Action Team 10; A Report to the Social Exclusion Unit: Arts and Sport* (London: DCMS).

Department for Culture, Media and Sport (2000a) *Centres for Social Change: Museums, Galleries and Archives for All* (London: DCMS).

Department for Culture, Media and Sport (2000b) *Creative Industries: The Regional Dimension* (London: DCMS).

Department for Culture, Media and Sport (2001) *Culture and Creativity: The Next Ten Years* (London: DCMS).

Department for Culture, Media and Sport (2002) *People and Places – Social Inclusion Policy for the Built and Historic Environment* (London: DCMS).

Department for Culture, Media and Sport (2004) *The DCMS Evidence Toolkit* (London: DCMS).

Department for Culture, Media and Sport (2005) *Autumn Performance Report: Achievement against 2002 and 2004 Public Service Agreement Targets and Efficiency Review Target* (London: DCMS).

Department for Culture, Media and Sport (2007a) *Heritage Protection for the 21st Century* (London: DCMS).

Department for Culture, Media and Sport (2007b) *Winning: A Tourism Strategy for 2012 and Beyond* (London: DCMS).

Department for Culture, Media and Sport (2008) *Creative Britain: New Talents for the New Economy* (London: DCMS).

Department for Culture, Media and Sport (2011) *Creative Industries Economic Estimates: Full Statistical Release* (London: DCMS).

Department for Culture, Media and Sport (2013) 'Maintaining World-Leading National Museums and Galleries, and Supporting the Museum Sector', Press Release, 27 February 2013 (London: DCMS).

Department for Culture, Media and Sport (no date) *Public Service Agreements (PSA) and Departmental Strategic Objectives (DSO)*, https://www.gov.uk/government/uploads/system/uploads/attachment_data/file/77835/Resource_Accounts_Annex_2__2009-10_Performance.doc (London: DCMS). Accessed 9th March 2014.

Department for Culture, Media and Sport and Department for Transport, Local Government and the Regions (2001) *Historic Environment: A Force for Our Future* (London: DCMS and DTLG).

De Propris, L. (2013) 'How Are Creative Industries Weathering the Crisis?' *Cambridge Journal of Regions, Economy and Society*, 6(1), 23–35.

Department for Education and Employment (1999) *Millennium Volunteers*, http://webarchive.nationalarchives.gov.uk/20090215180949/http://www.mvonline.gov.uk.

Department for Education and Skills (2003) 'Every Child Matters', *Green Paper CM 5680* (London: HMSO).

Department of National Heritage (1990) *Annual Report* (London: DNH).

Department of National Heritage (1993) *Annual Report* (London: DNH).

Department of National Heritage (1995) *Annual Report* (London: DNH).

Department of the Environment, Transport and the Regions (2000) *Our Towns and Cities: The Future. Delivering an Urban Renaissance*. Cm 4911 (London: Department of the Environment, Transport and the Regions).

Department of Trade and Industry (2001) *Business Clusters in the UK – A First Assessment* (London: DTI).

Diamond, P. and Kenny, M. (eds) (2011) *Reassessing New Labour: Market, State and Society under Blair and Brown* (Oxford: Wiley-Blackwell).

Dickinson, M. and Harvey, S. (2005) 'Film Policy in the United Kingdom: New Labour at the Movies', *Political Quarterly*, 76(3), 420–429.

Dight, C. (2007) 'Sponsorship Is a Fine Art', *The Times*, 10 May.

Donohue, M. (2013) 'Welfare and Cohesion Contested: A Critical Discourse Analysis of New Labour's Reform Programme', *British Politics*, 8(1), 79–100.

Doyle, G. (2014) 'Film Support and the Challenge of Sustainability: On Wing Design, Wax and Feathers and Bolts from the Blue', *Journal of British Cinema and Television*, 11(2), 129–151.

Drahos, P. and Braithwaite, J. (2002) *Information Feudalism: Who Owns the Knowledge Economy?* (New York: New Press).

Dresser, M. (2007) 'Set in Stone? Statues and Slavery in London', *History Workshop Journal*, 64, 162–199.

Driver, S. and Martell, L. (1997) 'New Labour's Communitarianisms', *Critical Social Policy*, 17(52), 27–46.

Driver, S. and Martell, L. (2006) *New Labour* (Cambridge: Polity).

Duelund, P. (2008) 'Nordic Cultural Policies: A Critical View', *International Journal of Cultural Policy*, 14(1), 7–24.

Eames, A., Benton, T., Sharp, C. and Kendall, L. (2006) *The Impact of Creative Partnerships on the Attainment of Young People* (Slough: NFER), http://www.nfer.ac.uk/nfer/publications/CPS03/CPS03.pdf.

Economist, The (2001) 'When Merchants Enter the Temple', *The Economist*, 19 April, p. 90.

Edwards, L., Klein, B., Lee, D., Moss, G. and Philip, F. (2013) ' "Isn't it just a way to protect Walt Disney's rights?" Media User Perspectives on Copyright', *New Media & Society*, 17(5), 691–707.

Edwards, L., Klein, B., Lee, D., Moss, G. and Philip, F. (2015) 'Discourse, Justification, and Critique: Towards a Legitimate Digital Copyright Regime?' *The International Journal of Cultural Policy*, 21(1), 60–77.

Elsheshtawy, Y. (2012) 'The Production of Culture: Abu Dhabi's Urban Strategies', in *Cultural Policy and Governance in a New Metropolitan Age, Volume 5, The Cultures and Globalization Series* (London: Sage).

English Heritage (1997) *Sustaining the Historic Environment: New Perspectives on the Future* (London: English Heritage).

English Heritage (2000) *Power of Place: The Future of the Historic Environment* (London: English Heritage).

English Heritage (2005) *Regeneration and the Historic Environment: Heritage as a Catalyst for Better Social and Economic Regeneration* (London: English Heritage).

English Heritage (2008) *Conservation Principles: Policies and Guidance for the Sustainable Management of the Historic Environment* (London: English Heritage).

English Heritage (2010) *Heritage Counts* (London: English Heritage).

English Heritage (2011a) *Annual Reports and Accounts 2010–11* (London: English Heritage).

English Heritage (2011b) *Outreach: Engaging New Audiences with the Historic Environment* (London: English Heritage).

English Heritage, National Trust, Heritage Lottery Fund, Historic Houses Association and Heritage Link (2007) *Valuing Our Heritage: The Case for Future Investment in the Historic Environment* (publisher unknown).

Etzioni, A. (ed) (1995) *The New Communitarian Thinking: Persons, Virtues, Institutions and Communities* (Charlottesville: University of Virginia Press).

European Parliament (2001) *Directive 2001/29/EC of the European Parliament and of the Council of 22 May 2001 on the Harmonisation of Certain Aspects of Copyright and Related Rights in the Information Society* (Brussels: European Parliament).

Evans, G. (2003) 'Hard-Branding the Cultural City – from Prado to Prada', *International Journal of Urban and Regional Research*, 27(2), 417–440.

Evans, G. (2009) 'Creative Spaces and the Art of Urban Living', in T. Edensor, D. Leslie, S. Millington and N. Rantisi (eds) *Spaces of Vernacular Creativity: Rethinking the Cultural Economy* (Abingdon: Routledge), pp. 19–32.

Evans, G. (2009a) 'Creative Cities, Creative Spaces and Urban Policy', *Urban Studies*, 46(5–6), 1003–1040.

Evans, G. and Shaw, P. (2004) *The Contribution of Culture to Regeneration in the UK: A Review of the Evidence* (London: DCMS).

Fairclough, N. (2000) *New Labour, New Language?* (London: Routledge).

Falconer, P. and McLaughlin, K. (2000) 'Public-Private Partnerships and the New Labour Government in Britain', in S. Osborne (ed) *Public-Private Partnerships: Theory and Practice in International Perspective* (London and New York: Routledge), pp. 120–133.

Falconer, P. K. and Blair, S. (2003) 'The Governance of Museums: A Study of Admission Charges Policy in the UK', *Public Policy and Administration*, 18(2), 71–88.

Fawcett, P. and Daugbjerg, C. (2012) 'Explaining Governance Outcomes: Epistemology, Network Governance and Policy Network Analysis', *Political Studies Review*, 10(2), 195–207.

Finlayson, A. (2003) *Making Sense of New Labour* (London: Lawrence and Wishart).

Flew, T. (2012) *The Creative Industries: Culture and Policy* (London: Sage).

Foster, P. (2010) 'Abbey Road Studios Given Listed Status', *The Times*, 24 February 2010, p. 11.

Frayling, C. (1987) *The Royal College of Art. One Hundred and Fifty Years of Art and Design* (London: Barrie & Jenkins).

Frayling, C. (2005) *'The Only Trustworthy Book...' Arts and Public Value* (London: Arts Council England), http://www.artscouncil.org.uk/media/uploads/documents/publications/Trustworthybook_phpv5Rbih.pdf.

Freedman, D. (2008) *The Politics of Media Policy* (Cambridge: Polity Press).

Frith, S. and Marshall, L. (2004) *Music and Copyright* (Edinburgh University Press).

García, B. (2004a) 'Cultural Policy and Urban Regeneration in Western European Cities: Lessons from Experience, Prospects for the Future', *Local Economy*, 19(4), 312–326.

García, B. (2004b) 'Urban Regeneration, Arts Programming and Major Events', *International Journal of Cultural Policy*, 10(1), 103–118.

Garnham, N. (2005) 'From Cultural to Creative Industries', *International Journal of Cultural Policy*, 11(1), 15–29.

Gates, C. and Booth, R. (2005) 'Preserving Listed Buildings – On Computer', *The Guardian*, 24 March.

Gerolymbos, A., Spedding, P. and Tuchner, J. (2013) *Where Is Private Investment to the Arts Going?* (London: Arts & Business).

Gibson, L. (2008) 'In Defence of Instrumentality', *Cultural Trends*, 17(4), 247–257.

Gibson, L. (2013) 'Piazzas or Stadiums: Towards an Alternative Account of Museums in Cultural and Urban Development', *Museum Worlds: Advances in Research*, 1(1), 101–112.

Giddens, A. (1999) *The Third Way: The Renewal of Social Democracy* (Cambridge: Polity Press).

Giddens, A. (ed) (2001) *The Global Third Way Debate* (Cambridge: Polity).

Gilmore, A. (2013) 'Cold Spots, Crap Towns and Cultural Deserts: The Role of Place and Geography in Cultural Participation and Creative Place-Making', *International Journal of Cultural Policy*, 22(2), 86–96.

Gilmore, A. (2014) *Raising Our Quality of Life: The Importance of Investment in Arts and Culture* (London: Centre for Labour and Social Studies).

Glaister, D. (1999) 'Hall Reveals Formation of 'Alternative' Arts Council', *The Guardian*, 13 February.

Glyn, A. (2007) *Capitalism Unleashed: Finance, Globalization, and Welfare* (Oxford: Oxford University Press).

Goldsmith, B., Ward, S. and O'Regan, T. (eds) (2010) *Local Hollywood: Global Film Production and the Gold Coast* (St Lucia: University of Queensland Press).

Goodwin, M., Jones, M. and Jones, R. (2005) 'Devolution, Constitutional Change and Economic Development: Explaining and Understanding the New Institutional Geographies of the British State', *Regional Studies*, 39(4), 421–436.

Government of the Commonwealth of Australia (1994) *Creative Nation: Commonwealth Cultural Policy* (Canberra: Government of the Commonwealth of Australia).

Gowers, A. (2006) *Gowers Review of Intellectual Property* (London: HMSO).

GPS Culture (2014) *Hard Facts to Swallow*, http://www.gpsculture.co.uk/, accessed 10 October 2014.

Graham, H. (2009) 'Department of Culture, Media and Sport's Peer Review Pilot', *Cultural Trends*, 18(4), 323–331.

Grant, W. (2000) *Pressure Groups and British Politics* (Basingstoke: Palgrave Macmillan).

Gray, C. (2000) *The Politics of the Arts in Britain* (Basingstoke: Palgrave Macmillan).

Gray, C. (2002) 'Local Government and the Arts', *Local Government Studies*, 28(1), 77–90.

Gray, C. (2003) 'The Millennium Dome: Falling from Grace', *Parliamentary Affairs*, 56, 441–455.

Gray, C. (2004) 'Joining-Up or Tagging On? The Arts, Cultural Planning and the View from Below', *Public Policy and Administration*, 19(2), 38–49.

Gray, C. (2007) 'Commodification and Instrumentality in Cultural Policy', *International Journal of Cultural Policy*, 13(2), 203–215.

Gray, C. (2009a) 'Museums, Galleries, Politics and Management', *Proceedings of the Public Administration Committee Annual Conference*, 7–9 September 2009, University of Glamorgan, Wales.

Gray, C. (2009b) 'Managing Cultural Policy: Pitfalls and Prospects', *Public Administration*, 87(3), 574–585.

Gregg, P. A., Hanson, K. and Wadsworth, J. (1999) 'The Rise of the Workless Household', in P. Gregg and J. Wadsworth (eds) *The State of Working Britain* (Manchester: Manchester University Press), pp. 75–89.

Grodach, C. (2010) 'Beyond Bilbao: Rethinking Flagship Cultural Development and Planning in Three California Cities', *Journal of Planning Education and Research*, 29(3), 353–366.

Hall, C. and Thomson, P. (2007) 'Creative Partnerships? Cultural Policy and Inclusive Arts Practice in One Primary School', *British Educational Research Journal*, 33(3), 315–329.

Hall, P. (1993) 'Policy Paradigms, Social Learning, and the State: The Case of Economic Policymaking in the UK', *Comparative Politics*, 25(3), 275–296.

Hall, S. (2005) 'Whose Heritage? Un-Settling "The Heritage": Re-imagining the Post-Nation', in J. Littler and R. Naidoo (eds) *The Politics of Heritage: The Legacies of 'Race'* (Abingdon: Routledge), pp. 23–35.

Hall, S. and Jacques, M. (eds) (1989) *New Times: The Changing Face of Politics in the 1990s* (London: Lawrence and Wishart).

Harris, J. (2003) *The Last Party: Britpop, Blair and The Demise of English Rock* (London and New York: Fourth Estate).

Hartley, J. and Cunningham, S. (2001) 'Creative Industries: From Blue Poles to Fat Pipes', in M. Gillies (ed) *The National Humanities and Social Sciences Summit: Position Papers* (Canberra: Department of Education Science and Training), 1–10.

Hatherley, O. (2014) 'In Praise of White Elephants', *Jacobin*, issue 13, https://www.jacobinmag.com/2014/01/in-praise-of-white-elephants/, accessed 7 January 2015.

Hay, C. (1999) *The Political Economy of New Labour: Labouring under False Pretences?* (Manchester and New York: Manchester University Press).

Henley, D. (2011) *Music Education in England* (London: Department for Culture, Media and Sport).

Herald, The (1998) 'Arts' £5m to Attract New Audiences', *The Herald (Glasgow)*, 18 March, http://www.heraldscotland.com/sport/spl/aberdeen/arts-5m-to-attract-new-audiences-1.350048, accessed 2 January 2015.

Heritage Link (2004) Letter to Tessa Jowell from John Sell and Anthea Case, 28 October 2004.

Heritage Link (2006a) Chairman's Report to the Annual General Meeting, 6 December 2006.

Heritage Link (2006b) Letter to Gordon Brown from Anthea Case, 2 March 2006.

Heritage Link (2007a) Letter to Margaret Hodge from Anthea Case, 18 December 2007.

Heritage Link (2007b) Chairman's Report to the Annual General Meeting, 11 December 2007.

Heritage Lottery Fund (2002) *Broadening the Horizons of Heritage, The Heritage Lottery Fund Strategic Plan 2002–2007* (London: HLF).

Hesmondhalgh, D. (2005) 'Media and Cultural Policy as Public Policy', *International Journal of Cultural Policy*, 11(1), 95–109.

Hesmondhalgh, D. (2008) 'Cultural and Creative Industries', in T. Bennett and J. Frow (eds) *The Sage Handbook of Cultural Analysis* (Sage Publications Ltd), pp. 553–569.

Hesmondhalgh, D. (2009) 'The Digitalisation of Music', in P. Jeffcut and A. Pratt (eds) *Creativity and Innovation in the Cultural Economy* (London: Routledge), pp. 57–73.

Hesmondhalgh, D. (2013a) *The Cultural Industries* (3rd edition) (London: Sage).

Hesmondhalgh, D. (2013b) *Why Music Matters* (Malden, MA: Wiley-Blackwell).

Hesmondhalgh, D., Nisbett, M., Oakley, K. and Lee, D. (2015) 'Were New Labour's Cultural Policies Neo-Liberal?' *International Journal of Cultural Policy*, 21(1), 97–114.

Hetherington, S. (2014) *The Rationales of New Labour's Cultural Policy 1997–2001* (PhD thesis, University of Birmingham).

Hewison, R. (1987) *The Heritage Industry: Britain in a Climate in Decline* (London: Methuen).

Hewison, R. (1993) 'State and the Arts', *The Sunday Times*, 23 May.

Hewison, R. (1995) *Culture and Consensus: England, Art and Politics since 1940* (London: Methuen).

Hewison, R. (2009) 'The Heritage Obsession: The Battle for England's Past' (Book Review), *Cultural Trends*, 18(1), 105–197.

Hewison, R. (2014) *Cultural Capital: The Rise and Fall of Creative Britain* (London: Verso).

Higgins, C. (2012) 'Nicholas Hytner: "The Arts Are on a Knife's Edge"', *The Guardian*, 30 November.

Hill, J. (2012). ' "This Is for the Batmans as well as the Vera Drakes": Economics, Culture and UK Government Film Production Policy in the 2000s', *Journal of British Cinema and Television*, 9(3), 333–356.

Hitchen, G. (2013) 'The New Landscape for Creative Industries Policy', http://bop.co.uk/blog/culture-and-creative-industries/the-new-landscape-for-creative-industries-policy, accessed 12 November 2013.

HM Treasury (1999) *Comprehensive Spending Review* (London: HMSO).

HM Treasury (2004) *Skills in the Global Economy* (London: HMSO).

HM Treasury (2006) *Investing in Britain's Potential: Building Our Long-term Future. Pre-Budget Report*, http://www.hm-treasury.gov.uk/media/5cc/43/, accessed 9 August 2013.

Hodge, M. (2010) Seminar Speech: 12 March 2010, https://www.gov.uk/government/uploads/system/uploads/attachment_data/file/272403/6984.pdf, accessed July 2013 (London: Demos).

Hogge, B. (2006) The Future of Intellectual Property: Andrew Gowers Interviewed, http://www.opendemocracy.net/media-copyrightlaw/gowers_4160.jsp, accessed 5 December 2014.

Holden, J. (2004) *Capturing Cultural Value: How Culture Has Become a Tool of Government Policy* (London: Demos).

Holden, J. (2006) *Cultural Value and the Crisis of Legitimacy* (London: Demos).

Holden, J. (2007) *Publicly-Funded Culture and the Creative Industries* (London: Demos).

Home Office (2001) *The Cantle Report – Community Cohesion: A Report of the Independent Review Team* (London: Home Office).

Hood, C. (1991) 'A Public Management for All Seasons?' *Public Administration*, 69(1), 3–19.

Hood, C. (1995) 'The "New Public Management" in the 1980s: Variations on a Theme', *Accounting, Organizations and Society*, 20(2–3), 93–109.

Hooper-Greenhill, E., Dodd, J., Philips, M., Jones, C., Woodward, J. and O'Riain, H. (2004) *Inspiration, Identity, Learning: The Value of Museums* (London: DCMS/DfES).

Horten, M. (2013) *A Copyright Masquerade: How Corporate Lobbying Threatens Online Freedoms* (London: Zed Books).

House of Commons Committee of Public Accounts (2004a) *Income Generated by the Museums and Galleries, Thirty-third Report of Session 2003–04* (London: The Stationery Office).

House of Commons Culture, Media and Sport Committee (2004b) *DCMS Annual Report: Work of the Department in 2002–03* (London: The Stationery Office).

House of Commons Culture, Media and Sport Committee (2011) *Funding of the Arts and Heritage* (London: The Stationery Office).

House of Commons Culture, Media and Sport Committee (2012) *Library Closures* (London: The Stationery Office).

House of Commons Culture, Media and Sport Committee (2013) *Supporting the Creative Economy* (London: The Stationery Office).

House of Commons Public Accounts Select Committee (2000) *The Arts Council of England: Monitoring Major Capital Projects Funded by the National Lottery* (London: The Stationery Office).

House of Commons, Science and Technology Committee (2002) *National Endowment for Science, Technology and the Arts: A Follow Up. Sixth Report of Session 2001–02* (London: The Stationery Office).

Hughes, J. (1998) 'Rattle to Quit Labour's Musical Desert', *The Independent*, 21 December, http://www.independent.co.uk/news/rattle-to-quit-labours -musical-desert-1193702.html, accessed 11 January 2015.

Hunt, J. (2008) 'First Keynote Speech on the Arts', 24 June 2008, http://www .jeremyhunt.org/news/jeremy-hunt-gives-his-first-keynote-speech-arts, accessed 20 May 2013.

Hunt, T. (2007) 'Heritage Funds Must Not Be Raided to Pay for the Olympics', *The Observer*, 14 January 2007, p. 25.

Hunt, T. (2011) 'We Need to Start Charging for Museums and Galleries Again', *The Observer*, 6 March, http://www.theguardian.com/commentisfree/2011/mar/06/ tristram-hunt-entrance-fees-museums, accessed 12 January 2015.

Hutchison, R. (1982) *The Politics of the Arts Council* (London: Sinclair Browne).

Hutton, W. (2010) *Them and Us: Changing Britain – Why We Need a Fairer Society* (London: Little, Brown).

Hytner, N. (2003) 'To Hell with Targets', *The Observer*, 12 January.

IDeA (2005) *Innovation in Public Services* (London: Improvement and Development Agency).

Imrie, R. (2004) 'Governing the Cities and the Urban Renaissance', in C. Johnstone and M. Whitehead (eds) *New Horizons in British Urban Policy: Perspectives on New Labour's Urban Renaissance* (London: Ashgate), pp. 129–141.

Ipsos Mori (2000) *Attitudes towards the Heritage: Research Studies Conducted for English Heritage* (London: English Heritage).

Ipsos Mori (2003) *The Impact of Free Entry to Museums* (London: Ipsos Mori).

IPSOS-RSL (2003) *Restoration QUEST Results*, IPSOS-RSL for the BBC.

Jakob, D. (2011) 'Constructing the Creative Neighbourhood: Hopes and Limitations of Creative City Policies in Berlin', *City, Culture and Society*, 1(4), 193–198.

James, O. (2004) 'The UK Core Executive's Use of Public Service Agreements as a Tool of Governance', *Public Administration*, 82(2), 397–419.

Jancovich, L. (2011) 'Great Art for Everyone? Engagement and Participation Policy in the Arts', *Cultural Trends*, 20(3–4), 271–279.

Jarvie, I. (1992) *Hollywood's Overseas Campaign: The North American Movie Trade, 1920–1950* (Cambridge: Cambridge University Press).

Jayne, M. (2005) 'Creative Industries: The Regional Dimension', *Environment and Planning C: Government and Policy*, 23, 537–556.

Jenkins, J. (1995) 'The Roots of The National Trust', *History Today*, 45(1), 3–9.

Jermyn, H. (2001) *The Arts and Social Exclusion: A Review Prepared for the Arts Council of England* (London: Arts Council England).

Jessop, B. (2002) *The Future of the Capitalist State* (Cambridge: Polity).

Jones, K. and Thomson, P. (2008) 'Policy Rhetoric and the Renovation of English Schooling: The Case of Creative Partnerships', *Journal of Education Policy*, 23(6), 715–727.

Jordan, B. (2005) 'New Labour: Choice and Values', *Critical Social Policy*, 25(4), 427–446.

Jowell, T. (2004) *Government and the Value of Culture* (London: DCMS).

Jowell, T. (2005) *Better Places to Live: Government, Identity and the Public Value of Heritage* (London: DCMS).

Jubb, M. (2004) 'Commentary: Research Activities and Strategies in the Cultural and Heritage Sectors', *Cultural Trends*, 13(4), 87–92.

Khan, N. (1976) *The Art Britain Ignores: The Arts of Ethnic Minorities in Britain* (London: Commission for Racial Equality).

King, D. S. (1999) *In the Name of Liberalism: Illiberal Social Policy in the USA and Britain* (Oxford: Oxford University Press).

Koch-Baumgarten, S. and Voltmer, K. (eds) (2010) *Public Policy and the Mass Media: The Interplay of Mass Communication and Political Decision Making* (London: Routledge).

Labour Party (1997a) *Create the Future* (London: Labour Party).

Labour Party (1997b) *New Labour: A Government for Entrepreneurs* (London: Labour Party).

Labour Party (1997c) *Labour Party General Election Manifesto 1997: Because Britain Deserves Better* (London: Labour Party).

Lanchester, J. (2010) *Whoops! Why Everyone Owes Everyone and No-One Can Pay* (London: Penguin).

Lapsley, I. (2009) 'New Public Management: The Cruellest Invention of the Human Spirit?' *Abacus*, 45(1), 1–21.

LDA (2003) *Creative London* (London: London Development Agency).

Leadbeater, C. (1999) *Living on Thin Air: The New Economy* (London: Penguin).

Leitch, S. (2006) *Prosperity for All in the Global Economy – World Class Skills: Final Report* (London: HMSO).

Leonard, M. (1997) *Britain TM: Renewing Our Identity* (London: Demos).

Lessig, L. (2001) *The Future of Ideas: The Fate of the Commons in a Connected World* (London: Random House).

Levitas, R. (2005) *The Inclusive Society? Social Exclusion and New Labour* (Basingstoke: Palgrave Macmillan).

Levitt, R. (2008) 'The Political and Intellectual Landscape of Instrumental Museum Policy', *Cultural Trends*, 17(4), 223–231.

Lewis, J. (1990) *Art, Culture and Enterprise: The Politics of Art and the Cultural Industries* (London: Routledge).

Leys, C. (2003) *Market Driven Politics: Neoliberal Democracy and the Public Interest* (London: Verso).

Littler, J. (2005) 'Introduction: British Heritage and the Legacies of "Race" ', in J. Littler and R. Naidoo (eds) *The Politics of Heritage: The Legacies of 'Race'* (Abingdon: Routledge), pp. 1–19.

Lloyd, R. D. (2006) *Neo-bohemia* (New York: Routledge).

Looseley, D. (1995) *The Politics of Fun: Cultural Policy and Debate in Contemporary France* (Oxford: Berg).

Lunt, P. and Livingstone, S. (2012) *Media Regulation: Governance and the Interests of Citizens and Consumers* (London: Sage).

Lyth, P. (2006) 'Selling History in an Age of Industrial Decline: Heritage Tourism in Robin Hood Country', in *Proceedings of the XIV International Economic History Congress* (Helsinki, Finland), 21–25 August 2006.

Maas, H. (2006) 'A Pragmatic Intellectual: Dutch Fabians, Boekman and Cultural Policy in the Netherlands, 1890–1940', *International Journal of Cultural Policy*, 12(2), 151–170.

MacPherson, G. (2002) *Shifting Power, Policy and Practice in a Local Authority Museum Service* (unpublished doctoral thesis, Glasgow Caledonian University).

Magor, M. and Schlesinger, P. (2009) ' "For This Relief Much Thanks": Taxation, Film Policy and the UK Government', *Screen*, 50(3), 299–317.

Malik, S. (2013) ' "Creative Diversity": UK Public Service Broadcasting after Multiculturalism', *Popular Communication*, 11(3), 227–241.

Mansfield, J. R. (2013) 'Heritage Protection in England: The New Labour Legacy', *Structural Survey*, 31(1), 6–20.

Marquand, D. (2004) *The Decline of the Public: The Hollowing Out of Citizenship* (Cambridge: Polity Press).

Marliere, P. (2010). 'Le déclin historique de la social-démocratie'. *La Démocratie. Histoire, théories, pratiques* (pp. 139–147). Paris: Editions Sciences Humaines.

Marsh, D. (2011) 'The New Orthodoxy: The Differentiated Polity Model', *Public Administration*, 89(1), 32–48.

Marsh, D. and Rhodes, R. A. W. (1992) *Policy Networks in British Government* (Oxford: Clarendon Press).

Marsh, D., Toke, D., Belfrage, C., Tepe, D. and McGough, S. (2009) 'Policy Networks and the Distinction between Insider and Outsider Groups: The Case of the Countryside Alliance', *Public Administration*, 87(3), 621–638.

Martin, R. (2010) 'Uneven Regional Growth: The Geographies of Boom and Bust under New Labour', in N. Coe and A. Jones (eds) *The Economic Geography of the UK* (London: Sage), pp. 29–46.

Maxwell, R. and Miller, T. (2012). *Greening the Media* (New York: Oxford University Press).

May, C. (2000) *The Global Political Economy of Intellectual Property Rights: The New Enclosures?* (London: Routledge).

McDonald, A. (2011) 'Down the Rabbit Hole: The Madness of State Film Incentives as a Solution to "Runaway" Film Production', *University of Pennsylvania Journal of Business Law*, 14(1), 85–165.

McGuigan, J. (2005) 'Neo-Liberalism, Culture and Policy', *International Journal of Cultural Policy*, 11(3), 229–241.

McGuigan, J. and Gilmore, A. (2002) 'The Millennium Dome: Sponsoring, Meaning and Visiting', *International Journal of Cultural Policy*, 8(1), 1–20.

McLellan, R., Galton, M., Steward, S. and Page, C. (2012) *The Impact of Creative Initiatives on Wellbeing* (London: CCE).

McMaster, B. (2008) *Supporting Excellence in the Arts* (London: DCMS).

McRobbie, A. (2011) 'Re-Thinking Creative Economy as Radical Social Enterprise', *Variant*, 41(Spring), 32–33.

Miles, A. and Sullivan, A. (2012) 'Understanding Participation in Culture and Sport: Mixing Methods, Reordering Knowledges', *Cultural Trends*, 21(4): 311–324.

Miles, S. (2005) ' "Our Tyne": Iconic Regeneration and the Revitalisation of Identity in Newcastle-Gateshead', *Urban Studies*, 42(5–6), 913–926.

Miliband, E. (2015) 'Text of Ed Miliband's Arts for All Speech', Labour Arts Alliance website, http://www.labourartsalliance.org.uk/text_of_ed_miliband_s_arts_for_all_speech, accessed 24 February 2015.

Millard, R. (2010) 'Why Have Costly Arts Projects That Were Supposed to Transform the Country's Cultural Landscape Flopped?' *The Independent*, 11 February.

Miller, D. (2008) 'The Uses of Value', *Geoforum*, 39(3), 1122–1132.

Miller, T. and Yúdice, G. (2002) *Cultural Policy* (London: Sage).

Miller, T., Govil, N., McMurria, J., Maxwell, R. and Wang, T. (2005) *Global Hollywood 2* (London: BFI Publishing).

Mirza, M. (2012) *The Politics of Culture: The Case for Universalism* (Basingstoke: Palgrave Macmillan).

Mitchell, S. (2001) 'Upstairs, Downstairs: The National Trust Is in a State of Upheaval, with a New Director General and a Shift of Emphasis from Stately Homes to Workhouses. Sandy Mitchell Questions Whether It Has Got Its Priorities Right', *The Telegraph*, http://www.telegraph.co.uk/gardening/4793957/ Upstairs-downstairs.html, accessed 10 January 2015.

Moir, L. and Taffler, R. J. (2004) 'Does Corporate Philanthropy Exist? Business Giving to the Arts in the U.K.', *Journal of Business Ethics*, 54(2), 149–161.

Moss, L. (2000) 'Constructing White Elephants: Why Have So Many Arts Lottery Funded Projects Failed To Meet Expectations?' Working Papers, School of Leisure and Sport Management, Sheffield Hallam University.

Mulcahy, K. (2006) 'Cultural Policy', in B. Peters and J. Pierre (eds) *Handbook of Public Policy* (London: Sage), pp. 265–279.

Mulgan, G. (2007) *Ready or Not? Taking Innovation in the Public Sector Seriously* (London: Nesta).

Mulgan, G. and Worpole, K. (1986) *Saturday Night or Sunday Morning? From Arts to Industry – New Forms of Cultural Policy* (London: Comedia).

Museums, Libraries and Archives Council (2005) *New Directions in Social Policy: Developing the Evidence Base for Museums, Libraries and Archives in England* (London: MLA).

Myerscough, J. (1988) *The Economic Importance of the Arts* (London: Policy Studies Institute).

National Advisory Committee on Creative and Cultural Education (1999) *All Our Futures: Creativity, Culture and Education* (London: DFEE).

Narain, J. (2009) 'Fasten Your Seat Belts, Children, Your New Geography Classroom Has Landed in the Playground', *Daily Mail*, 31 March.

National Audit Office (2002) *Winding-up The New Millennium Experience Company Limited* (Report by the Comptroller and Auditor General), http://www.nao.org .uk/wp-content/uploads/2002/04/0102749es.pdf.

National Museum Directors' Conference (2013). *Museums and Tourism* (London: NMDC).

National Trust (2014) *Annual Report 2013/14* (Swindon: National Trust).

Neal, S. (2002) 'Rural Landscapes, Representations and Racism: Examining Multicultural Citizenship and Policy-Making in the English Countryside', *Ethnic and Racial Studies*, 25(3), 442–461.

Needham, A. (2012) 'Big Hitters Dominate Arts Council Capital Funding Awards', *The Guardian*, 29 March, http://www.theguardian.com/culture/2012/mar/29/ big-hitters-arts-council-funding, accessed 3 January 2014.

Needham, C. (2003) *Citizen-Consumers: New Labour's Marketplace Democracy* (London: Catalyst Forum).

Negroponte, N. (1995) *Being Digital* (London: Hodder and Stoughton).

Nesta (2006) *Creating Growth: How the UK Can Create World Class Creative Business* (London: Nesta).

Nesta (2010) *Creative Clusters and Innovation: Putting Creativity on the Map* (London: Nesta).

Nesta (2012) *A Brief History of NESTA* (London: Nesta).

Nesta (2013) 'About Us', http://www.Nesta.org.uk/about_us, accessed 7 January 2013.

Nesta Working Group (1997) *From Pledge to Policy: A Way Forward for the Labour Government* (London: Nesta).

Newbigin, J. (2011) 'A Golden Age for the Arts?' *Cultural Trends*, 3(4), 231–234.

Newman, A. and MacLean, F. (2004) 'Presumption, Policy and Practice: The Use of Museums and Galleries as Agents of Social Inclusion in Great Britain', *International Journal of Cultural Policy*, 10(2), 167–181.

Newman, J. (2001) *Modernizing Governance: New Labour, Policy and Society* (London: Sage).

Newsinger, J. (2009) *From the Grassroots: Regional Film Policy and Practice in England* (PhD thesis, University of Nottingham).

Newsinger, J. (2011) 'The Politics of Regional Audio-Visual Policy in England: Or, How We Learnt to Stop Worrying and Get "Creative"', *International Journal of Cultural Policy*, 18(1), 111–125.

Oakley, K. (2004) 'Not So Cool Britannia: The Role of the Creative Industries in Economic Development', *International Journal of Cultural Studies*, 7(1), 67–77.

Oakley, K. (2006) 'Include Us Out: Economic Development and Social Policy in the Creative Industries', *Cultural Trends*, 15(4), 255–273.

Oakley, K. (2009a) 'The Disappearing Arts: Creativity and Innovation after the Creative Industries', *International Journal of Cultural Policy*, 15(4), 403–413.

Oakley, K. (2009b) 'From Bohemia to Britart – Art Students over 50 Years', *Cultural Trends*, 18(4), 281–294.

Oakley, K. (2011) 'In Its Own Image: New Labour and the Cultural Workforce', *Cultural Trends*, 20(3–4), 281–289.

Oakley, K. (2012) 'Not the New, New Thing: Innovation and Cultural Policy in the EU', in I. Elam (ed) *Artists and the Arts Industries* (Stockholm: The Swedish Arts Grants Committee), pp. 56–66.

Oakley, K. (2014) 'Good Work? Rethinking Cultural Entrepreneurship', in C. Bilton and S. Cummings (eds) *Handbook of Management and Creativity* (Cheltenham: EE Publishing), pp. 145–159.

Oakley, K. and O'Brien, D. (2014) *Cultural Value and Inequality: A Critical Literature Review* (Swindon: Arts and Humanities Research Council).

Oakley, K., Hesmondhalgh, D., Lee, D. and Nisbett, M. (2014) 'The National Trust for Talent? NESTA and New Labour's Cultural Policy', *British Politics*, 9, 297–317.

O'Brien, D. (2010) *Measuring the Value of Culture: A Report to the Department for Culture, Media and Sport* (London: Department for Culture, Media and Sport).

O'Brien, D. (2013) *Cultural Policy: Management, Value and Modernity in the Creative Industries* (London: Routledge).

O'Connor, J. (2004) ' "A Special Kind of City Knowledge": Innovative Clusters, Tacit Knowledge and the "Creative City" ', *Media International Australia*, 112, 131–149.

O'Connor, J. and Gu, X. (2010) 'Developing a Creative Cluster in a Postindustrial City: CIDS and Manchester', *The Information Society*, 26(2), 124–136.

Office of the Deputy Prime Minister (2001) *New Deal for Communities. Neighbourhood Renewal Unit* (London: Office of the Deputy Prime Minister).

Office for National Statistics (2006) *International Passenger Survey, Office for National Statistics: Social and Vital Statistics Division* (London: HMSO).

Office for National Statistics (2010) *Creative Industries in the Regions: An Analysis of Data from Inter Departmental Business Register* (London: ONS).

O'Neill, M. (2008) 'Museums, Professionalism and Democracy', *Cultural Trends*, 17(4), 289–307.

One North East (2012) *Legacy of the Agency*, http://www.onenortheastlegacy.co .uk/file.aspx?id=6, accessed 16 October 2013.

Paschalidis, G. (2009) 'Exporting National Culture: Histories of Cultural Institutes Abroad', *International Journal of Cultural Policy*, 15(3), 275–289.

Pautz, H. (2011) 'New Labour in Government: Think-tanks and Social Policy Reform, 1997–2001', *British Politics*, 6(2), 187–209.

Pearce, G. and Ayres, S. (2009) 'Governance in the English Regions: The Role of the Regional Development Agencies', *Urban Studies*, 46(3), 537–557.

Peck, J. and Theodore, N. (2010) 'Mobilizing Policy: Models, Methods, and Mutations', *Geoforum*, 41(2), 169–174.

Pendlebury, J. (2000) 'Conservation, Conservatives and Consensus: The Success of Conservation under the Thatcher and Major Governments, 1979–1997', *Planning Theory & Practice*, 1(1), 31–52.

Pendlebury, J. (2002) 'Conservation and Regeneration: Complementary or Conflicting Processes? The Case of Grainger Town, Newcastle Upon Tyne', *Planning Practice & Research*, 17(2), 145–158.

Pendlebury, J., Townshend, T. and Gilroy, R. (2004) 'The Conservation of English Cultural Built Heritage: A Force for Social Inclusion?' *International Journal of Heritage Studies*, 10(1), 11–31.

Phillips, D. and Whannel, G. (2013) *The Trojan Horse: The Growth of Commercial Sponsorship* (London: Bloomsbury).

Pickernell, D., Brown, K., Worthington, A. and Crawford, M. (2004) 'Gambling as a Base for Hypothecated Taxation: The UK's National Lottery and Electronic Gaming Machines in Australia', *Public Money & Management*, 24(3), 167–174.

Pickford, J. (2014) 'Arts and Culture Spending Crunch Prompts New Ways of Working', *Financial Times*, 9 March.

Platt, E. (2012) 'Multi-Million-Pound Makeover for Sheffield's Notorious Park Hill Estate', *The Daily Telegraph*, http://www.telegraph.co.uk/culture/ art/architecture/9551327/Multi-million-pound-makeover-for-Sheffields-notorious-Park-Hill-estate.html.

Pollitt, C. (2003) 'Joined-up Government: A Survey', *Political Studies Review*, 1(1): 34–49.

Ponzini, D. (2012) 'Competing Cities and Spectacularizing Urban Landscapes', in H. K. Anheier, Y. R. Isar, M. Hoelscher (eds) *Cultures and Globalization Series*, Vol. 5 (London: Sage), pp. 99–110.

Porat, M. (1977) *The Information Economy* (Washington, DC: Department of Commerce).

Porter, M. E. (1998) *Clusters and the New Economics of Competition* (Boston: Harvard Business Review).

Porter, M. E. (2000) 'Location, Competition, and Economic Development: Local Clusters in a Global Economy', *Economic Development Quarterly*, 14(1), 15–34.

Power, M. (1997) *The Audit Society: Rituals of Verification* (Oxford: Oxford University Press).

Pratt, A. C. (1997) 'The Cultural Industries Production System: A Case Study of Employment Change in Britain, 1984–1991', *Environment and Planning A*, 29(11), 1953–1974.

Pratt, A. C. (2004) 'Creative Clusters: Towards the Governance of the Creative Industries Production System?' *Media International Australia*, 112, 50–66.

Pratt, A. C. (2009) 'The Challenge of Governance in the Creative and Cultural Industries', in B. Lange, A. Kalandides, B. Stober and I. Wellmann (eds) *Governance der Kreativwirtschaft: Diagnosen und Handlungsoptionen*. Transcript-Verl., Bielefeld, pp. 271–288.

Pratt, A. C. (2010) 'Creative Cities: Tensions within and between Social, Cultural and Economic Development: A Critical Reading of the UK Experience', *City, Culture and Society*, 1(1), 13–20.

Prince, R. (2010a) 'Globalizing the Creative Industries Concept: Travelling Policy and Transnational Policy Communities', *The Journal of Arts Management, Law, and Society*, 40(2), 119–139.

Prince, R. (2010b) 'Fleshing Out Expertise: The Making of Creative Industries Experts in the United Kingdom', *Geoforum*, 41(6), 875–884.

Pringle, E. and Harland, J. (2008) *Creative Partnerships: An Audit of Practice. Final Report* (London: Arts Council England/Creative Partnerships).

Putnam, R. (2000) *Bowling Alone: The Collapse and Revival of American Community* (New York: Simon and Schuster).

PWC (2009) *Impact of RDA Spending. National Report – Volume 1* (London: Department for Business, Enterprise & Regulatory Reform).

Rhodes, R. A. W. (1994) 'The Hollowing Out of the State: The Changing Nature of the Public Service in Britain', *Political Quarterly*, 65(2), 138–151.

Rhodes, R. A. W. (1997) *Understanding Governance: Policy Networks, Governance, Reflexivity and Accountability* (Milton Keynes: Open University Press).

Rhodes, R. A. W. (2007) 'Understanding Governance: Ten Years On', *Organization Studies*, 28(8), 1243–1264.

Rickey, B. and Houghton, J. (2009) 'Solving the Riddle of the Sands: Regenerating England's Seaside Towns', *Journal of Urban Regeneration and Renewal*, 3(1), 46–55.

Ritzer, G. and Jurgenson, N. (2010) 'Production, Consumption, Prosumption', *Journal of Consumer Culture*, 10(1), 13–36.

Romer, P. M. (1994) 'The Origins of Endogenous Growth', *Journal of Economic Perspectives*, 22(1), 3–22.

Ross, A. (2009) *Nice Work If You Can Get It: Life and Labor in Precarious Times* (New York & London: New York University Press).

Ross, M. (2004) 'Interpreting the New Museology', *Museum and Society*, 2(2), 84–103.

Ruiz, J. (2004) *A Literature Review of the Evidence Base for Culture, the Arts and Social Policy* (Edinburgh: Scottish Executive Education Department).

Samuel, R. (1994) *Theatres of Memory: Past and Present in Contemporary Culture* (London: Verso).

Sandell, R. (2002) *Museums, Society, Inequality* (London: Routledge).

Sandell, R. (2003) 'Social Inclusion, the Museum and the Dynamics of Sectoral Change', *Museum and Society*, 1(1), 45–62.

Sandford, M. (2005) 'Devolution Is a Process Not a Policy' (briefing no. 18), *ESRC Devolution and Constitutional Change Programme* (Edinburgh: University of Edinburgh).

Sassoon, D. (2014) *One Hundred Years of Socialism: The West European Left in the Twentieth Century*, 2nd edition (London: I.B. Tauris).

Sayer, D. (2014) *Rank Hypocrisies: The Insult of the REF* (London: Sage).

Schaffner, D. J. (2004) 'Digital Millennium Copyright Act: Overextension of Copyright Protection and the Unintended Chilling Effects on Fair Use, Free Speech, and Innovation', *The Cornell Journal of Law and Public Policy*, 14, 145.

Schlesinger, P. (2009) 'Creativity and the Experts: New Labour, Think Tanks, and the Policy Process', *International Journal of Press/Politics*, 14(1), 3–20.

Schlesinger, P. (2015) 'The Creation and Destruction of the UK Film Council', in K. Oakley and J. O'Connor (eds) *The Routledge Companion to Cultural Industries* (London and New York: Routledge).

Seltzer, K. and Bentley, T. (1999) *The Creative Age: Knowledge and Skills for the New Economy* (London: Demos).

Selwood, S. (ed) (2001) *The UK Cultural Sector* (London: Policy Studies Institute).

Selwood, S. (2006) 'Unreliable Evidence: The Rhetorics of Data Collection in the Cultural Sector', in M. Mirza (ed) *Culture Vultures: Is UK Arts Policy Damaging the Arts?* (London: Policy Exchange), pp. 38–52.

Selwood, S. (2010) *Making a Difference: The Cultural Impact of Museums* (London: NMDC).

Selwood, S. and Davies, M. (2005) 'Capital Costs: Lottery Funding in Britain and the Consequences for Museums', *Curator: The Museum Journal*, 48(4), 439–465.

Serota, N. (2010) 'A Blitzkrieg on the Arts', *The Guardian*, 5 October.

Shaw, E. (2007) *Losing Labour's Soul? New Labour and the Blair Government 1997–2007* (London: Routledge).

Siddique, H. (2013) 'Government Has Failed on Library Closures, Says Children's Laureate', *The Guardian*, 22 September.

Simpson, J. (1976) *Towards Cultural Democracy* (Strasbourg: Council of Europe).

Skillset (2011) *Sector Skills Assessment for the Creative Industries of the UK* (London: Skillset).

Smith Institute (2013) *Where Next for Local Enterprise Partnerships?* (London: Smith Institute).

Smith, C. (1997) 'Ministry of All the Talents', *The Times*, 15 July.

Smith, C. (1998) *Creative Britain* (London: Faber & Faber).

Smith, L. (2006) *The Uses of Heritage* (Abingdon: Routledge).

Smith, L. (2009) 'Class, Heritage and the Negotiation of Place', *Proceedings of the Missing Out on Heritage: Socio-Economic Status and Heritage Participation Conference*, March 2009.

Stanziola, J. (2007) 'Measuring the Size and Concentration of Business Funding of Culture in the UK: Closing the Gap between Advocacy and Theory', *Cultural Trends*, 16(2), 75–98.

Stanziola, J. (2012) 'Private Sector Policy for the Arts: The Policy Implementer Dilemma', *Cultural Trends*, 21(3), 265–269.

Stark, P., Gordon, C. and Powell, D. (2013) *Rebalancing our Cultural Capital*, http://www.gpsculture.co.uk/downloads/rocc/Rebalancing_FINAL_3mb.pdf, accessed 5 February 2014.

Stevenson, D. (2014) 'Tartan and Tantrums: Critical Reflections on the Creative Scotland "Stooshie" ', *Cultural Trends*, 23(3), 178–187.

Stevenson, D., McKay, K. and Rowe, D. (2010) 'Tracing British Cultural Policy Domains: Contexts, Collaborations and Constituencies', *International Journal of Cultural Policy*, 16(2), 159–172.

Stoker, G. (2004) *Transforming Local Governance: From Thatcherism to New Labour* (Basingstoke: Palgrave MacMillan).

Stolarick, K. and Currid-Halkett, E. (2013) 'Creativity and the Crisis: The Impact of Creative Workers on Regional Unemployment', *Cities*, 33, 5–14.

Strom, E. (2003) 'Cultural Policy as Development Policy: Evidence from the United States', *International Journal of Cultural Policy*, 9(3), 247–263.

South West Regional Development Agency (2011) *South West RDA: Reflections and Lessons* (Bristol: SWRDA).

Swinford, S. (2007) 'Disillusioned tycoon donors desert Brown', *The Sunday Times*, 14th October, available online at http://www.thesundaytimes.co.uk/sto/Test/politics/article73488.ece, accessed 20 November 2014.

Symon, P. and Williams, A. (2002) 'Urban Regeneration Programmes', in S. Selwood (ed) *The UK Cultural Sector* (London: Policy Studies Institute), pp. 54–65.

Tawney, R. (1952/1931) *Equality*, 4th edition (London: Allen and Unwin).

Taylor, A. (1997) ' "Arm's Length But Hands On" Mapping the New Governance: The Department of National Heritage and Cultural Politics in Britain', *Public Administration*, 75(3), 441–466.

Thomas, K. (2010) 'Creating Regional Cultures of Innovation? The Regional Innovation Strategies in England and Scotland', *Regional Studies*, 34(2), 190–198.

Thomson, P. (2010) *Whole School Change: A Literature Review*, 2nd edition. (Newcastle: Creativity, Culture and Education).

Throsby, C. D. (2010) *The Economics of Cultural Policy* (Cambridge: Cambridge University Press).

Thurley, S. (2009) 'From Boom to Bust: The Politics of Heritage 1997 to 2009', December 2009 Gresham College Speech, http://www.gresham.ac.uk/lectures-and-events/from-boom-to-bust-the-politics-of-heritage-1997-to-2009, accessed 22 December 2014.

Toffler, A. (1970) *Future Shock* (London: Pan).

Toynbee, M. and Walker, D. (2010) *The Verdict: Did Labour Change Britain?* (London: Granta Books).

Toynbee, P. (2011) 'A Great Act of Vandalism That Will Impoverish Us All', *The Guardian*, 29 March.

Trimm, R. S. (2005) 'Nation, Heritage and Hospitality in Britain after Thatcher', *CLCWeb: Comparative Literature and Culture*, 7(2), 1–10.

Turner, A. (2009) *The Turner Review. A Regulatory Response to the Global Banking Crisis* (London: Financial Services Authority).

Turnpenny, M. (2004) 'Cultural Heritage, an Ill-defined Concept? A Call for Joined-up Policy', *International Journal of Heritage Studies*, 10(3), 295–307.

Tusa, J. (1999) *Art Matters: Reflecting on Culture* (London: Methuen).

UK Film Council (2000) *Towards a Sustainable Film Industry* (London: UKFC).

UK Parliament (2010) *Digital Economy Act* (London: HMSO).

UNESCO (2003) *Convention for the Safeguarding of Intangible Cultural Heritage* (New York: UNESCO).

Vestheim, G. (1994) 'Instrumental Cultural Policy in Scandinavian Countries: A Critical Historical Perspective', *International Journal of Cultural Policy*, 1(1), 57–71.

VisitBritain (2010) *Culture and Heritage: Topic Profile*, http://www.visitbritain .org/Images/Culture%20%26%20Heritage%20Topic%20Profile%20Full _tcm29-14711.pdf, accessed 22 December 2014.

VisitEngland (2006–2011) *Attractions Business Monitor* http://www.visitengland .com/biz/resources/insights-and-statistics/research-topics/attractions-research/ attractions-business-monitor, accessed 14 May 2015.

Warwick Commission (2015) *Enriching Britain: Culture, Creativity and Growth*, http://www2.warwick.ac.uk/research/warwickcommission/futureculture/ finalreport/, accessed 27 March 2015.

Waters, C. (1990) *British Socialists and the Politics of Popular Culture, 1884–1914* (Manchester: Manchester University Press).

Waterton, E. (2010) *Politics, Policy and the Discourses of Heritage in Britain* (Basingstoke: Palgrave Macmillan).

Watson, D. (2007) 'A Very British Coo: Pigeon Men Battle Developer to Save World's Only Listed Loft', *The Daily Mirror*, 22 December 2007, p. 16.

Wells, P. (2011) 'Prescriptions for Regional Economic Dilemmas: Understanding the Role of Think Tanks in the Governance of Regional Policy', *Public Administration*, 90(1), 211–229.

White, M. (1994) 'The Gift of Tired Tongues', *The Guardian*, 30 September.

Wighton, D. (1998) 'Mandelson Plans a Microchip Off the Old Block', *Financial Times*, 23 October.

Wilks-Heeg, S. (2009) 'New Labour and the Reform of English Local Government, 1997–2007: Privatizing the Parts That Conservative Governments Could Not Reach?' *Planning, Practice & Research*, 24(1), 23–39.

Wisman, J. D. (2006) 'State Lotteries: Using State Power to Fleece the Poor', *Journal of Economic Issues*, 40(4), 955–966.

Witts, R. (1998) *Artist Unknown: An Alternative History of the Arts Council* (London: Warner).

Work Foundation (2007) *Staying Ahead: The Economic Performance of the UK's Creative Industries* (London: DCMS).

Work Foundation (2012) *People or Place? Urban Policy in an Age of Austerity* (London: Work Foundation).

Wright, P. (1985) *On Living in an Old Country: The National Past in Contemporary Britain* (London: Verso).

Wu, C. T. (2002) *Privatising Culture: Corporate Art Intervention since the 1980s* (London and New York: Verso).

Yoon, O. K. (2010) *Intrinsic and Instrumental Rationales in Contemporary UK Cultural Policy: Negotiating Cultural Values in the Climate of Neoliberalism* (PhD thesis, University of Loughborough).

Index